W9-CNC-333

# The Circus at the Edge of the Earth

# The Circus at the
# Edge of the Earth

*Travels with the Great Wallenda Circus*

CHARLES WILKINS

**M&S**

Copyright © 1998 Charles Wilkins

All rights reserved. The use of any part of this publication reproduced, transmitted in any form or by any means, electronic, mechanical, photocopying, recording, or otherwise, or stored in a retrieval system, without the prior written consent of the publisher – or, in the case of photocopying or other reprographic copying, a licence from the Canadian Copyright Licensing Agency – is an infringement of the copyright law.

**Canadian Cataloguing in Publication Data**

Wilkins, Charles
    The circus at the edge of the earth : travels with the Great Wallenda Circus

ISBN 0-7710-8847-7

1. Great Wallenda Circus.    I.  Title.

GV1821.G7W55  1998      791.3      c98-931845-1

We acknowledge the financial support of the Government of Canada through the Book Publishing Industry Development Program for our publishing activities. We further acknowledge the support of the Canada Council for the Arts and the Ontario Arts Council for our publishing program.

Set in Goudy by M&S, Toronto
Printed and bound in Canada

McClelland & Stewart Inc.
*The Canadian Publishers*
481 University Avenue
Toronto, Ontario
M5G 2E9

1  2  3  4  5    02  01  00  99  98

*For Betty*

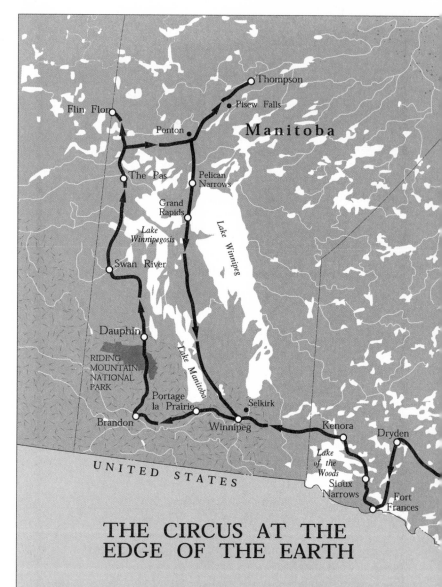

Flin Flon

Thompson

Pisew Falls

Ponton

Manitoba

The Pas

Pelican
Narrows

Grand
Rapids

*Lake
Winnipegosis*

*Lake
Winnipeg*

Swan River

Dauphin

RIDING
MOUNTAIN
NATIONAL
PARK

*Lake
Manitoba*

Portage
la Prairie

Selkirk

Brandon

Winnipeg

Kenora

Dryden

UNITED STATES

*Lake
of the
Woods*

Sioux
Narrows

Fort
Frances

# THE CIRCUS AT THE
# EDGE OF THE EARTH

0        100        200 km

0             100 mi.

Scale

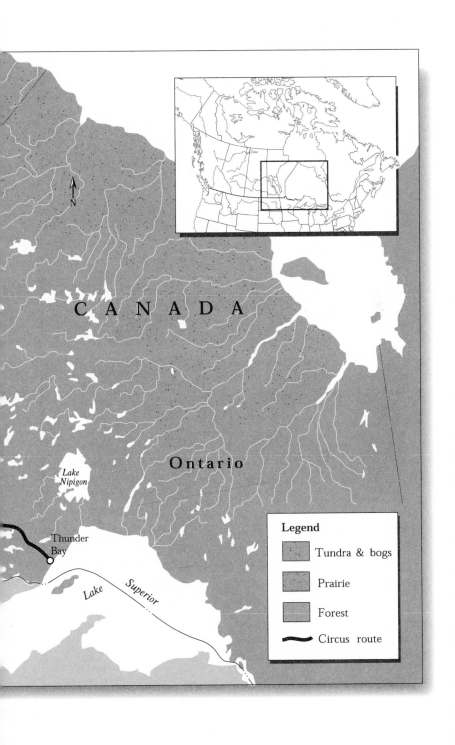

# I

THE EVENING OF May 13, 1997, was not the worst in Wilson Barnes's career as a tiger trainer, but it was within hailing distance of the worst. His joints ached, his eyes watered, and his inner throat resembled a paste of crushed raspberries. In the hours since the afternoon show, he had battled surges of intense chills, his particular response to a germ that, over the past few days, had reduced half the circus to moaning and fever and long disquieting sleeps.

For Wilson, the virus had rooted during a week of extraordinary demands on his energy. Six days earlier, his co-worker on the show, a Barnumesque elephant trainer named Bobby Gibbs, had blown the engine in his aging diesel Freightliner on the highway at Sioux Narrows, Ontario. The result was that Wilson, besides doing two performances a day and raising his three-year-old daughter, Connie, was hauling his tigers from one stop to the next, then doubling back to haul the elephant trailer over highways perilously heaved by the frosts of the Canadian winter. On the jump north from Brandon the previous day, he had been obliged to detour a hundred kilometres around Riding Mountain

National Park to comply with laws forbidding the transport of exotic animals through Canada's federal preserves.

On the repeat run with the elephant, he had stopped at the park gate, where the same attendant who had forced him to detour earlier asked jauntily if he had another load of tigers on board. "Nothin this time but a dozen bales of hay!" hollered Bobby Gibbs from the passenger seat. And they had been waved on into the sanctified forest, hauling a nine-thousand-pound Asian elephant.

Had there been so much as a day of sunshine, of seasonable warmth, as the tour pressed north and west, Wilson's weariness would have been soothed. But for two weeks straight, the wind had come hard out of the Arctic, bringing daily snow and skies the colour of old asphalt during a month when, even on the Fiftieth Parallel, crocuses and daffodils should have been coming into bud. The spring to date had been the coldest of the century. But few northerners were of a mind to complain, knowing that, in the distance to the south, ten thousand of their countrymen in the Red River Valley had seen their farms and villages disappear under a flood deemed the worst in five hundred years. The circus's date in Selkirk, just north of Winnipeg, had been cancelled because the arena booked for the occasion had been commandeered to house soldiers brought in to protect what could still be protected.

On top of all this, in the frigid arena on the eastern boundary of Dauphin, Manitoba, the anticipated crowd had not materialized. A few dozen schoolchildren who had missed the afternoon show, or had returned with their parents, sat in a loose aggregation behind the players' benches. Below and in front, a double line of wheelchair occupants – some barely above the threshold of sensibility – had been rolled into place on a plywood riser along the arena's north boards. They huddled in blankets and parkas as the Grand Potentate of the Khartum Temple of Shriners, the esteemed Bob Bridgewater, introduced the local "nobles" and, with merciful brevity, touted the efforts of the Shrine in bringing the Great Wallenda Circus from Sarasota, Florida *"All the way to Dauphin, Manitoba. And now ladies and gentlemen, boys and girls,"* shouted the Potentate, *"will you please join me in welcoming one of the great ringmasters of all time, the* singing *ringmaster . . . Misterrr . . . Billlll . . . Borrrren!"*

As the three-piece band blew a brisk rendition of "Oh, What a Feeling," and a motorized mirror-ball threw silver dollars across the overhead trusses, Wilson shucked his buckskin jacket, flung it into the penalty box, and stepped onto the arena floor. He had performed for seventy thousand fans in the Kingdome in Seattle, had played the Cotton Bowl in Dallas and the Los Angeles Shrine Auditorium. But in one respect at least, his performance tonight in front of 120 people was no different from those he had given in the largest cities on the continent. On that account, as always, he paused in the darkness by the ring curb and uttered a brief, silent prayer. Two nights earlier, in Brandon, I had asked him what he prayed for when he entered the steel cage. Raised in Newfoundland but a sixteen-year resident of Dallas, his voice combines the nasal twang of the Rock with the taffied drawl of central Texas. "I pray," he said softly, "that I'll come out alive."

Wilson is not given to dramatics or hyperbole. He is simply aware of the realities of his chosen work.

Under cover of darkness and the diversion of the ringmaster's singing, he slipped through the door of the circular pen that is his office, latched it behind him, and stood in the shadows awaiting his introduction. Unapparent yet to the audience, he was costumed in a one-piece lime-coloured suit, adorned with curlicues of black sequins and cut to the navel, revealing his thickening torso and generous thatching of chest hair. He had a buggy whip in one hand, a "bait stick" in the other, and on his feet a pair of silvered dingo boots.

In the moments that remained, he slowed his breathing, distanced his surroundings, and focused his energy on the exceptional requirements at hand.

And then he was on, no longer the flu-ridden circus cowboy but *"The one and only Wilson Barnes,"* floodlit commando, as dauntless as Daniel, with a smile as glittering as his nerve.

As the opening strains of "The Jungle Rumba" rattled through the empty arena, Wilson turned on his heel to face his assistant, Rick Robinson, who from outside the ring pulled the lock pin on the slide-gate and yanked it back, allowing a four-hundred-pound Bengal named Kismit to glide into the spotlight. Like the other tigers, she had spent much of the day in the frigid arena, sending up a keening yowl, and was in no mood to be trifled with or pushed around. She feinted toward Wilson, showed him four inches of ivory, and, as he cracked his whip, leapt peevishly onto her seat. Unlike lions, which live in prides and hunt in numbers, tigers are solitary animals, territorial isolationists, that will fight one another, sometimes to death, if they are allowed into unsupervised proximity. For that reason, they are brought briskly into the ring through the chute formed by their aligned cages, and hustled onto their perches, which are located equidistant around the periphery of the circular pen: Kismit, Lokme, Robin, Pasha, Seanna – all females except Pasha, all Bengals except the big Siberian, Seanna.

When all five tigers were securely on their seats, Wilson styled to the audience, accepted a scrap of applause, and, as the band pounded into an old Count Basie tune called "Jungle Voodoo," raised an aluminum hoop as high over his head as he could reach. He brought Robin off her seat, and, by cracking his whip within inches of her backside, directed her onto an ornate pedestal, from which she bounded through the hoop onto an identical pedestal eight feet away. He repeated the trick with a cotton-wrapped hoop that had been soaked in lighter fluid and set on fire.

Wilson normally worked eight tigers, but when he had attempted to get clearance to leave the United States on April 29 he learned that he had inadvertently muddled the exacting paperwork required to bring an endangered species across an international border. When the error was detected by an astute federal agent in Minneapolis, three of the tigers – Baby, Sheba, and India – were refused exit from the country. With the circus opening the following day in Thunder Bay, Ontario, and no time for adjustments, Bobby Gibbs, who handles business for both the tigers and elephants, had no choice but to rent a twenty-six-foot U-Haul and send the tigers home to Seagoville, Texas. "I didn't tell the rental lady what we were gonna use the truck for," Bobby told me. "She kept saying, 'You sure you don't want packing blankets or anything to protect your furniture?' I said, 'No, no, we'll be okay. We're not hauling anything delicate.' Lucky I knew a cop in Minneapolis, a guy who used to work for me. I got him to drive the truck."

Wilson is something over six feet tall, with high dimpled cheeks and straight brown hair that touches his eyebrows in front, his collar behind. His nose travels half the length of his face and has the contour of a dolphin's back. He professes to have loved tigers since he was a boy back in Fortune, Newfoundland, where his family has fished cod for nearly seventy-five years. But despite his longstanding relationship with the cats, his love for them remains radically unrequited. Any of the twenty or more he has worked during his years as a tiger trainer would have torn out his throat had he betrayed even the slightest sign of vulnerability. In the cage, he moves constantly forward. He is bigger than they are, or so they are led to believe. But the illusion can be maintained only as long as he is standing, advancing, overshadowing, subduing not by force but by superior confidence and intelligence. "You never take a step back," he told me one afternoon on the lot, "and if they're challenging you, you sure as hell don't turn and take off.

Once they have you on the run, they'll have their claws and teeth into you within seconds."

It is only in recent decades that tigers have appeared in the circus at all. For more than 150 years after the emergence of the modern circus during the late 1700s in England, they were considered too mean, too dangerous, too independent to be trusted in the ring. Until well into the twentieth century, only legendary cat trainers such as Mabel Stark and Clyde Beatty possessed the jam to take them on. And they paid for their insolence. Asked once by a journalist what it took to be a tiger trainer, Mabel Stark, in a melodramatic pique, threw open her robe, revealing a lower body all but covered in a dense embroidery of suture marks and scar tissue. "That's what it takes," she said.

"When Clyde Beatty died," Bobby Gibbs told me, "he was just one big mass of scars. He'd been beaten up so many times he couldn't even remember them all." By his own estimate, Bob has seen "every cat act in America" and some "unforgettable bloodlettings" in the ring. "A tiger attack is almost impossible to repel," he said one day as we watched Wilson work. "If his adrenaline's pumping and he's serious about getting you, you're not gonna stop him with a crowbar; he'll come through a gun blast to get you. A lion on his own can be stopped; he's a coward, just like in the storybook. Besides, you can see a lion's attack coming – he'll start barking if he's getting ready to challenge you. A tiger just sits there glaring – then he's in the air."

Wilson himself has been "hit," as they say in the circus – "torn up," to use his own picturesque phrase. Three years ago in Nebraska, working outdoors, he momentarily lost his footing on fine gravel during what he calls the "go-home" trick, a charade in which he attempts to get the apparently reluctant Kismit to leave the ring after the others have departed at the end of the act. "I slid a few inches toward her," he told me, "and in the moment I was off balance, I saw her paw coming for my face with the claws bared." He managed to get his arm up for protection but, in the process, received deep lacerations to the muscles and tendons in his forearm. "A tiger's swipe is so powerful," he said, "that if it catches you low on the arm, it can destroy connected muscle and skin away up on the biceps. Since the act was over, I styled, wrapped my arm up and headed for the hospital. She'd hit an artery, so the blood was everywhere."

On another occasion, a tiger about to jump through the fire hoop stopped on the pedestal before leaping. "You don't want them parked up there, because they can come down on you," Wilson said. "But when I tried to coax her along, she bit me on the hand, drove an eye tooth right through the palm and out the other side. Chomp – and she let me go. But with the shock of it, I didn't feel a thing – I finished the act, and it wasn't for a couple of hours that it really started to hurt."

Wilson's worst accident came in 1992 during what he calls the "lay down," a trick in which he gets eight tigers to stretch out side by side on the floor, so that their combined mass resembles a luxurious log raft or plush corduroy road. With the tigers down during a performance in Lawrence, Kansas, he turned to receive the audience's applause, taking his eyes off the cats just long enough for an aging male – "a real nice tiger" – to rise, step forward, and put its teeth through the calf of his leg. "He hung on like it was the last meal he was ever gonna get," Wilson said in a voice verging on nostalgia. "I knew if I went down, I was finished – he'd have been all over me. So I dropped my whip, concentrated my strength, and hit him in the face with my fist – and I'll tell ya, it was fully loaded. I guess it surprised him, because he let go and just looked at me, as if he were gonna cry, and I was able to get the bunch of them back on their seats."

On that occasion, too, Wilson finished the act in shock, leaving the ring at about the same time as the collected blood began to overflow the top of his boot.

"I'm lucky," Wilson says. "I've never been seriously taken apart."

And he is undisturbed by the fact that, if he were, there is no contingency plan for his rescue – nobody stationed near the cage with a gun, a can of mace, or a $CO_2$ fire extinguisher, the deterrent of choice for repelling an attacking tiger (the cat cannot stand the smothering cold around its nostrils and eyes). At one time, years ago, guards with rifles were stationed outside the ring during the more sensational cat acts. Clyde Beatty carried a pistol *inside* the ring. But in each case the weapons were for effect only; Beatty's pistol fired blanks, and the rifles were not loaded. "You couldn't shoot a gun in a crowded arena," scoffs Bobby Gibbs. "We're not even allowed to carry tranquillizer guns. Then again, what good would they do? They take time to work. A tiger can kill you in a fraction of a second."

Wilson says, "I guess I just figure that if I was ever being dragged around, there are people who'd come into the ring to save my life."

Perhaps forfeiting their own in the process.

One night as I stood with the prop boss, David Connors, watching Wilson's act, I asked him what *would* happen if one of the tigers turned on Wilson in the cage. "I don't even like to think about it," he said. "I saw Oakie Carr get taken apart by a big old lion in the sixties, when I was with Carson and Barnes – carved 'im up so bad I wouldn't't'a dreamed they'd put him back together. But people I never thought had the guts went into that cage to save his life – little Mexican jugglers, acrobats, people who didn't owe him a thing."

It is hardly surprising that, among circus acts, tiger training stands foremost, if not alone, in its imperviousness to comedy. "In fifty years," says Bobby Gibbs, "I've seen clowning in just about everything you can do in a circus: high wire, flying acts, cycling, trampoline, teeter board, elephants, horses, bears, lions, alligators. Even something as dangerous as the human cannonball has a funny side. But no matter how they dress it up, there is no such thing as a comedy tiger act."

Even in their cages, tigers pose a formidable menace to anyone ignorant of, or careless about, their lethal temperaments and capabilities. Depending on the design of a cage, a tiger will sometimes be able to extend a forepaw as much as ten or twelve inches through an open feeding slot at floor level. "Because a tiger hunts alone," Bobby Gibbs told me, "every weapon it's got has to be deadly efficient." Each of its retractable claws, for example, is independently articulated, so that, having grabbed its prey, it can drag it in, as if on a conveyor belt, without having to release its grip. "A lion can't do that, because its claws aren't fully retractable and because they all work together. If it grabs you through the cage bars and wants to pull you in, it has to release its grip every time it moves farther along your arm or leg, so you have a chance to escape. If a tiger gets even a thread of your clothing, it can have your arm or leg through the slot in an instant." As he spoke, Bobby grabbed my arm and, with great force, walked the fingers of his right hand from my elbow to my shoulder. "That's how they do it," he said. "You watch out around them tiger cages. One year in Oklahoma I saw a cat hook a seventy-pound dog by the lip and shred him through a four-inch slot in its cage. It'll do the same to you."

As if Wilson's job that night in Dauphin was not difficult enough, two of the female cats, Robin and Seanna, had "come in" that morning and were exhibiting the testiness typical of tigers in heat. The cats' twenty-eight-day fertility cycle corresponds exactly to that of human beings. Like the cycles of women who live together, those of the cats will tend, over time, to align. "When one comes in, they all do," said Wilson. "During the four or five days they're in heat, all they wanta do is make babies. With a male in the ring, they'll go right at it if you give them the chance. Even when they're in their cages, I can always tell if they're in heat, because instead of growling they'll just purr at me. In the ring, of course, they're more interested in the other cats – the females don't like one another at all. And their periods make them snarlier than ever."

In the ongoing imminence of chaos – or of an outbreak of the natural "order" of things – Wilson does his best never to take his eyes off any single cat for more than a few seconds. "I can't watch all of them all the time," he said, "but I have Rick's eyes working for me, too. If I'm not looking, and, say, Seanna starts coming off her seat, Rick'll yell *'Seanna'* and I'll turn to her and put her back up before she gets into trouble." Suddenly Wilson was laughing. "What she's thinking when she comes down is, *Isn't this nice; he ain't lookin at me – I'll just step over there and eat him.*"

Wilson is asked regularly whether his cats have had their claws or teeth removed, or whether they are drugged. "First off," he says, "I'd never destroy a tiger by removing its claws or teeth. How's it going to eat or defend itself? And if you drugged them, you'd never get them to do anything. They sleep sixteen hours a day as it is. The only way to keep 'em in their place is to get their respect – there's no substitute for it, no gimmicks."

"What about the whip?" I asked.

"I never touch them with it. It's just to get their attention. If I whipped them, they'd have had me for lunch years ago."

Wilson's concern for the integrity of his animals extends to their (eminently saleable) carcasses. "I had a tiger die on me last year in St. Paul, Alberta," he told me, "and because tigers are an endangered species, we had to have a couple'a vets certify that it had died. They saw it, and they wanted to skin it out – stuff it and so on. But I wasn't havin any part of that. If we'd been at home we woulda buried it – that's what we do. But we couldn't really do that on the road, and, even if we could have, I didn't know but what somebody might dig it up for the bones or something. So, I phoned up the local funeral home, and told 'em I had a tiger that I wanted to have cremated. The guy didn't say anything for a few seconds; then he said, 'We don't usually do tigers here, sir. We just do humans.'

"I said, 'What's the difference, you're just burning it up? We don't want a funeral or nuthin.' Finally, they agreed to do it."

"Problem was," said Bobby Gibbs, "that before we got it over there, the vet had already pulled out some of the claws and teeth; he told us he had to do an autopsy. I said, 'You don't hafta yank the eye teeth to do an autopsy.' He was gonna keep them. So we phoned the Department of Agriculture, and they put a stop to that. They were gonna prosecute the guy."

Of all the factors affecting Wilson as he put the tigers through their routines that night in Dauphin, the most insidious, the least quantifiable, was an occurrence that, two days earlier, had sent a tremor through the entire North American circus community. The news had reached our own miscellaneous troupe on Saturday afternoon in the windy parking lot of the Keystone Centre in Brandon, where the animal trucks and the mobile homes of the performers were parked in a temporary cluster of the sort that passes for a neighbourhood among circus people on the road. The initial word was that Brian Franzen, son of Wayne Franzen, owner of the respected Franzen Brothers Circus, had been killed working tigers somewhere in North Carolina. Pat Delaney, a Chicago Irishman who ran the concessions for the Great Wallenda Circus, had caught the end of a television report on the incident as he was leaving his hotel room, and had stopped by the animal trailers with the news on his way into the Keystone Centre an hour before the evening performance.

Among circus people, all of whose fates are glimpsed in the fates of all other circus people, the response was a predictable mixture of dismay and calculated refusal to deal too deeply with the implications of the news.

"You can train 'em, but you can't tame 'em," said David Connors, whose own life had taken a fateful turn when his wife, Sissy, had been thrown from her aerial apparatus during a performance in Marquette, Michigan, in 1991, and had landed dead on the floor just metres from where David was standing.

Within minutes, Bobby Gibbs had passed the news of Franzen's death to Rick Robinson, urging him not to tell Wilson, at least until after his performance in a little over an hour. "You never know how he's gonna take something like that," he said. "Same thing could happen to him any time he goes in the ring. You remind a guy of that too often and he can get spooked."

The talk among veterans on the lot was that the younger Franzen had been inexperienced. "I doubt it woulda happened to his dad," shrugged Pat Delaney.

But the tone changed later that night when an Associated Press report divulged that it was not Franzen's son who had been killed but the veteran himself, a man who had spent twenty-three of his fifty years training tigers. He had been killed not in North Carolina but in Broad Top City, Pennsylvania.

Franzen's story was well known. He had quit his job as a high-school teacher in Madison, Wisconsin, in 1973, after watching a circus program on television, and had founded a one-ring tent circus with his brother. "He had a real nice little show," said Bobby Gibbs. "Everybody knew him."

The AP report suggested that the tiger that killed him, a six-year-old, four-hundred-pound Bengal named Lucca, had been confused by a bright new costume Franzen was wearing, and had perhaps not recognized him. But given that a tiger can detect the smell of its trainer a hundred feet away in an arena crowded with sixteen thousand people, it seemed unlikely that Lucca would have failed to recognize Franzen at a distance of six feet in familiar surroundings.

When the show ended that night, and the trucks were being loaded for the jump to Dauphin, I asked Wilson what he thought about the fate of his fellow trainer, and whether it had bothered him to go into the cage with the news so fresh in his mind (it turned out he had been told of Franzen's death minutes before he went on). He was reluctant to disparage a colleague, especially under the circumstances, but volunteered that, where Franzen was concerned, mistakes could have been made. Wilson took a pull on a freshly lit cigarette, exhaled a cubic metre of smoke, and said, "He may have been tired – may not have had his concentration. One thing I know is, you can't turn your back on 'em for long." In front of us on the arena floor, the prop hands, a trio of muscular Texans, laughed and kibitzed as they loaded ring curbs and floodlights into a white ten-ton truck bearing the insignia of the Great Wallenda Circus.

"Did it bother you tonight?" I asked again.

"Not really," he shrugged. "I have to know before I go in there that *I'm* not gonna make mistakes, no matter what's going on. Don't get me wrong, I'm not overconfident. I know how dangerous it is. In fact, if I'm not scared when I go in there, I'm not gonna be alert, and then I *am* gonna make mistakes."

"Every animal guy who ever lived will tell you exactly the same thing," said Bobby Gibbs when we spoke the following morning. "When somebody gets mauled, it's because he screwed up. The high-wire guys say it, too – somebody goes down, he's not concentrating. If Wilson believed that no matter how well he performed there was gonna come a day when, outta the blue, some tiger was gonna take his head off, sooner or later it'd get to him, and he wouldn't go back in. Nobody who hopes to survive is gonna play Russian roulette for very long."

By the time we got to Dauphin, I had seen Wilson perform twenty-two times in thirteen days. But far from growing inured to his efforts, I had grown intrigued to the point that, that night, in the drafty, near-vacant arena, I abandoned my usual seat behind the boards, moved out onto the floor, and crouched by the low metal table on which, two acts later, Jill Gonçalves would do her sword-balancing routine. Wilson urged the cats onto the cage furniture in a reluctant version of their three-level pyramid. As he returned them to their seats I edged forward in the darkness so that I was now within a step of the ring curb, just two or three metres from where Seanna, the big Siberian, sat awaiting her next cue. Several times over the past few days I had wondered where, amidst the numerous forms of courage, you might place that of a guy who of his own volition puts his life on the line daily in the interest of making a living. What arcane equation might connect such activity to the courage required to face disease or torture or political oppression – or, more obscurely, to hold the courage of one's convictions?

"Maybe it's not courage at all," I was told by a psychologist friend. "Maybe it's just exaggerated risk-taking. Then again," he shrugged, "maybe courage isn't courage."

Whatever it is, there is something daunting, even agonizing, but also something deeply poignant, about the notion of a man willing to risk his life so that others will be entertained. "I don't know what it is inside that allows me to do it, when the next guy won't go near it," Wilson says. "But I do know it can run out. I've heard of guys who've done ten thousand performances getting up one morning, looking at the cats, and knowing they're not going back in the ring."

Wilson comes from what he calls a very close family. His parents, however, have never seen him perform. "I've sent them a video," he says, "and they don't like it. They think I should get out of this line of work." Nor have his three brothers seen him in the cage, although his younger sister spent four days with him while he was performing in New Brunswick during the spring of 1996. "She saw me work once," he says, "and after that she

*Wilson Barnes left Fortune, Newfoundland, as a teenager during the mid-1970s to learn the circus's deadliest art, tiger training, in Seagoville, Texas. His daughter, Connie, was with him on tour in northern Canada.*

couldn't even be in the building when I was with the cats. She had to leave."

Back in Dauphin, the band chorded smoothly out of "Arabia Chase" into a precipitous version of "Gallop Go." Rick Robinson, who had been sidling in the shadows, stepped to the cage and tugged back the plywood door at the cat entrance, signalling to the tigers that another night in show business had come to an end. Their entire routine had taken nine minutes. Wilson pointed his bait stick and twirled his whip, snapping the cats from the ring. Experienced show tigers respond to the bait stick not because it carries bait but because it did when they were youngsters learning their routines. "You put a little piece of meat on the end," Wilson told me, "and they go where *it* goes."

Within seconds, only Kismit, an eleven-year-old female, was still in the ring, sitting obstinately on her seat on the opposite side of the cage to the cat exit. Wilson marched to within a metre of her – just out of claw range – and in gestures broad enough to be read in the next town urged her to vamoose. She threw a half-hearted roundhouse at him, then, on cue, rose on her haunches, growled convincingly, and made a series of wild swipes at the tip of the bait stick, which Wilson had extended to a point a foot or so above her brow.

Up came the spotlight on Bill Boren, who was approaching the ring in his patent leather shoes and blue sequined tux. Bill is an enamel-voiced cracker who as a teenager sang for four consecutive weeks on the Ted Mack Amateur Hour in New York City and was present in the radio studio in his home town of Tupelo, Mississippi, when Elvis Presley gave his earliest public performances.

"What seems to be the problem?" Bill asked, as the band relaxed into a low-level vamp.

"I can't get her to go home," shouted Wilson without the benefit of a mike.

"Maybe if you said *please* it'd help," Bill suggested, to which Wilson made him a mock offer of the whip and bait stick.

"No, no, that's *your* job," demurred the ringmaster, cueing Wilson to turn to the cat, lower himself to one knee, and attempt unsuccessfully to "*pleeease*" her into cooperating.

"How about pretty please?"

"*Pretty* please," said Wilson, terminating the cloying exercise with a gesture of the bait stick that sent Kismit loping across the ring to the exit chute.

By the halfway point of the next act – an aerial ballet choreographed to the ringmaster's rendition of "Wind Beneath My Wings" – the tiger cage had been dismantled, the tigers were aboard the well-louvred semi trailer that is their road home, and Wilson was standing in his jeans and T-shirt in the tiny apartment that he has furnished for himself in the front end of the trailer. His lime-green costume was pooled on the chesterfield, and the leg of his black "dress" costume dangled from an overhead shelf where he had tossed it following the performance that afternoon. Out of habit, not thirst, he took a beer from a case on the floor, opened the door a crack, and threw the bottle cap into the parking lot. Outside, it had begun to snow.

He went back into the arena, located Connie, and bought her a Pepsi and a bag of chips to make up for the supper she had missed. Then he bought her a Caramilk bar, her fourth of the day. He sat in the dressing room, inhaling the residue of last winter's hockey, and smoked a cigarette. If there was one thing he did not feel like doing that night it was driving. But if he was to be back in the morning to haul the elephant, he had little choice.

When the show was over he put Connie to bed in the trailer. For a few minutes, he lay in his own bed in a plywood loft above the tigers, at one point hollering at them to keep the noise down.

When it was clear sleep wouldn't come, he got up, started the truck, and sat in the cab with Rick Robinson, each of them sipping a Labatt's Blue. Their love of beer, Rick told me one day, was what had brought them together a couple of years earlier when Rick was working props with another show. "And of course we both love the tigers," he said. "I consider those cats a part of my family."

Wilson took a Kleenex from a box on the cab floor, evacuated his sinuses, and stuffed the tissue into a potato chip bag that, for the past couple of days, he had been using for that purpose. When the heat from the blowers was warm enough to soothe his joints, he released the brakes, slipped the gearbox into low, and ever so gently engaged the clutch.

# 2

On the last morning of April 1997, I drove from my home in the north end of Thunder Bay, Ontario, to the city's south side, where I plugged a meter on Miles Street and entered the thirty-five-hundred-seat Fort William Gardens. The place is not a "garden" in the strictest sense of the word but, rather, a windowless old crypt where, with the possible exception of drain moulds or eavestrough weeds, no living plant has taken root in decades. Nevertheless, it serves with lumpish adequacy as the city's main hockey rink and, once a year, for two days in spring, shelters the visiting Shrine Circus.

This year's version of the event was to open late that afternoon – the first performance in a month-long tour – and as I walked through the lobby on the arena's southeast corner, aging Shriners in flowerpot hats were readying enormous pallets of the sort of merchandise that is revered by circus-going children but that the people who sell it refer to unapologetically as "garbage" or "slum" – glow-in-the-dark jewellery, inflatable animals and hammers, plastic swords and ray-guns.

On the floor of the arena, a trio of well-nourished prop men in blue cotton coveralls mopped ring mats, positioned ring curbs, and adjusted speakers and light standards. Occasionally one of them shot a glance at a dark-complexioned young woman with a vesuvial hairdo who squinted into the rafters as she made exhaustive fractional adjustments to the turnbuckles and ratchets on an overhead rigging to which a few hours hence she would entrust her life. Five adult tigers lounged in their cages along the north boards, and at the opposite end of the arena a pair of slim-hipped trampolinists executed an endless number of bounding dance steps that seemed no less perfect on the first bounce than the fortieth.

I had come to the arena, in effect, to join the circus – and in a middle-aged reprise of the school kid's dream, to run away with it. And my motive was as simple as any kid's: I craved a little risk and excitement, needed to do something different. For the past three months, I had occupied my desk in much the way a dead man occupies a box – without sense, without humour, and, most certainly, without plans. My activities as a writer had been all but swallowed up by a kind of personalized version of the big black smudge that the French call *la grande noirceur*. By mid-April, the sum of my winter's productivity had been a sheaf of desultory promo for an American parks agency, a dreary magazine piece for a dreary magazine, and a couple of abortive book proposals. I had passed numerous mornings asleep at my PowerPC, or moving commas or semicolons from one part of the screen to another, or paper clips across my desk. Or simply staring out the window at Lake Superior – an appreciable alternative to whatever I might have been doing at the best of times, an irresistible attraction during the early months of 1997. I had been, at best, a defective husband, lacklustre dad, and delinquent son and friend. As bad as it was, my wife and kids had remained the warm, bright hope of my existence. Viewed from my "work" room at the top of the house, they were for me what Henry Miller called "the smile at the bottom of the ladder." And their faith in my flagging endeavours had kept me going at a time when other reasons for keeping going had become increasingly hard to identify.

In my lassitude – or more precisely *out* of my lassitude – my thoughts turned one afternoon to an old and reliable interest, and I wondered if, these days, there might yet be in the circus a fresh piece of writing, a magazine article or essay or broadcast documentary. Or at least a few days of enjoyable and educational travel. At one time, my parents had thought nothing of motoring a hundred miles with their kids for the matinee of some trifling tent circus, because we had heard they had a good trapezist or clown – or magician, or elephants, or teeterboard act. Invariably, the reward made the journey seem brief.

As the notion took root, I turned to books and movies, one night going so far as to sit twice through Cecil B. DeMille's *The Greatest Show on Earth*, a film about the Ringling Brothers and Barnum & Bailey circus during the early 1950s. I fantasized lengthier travels, lengthier writing. Yet even as I doped out a proposal for the extraordinary book it would all make, I had difficulty feeling confident about my chances for success in such a venture. I had once inquired about riding a grain freighter through the St. Lawrence Seaway in the interest of writing an article, and had been summarily shut down by a ship owner over considerations about insurance and union regulations and international law. Some part of me assumed there would be equally prohibitive reasons for circuses to stay clear of interlopers or parasites.

But the idea did not go away, and in the ensuing days I experienced the return of a childhood dream in which I swung on a mile-high trapeze, back and forth in immense liberating arcs, eventually releasing myself not to a catcher's hands but to somersaults through space, and then to a long spiralling flight in which I carefully avoided rigging and guy wires as I swept gradually downward into a stadium of cheering fans.

One evening after dinner, my wife, who was well aware not only of my evolving reverie but of my winter-long funk, was glancing through the local newspaper when she said, "Hey, the circus is coming."

"Oh, yeah?" I said. I took the paper and glared at it, roused by the imminence of opportunity but in a curious way resentful that what had been an essentially comfortable little whim would now have to be put to a test. And as I crossed the arena floor on the morning of April 30, the outcome of that test could hardly have been less predictable to me. Whatever hope I had of pursuing my plan depended on the decision of the circus's owner, Enrico "Ricky" Wallenda, whom I had tried unsuccessfully to reach by phone at the Airline Hotel the previous night. The closest I had come was to reach the local Shrine Circus chairman, Art Stephenson, who had promised he would give Rick my message, tell him of my desire for a meeting, the moment he got to town.

From my acquaintanceship with the circus, I knew that Enrico was the grandson of the celebrated Karl Wallenda, who had died in a fall from the high wire in 1978, and whose Great Wallenda troupe had for fifty years until his death been the most famous, daring, and ill-fated circus act in the world. During the heyday of the act, no fewer than six family members had died performing – Rick's uncles, cousins, aunt, grandfather, and stepfather. As a child during the late 1950s, I had seen them perform on the grandstand at the Canadian National Exhibition in Toronto and remembered well the paralysed silence of the crowd as their gangly pyramid, unprotected by safety nets, inched across the sky into a steady breeze off Lake Ontario. I remembered just as well the morbidly fascinating newspaper account of how the human pyramid had collapsed during a show in Detroit on January 30, 1962, leaving two aerialists dead, a third paralysed for life, and a fourth with internal and head injuries. The *Toronto Telegram* had carried preposterous photos of the dead and dying on the floor, the survivors clinging like monkeys to the rigging, and had printed a story a few days later describing how the grieving Karl, whose pelvis had been shattered in the accident, had left his hospital bed, against doctor's orders, to rejoin the troupe as it mounted a scaled-down version of the act just forty-eight hours after the accident.

I knew, too, that Ricky's own estimable career as a high-wire performer had ended eleven months earlier when he fell from his rigging in the tiny town of Arnold's Park on West Okoboji Lake in the northwest corner of Iowa. The crash, which broke his back and powdered the bones in his heels, had (I would soon learn) left him with a severe limp, a significantly altered physique, and a permanent burden of pain.

I did *not* know at the time, but would within hours, that he had recently emerged from a decade of alcoholism; that he had lost his wife and children (and temporarily his mental equilibrium) to divorce in 1993; had lost his brother Mario to AIDS in 1995 and then, within the year, his beloved grandmother, Helen Wallenda, Karl's wife and one-time performing partner, who had done much to raise Rick while the rest of the family was out on tour during the 1950s and '60s.

Perhaps to my advantage as I entered the arena that morning, I was blissfully uninformed about the circus's historic scepticism toward writers or any other strangers who might make it their business to go snooping around a show's back lot and dressing rooms. "If you showed up on Ringlings looking to write a book about them," Pat Delaney told me later, "they'd kick your can to Alaska. If anything's gonna get written about that buncha pinkos, it's gonna get written by their own flunkies."

In the old days, the book-writing stranger often turned out to be a tax inspector looking for evidence of questionable or non-existent bookkeeping, untraceable cash transactions, or the mysterious pay levels of the circus's employees and performers. Or he might have been an undercover cop, looking into grift, or gambling, or bootlegging, or pursuing an out-and-out criminal, a fugitive from the straight life, camouflaged in a world where a man's name was what he said it was, where surnames were irrelevant, and where a drifter could function for weeks or even years under a dub no more elaborate than Hambone or Stubby or Pug.

The despised cousins of the circus, the travelling carnivals, went to significant lengths to protect themselves from the scrutiny of outsiders, an effort that included the invention of a "carny" language, a kind of pig Latin, so elaborate and difficult to penetrate that its mastery took months if not years of practice. The circus, too, had its language, a private idiom that, while perhaps more poetic than carny lingo, focused on fewer words and phrases, many of them still heard on circus lots among veterans of the business. A representative glossary of them would be confided to me within hours of my walking into the Gardens – not because there was any thought that I would need such terminology to get along, but as a foundation block in my circus education. "Your 'donniker' is your shithouse," Pat Delaney would explain with considerable ceremony as we sat in the Fort William Curling Club, a building joined to the Gardens, where we had gone to escape the escalating noise and commotion that invariably precedes a performance. "The kids who sell popcorn, drinks, that sorta stuff, are called 'candy butchers,' and the guy who sells the balloons is a 'rubber' man. A newcomer like yourself is referred to as a 'first-of-May,' because most circuses start touring at about that time of year."

A "larry," he took pains to explain, is any piece of defective or damaged merchandise – say, the candy apple that has begun to turn, or the punctured inflatable toy. "If you're selling the stuff," he said, "and a customer gets abusive or something, you'll hear somebody say, 'Give 'im a larry,' which means give him the defective one, give him the one that's headed for the trash."

Pat was in Thunder Bay and heading out with the troupe partly to do business, but more pointedly out of nostalgia for his childhood, when he had travelled the continent first with the

Cole Brothers Circus and then with King Brothers, for whom his parents handled concessions, just as Pat was now handling them for the Great Wallenda Circus. His interest in this particular route lay in the fact that, as a preschooler during the mid-1940s, he had travelled to Flin Flon with the King show, the farthest north he or any family member had ever been. The eccentrically named mining town, seven hundred kilometres north of Winnipeg, was, in fact, the farthest north any circus ever went in the days before tubeless tires and paved rural highways.

"Oh, Flim Flam is legendary with us," Pat enthused. "Occasionally you'll hear old circus guys swapping lies about all the remote places they've been. Some guy'll have been to Bora Bora, some guy'll have been to some crazy little hillbilly town in Tennessee, another guy'll have taken a boat to Bimini with two elephants and a llama. But the guy who's been to Flin Flon, Manitoba, trumps everybody; he's *been* somewhere, because in the old days Flin Flon was the end of the highway, the end of civilization. Clyde Beatty once told me that the only things beyond Flin Flon were savages and the edge of the earth."

Pat went on to say that, in the old days, the route had been a "power run," with profits to be made just for showing up. "The tent'd be packed with Indians," he said. "You couldn't *get* 'em to stop spending money." Over the years, Pat's original trip had been so mythologized by his mother that he had come to view its recapitulation as an adventure on the order of Amundsen's or Peary's heroic trips into the high Arctic.

"To 'gilly' something," he continued, "is to move it from one place to another, and to 'red-light' something is to get rid of it."

Pat is a bulgy, natty little man, with reptilian eyes, TV-shaped glasses, and a thin white moustache, the ends of which are waxed, rolled, and meticulously curled toward heaven. As we sat there on folding chairs, on the ice-free floor of the curling club, he took one pistachio nut after another from a bag in his jacket pocket, chiselled them open with his bottom teeth, and pried out their meats. "The term you're gonna like," he said as he chewed, "is 'jackpotting,' or 'cutting up jackpots,' which is what they call it when a buncha show people are sitting around bullshitting about their experiences in the circus. As a writer, that's what you wanta get in on, 'cause if you keep your ears open around these people, you're gonna hear some unbelievable stuff. You *are* a writer, aren't you?" he laughed. "You're not a cop or a tax inspector, or something?"

These days, an infiltrator on the circus is less likely to be a cop or tax dick than an animal-rights activist, observing the means and manner of the treatment of the elephants, tigers, and horses. But even at face value a writer is not necessarily a welcome visitor to the circus lot. "Ya never know what he's gonna write," Bobby Gibbs told me later that day. "A couple of years ago the Beatty show let a guy travel with them all up and down the east coast, showed him every courtesy. And when it came time to write his book he turned on them, wrote all sortsa shit about who screwed who, how drunk they got on pay day – just a buncha nonsense that he coulda written about any old suspects, circus or not. He missed the whole point."

When I asked what the point might have been, Bob told me that, as institutions went, the American circus had more to say about the meaning of U.S. culture than did any institution – educational, religious, or governmental. "Think of it as a textbook," he said, and he reeled out a hypothetical chapter index, the themes of which ranged from transportation, business, and nationhood to public taste, athleticism, geography, animal husbandry, and science. "You could teach a kid more about physics and biology on a visit to the circus than you could in a month in the lab," he said. "We're the New World in a nutshell. Frontier society. And besides that, we have humour – we're survivors. Circus people are harder to kill than cockroaches."

He proceeded to tell me that in 1912, Kaiser Wilhelm, realizing that even his foremost engineers and military tacticians had no sense whatever of how to move a modern army quickly across a continent, asked John Ringling if he'd send some of his circus foremen to Berlin to instruct the German military in the logistics of large-scale travel. When Ringling refused, the Kaiser secretly sent engineers to America, where they infiltrated the circus, learning everything there was to know about transporting thousands of people and tons of equipment and animals across all kinds of terrain, in all kinds of weather, while simultaneously feeding and accommodating them, as well as building and dismantling a temporary village for as many as six thousand people, once a day, seven days a week. "Ringlings were feeding fifteen hundred employees in those days," Bob said. "Seven hundred draft horses. Nearly a hundred elephants. They were so far ahead of themselves, their cooks'd be stirring up pancake batter in Biloxi for the next morning's breakfast, before the tent was even down in New Orleans."

It hadn't helped the Kaiser win the war, I was impolite enough to point out.

"If it had been up to circus people, there wouldn't have *been* a war," he shot back. "The circus was taking political boundaries in stride before anybody ever heard of the League of gawdam Nations."

"Where could I find Rick Wallenda?" I had asked a sinewy Shriner a few hours earlier, and had been aimed across the floor in the direction of an unlikely-looking impresario in blue jeans and an outsized black leather jacket. I walked to within a few feet of where he was talking to a group of Shrine officials and, as he glanced up, held out my hand and told him who I was. Before I had so much as aired my full name, he said, "I know who you are, I'm sorry I didn't call, I've been extremely busy and will be for the next couple of days, you're welcome to tag along, please make yourself at home, I look forward to talking to you the first chance I get."

It was that simple, and in the moment of my transformation from supplicant scribbler to rolling writer-in-residence I felt a rush of childlike excitement of the sort that I once felt, say, at bedtime on Christmas Eve, or on the cusp of summer holidays when I would awaken with anticipatory tremors from dreams set in landscapes identical to those I would now be travelling with the Great Wallenda Circus.

Feeling faintly etherized, I located a pay phone in the lobby and called home, disappointed to hear nothing but my own recorded voice. At the instant I started my message, however, my wife picked up the receiver and said, "When do you leave?"

"On Saturday," I told her. "How did you know?"

"I've known all along," she said.

For the better part of the next hour, I wandered the arena doing my best to look purposeful and professional, when in fact I felt gawkish and ungainly, almost totally at a loss as to when to step and when to glide. I chatted briefly with David Perry, the circus chairman of the Khartum Temple, a division of the Shrine that encompasses northwestern Ontario and the province of Manitoba. David is kindly, birdlike man, a retired cartographer, who, like other Shriners, wears a burgundy felt fez but is distinguished from the rest by a beige cotton windbreaker emblazoned with the words Circus Chairman and bearing the vividly embroidered likeness of a Bengal tiger jumping through an equally vivid flame. David joined the Shriners during the mid-1970s with the express intent of working with hospitalized children, and was devastated when, a few months later, Winnipeg's Shrine Hospital was sold for a dollar and closed. "At that point, I thought I'd made a mistake. But my wife persuaded me to stick with it, and today," he said, "my fulfilment is in the circus," which he is happy to reveal generates yearly regional proceeds of $150,000 for the children's hospitals in Montreal and throughout the United States.

When I crossed paths with Rick Wallenda in the alley beneath the stands, he said, "I shoulda mentioned I've got a meeting here at one o'clock with the performers. If you want to be there I'll introduce you to them." Rick was never a tall man, and his broken back and crushed heels have left him not only measurably shorter but with a springless, grinding gait. To watch him walk any distance at all is to know a vicarious discomfort all but palpable in the hips and knee joints and feet. He has wavy brown hair, a lieutenant's moustache, and, from decades of hefting a thirty-five-pound balance pole, husky shoulders and chest. An incipient thickness in his jowls and waist did not exist during his days on the wire. He is well read and spoken, and is both open and philosophic about the pain he has suffered and the pain he may have caused. He is equally philosophic about the preposterous career path that was presented to him, pretty much as a *fait accompli*, from the time he was three or four years old. So commonplace were the risks that daily confronted the family in their work, and the accidents that Rick heard about, read about, and witnessed – accidents that were as intrinsic to the meaning of the family as were the daring and conquests and fame – that, today, he can speak with almost preternatural calm about the deaths and losses, and about the shadow of fatality that for more than half a century has hung inescapably over the family's professional activities. It requires the smallest part of his impressive equanimity to describe, for example, the fall in Ohio, during the 1940s, in which his grandmother caught a guy wire with her leg and rode it to the ground, slicing so severely through the tendons in the back of her knee that it was initially thought her career was over. Or to acknowledge the macabre coincidence that when the Hartford circus fire broke out in 1944 – a calamity that burned 168 people to death, most of them children, and is remembered as the greatest circus tragedy of all – it was the Wallendas who were in the middle of their act, forty feet above the rings.

*Ricky Wallenda, scion of the most famous performing family in the history of the American circus.*

Despite the nonchalance with which he addresses the family's travails, Rick confides that a day does not go by in which he is not "in some way affected" by the deaths and suffering of the past. "I don't agonize over it," he told me one night. "It's just there in the back of my head."

I said, "Specific images?" and he shrugged and said, "Sometimes I'll just be driving down the highway, or something, and suddenly it'll just be there – you know, Detroit, the accident, the deaths."

"Specific images?" I asked again, to which he responded that, where Detroit was concerned, he tended to return to the point at which the pyramid had started to disintegrate. "I've fallen off a wire," he said, "and I can't even imagine what must have been going on in their heads as they realized they were going down. My Aunt Jenny watched her husband die. She was right up there on the pedestal. In fact, a few minutes before they formed the pyramid, she'd offered to take Jana Schepp's place up top. It could have been her. It could have been my mom up top. I think about all that stuff – about Aunt Yetty on the sway-pole. Seventy-five feet up. Did a perfect handstand and then for no apparent reason toppled. . . . I guess if I seem casual, it's just that, like the rest of the family, I've had to put it all in perspective if I'm going to move on and get something done."

Rick's own injuries have forced a considerable change of perspective on at least one important facet of the complicated Wallenda gestalt: namely, their sense that the nightmarish accidents and deaths were not so much "tragedies" as failures, misfires, that, for the honour of the family name and reputation, had to be put right. He claims this attitude belonged more to his grandfather than to the younger generations of Wallendas. Although in 1983, he went to San Juan, Puerto Rico, and, in an effort that could hardly have been all business, successfully recreated the sky walk that had killed the family patriarch five years earlier.

"Right now," he says, "I couldn't put anything right if I wanted to – at least not on the wire. And I don't care. I did it for twenty-five years, and it's not going to hurt me again."

If there is a failure that Rick would like to reverse – although any opportunity to do so is now gone – it is that of his marriage to his former high-wire partner, Debbie Wallenda. "That caused me more pain than all this pain that I carry around from my fall," he told me on at least three occasions during the weeks I spent with the troupe. "Physical pain you can block out – the other you have to live with."

Rick's capability for blocking physical pain is, like his grand-father's, a study in almost incomprehensible forbearance. "You don't survive two five-storey falls onto concrete if you're made out of plastic," says Bobby Gibbs. "And you don't survive what he's been through if you ain't mentally tough."

Rick needed every shred of his physical and mental toughness to get off the ground in Arnold's Park, Iowa, in June 1996, and then to get out of his hospital bed a few weeks later, convinced not just that life was worth living but that it was worth living as a full-time circus producer, in its way a more stressful role even than that of the wire walker.

Six months after the fall, between visits to the operating room, he began this new phase of his career by putting together a medium-sized troupe for a couple of shows near his home in Sarasota, Florida. Then in March, just two months before he came to Thunder Bay, he mounted a sixteen-day spectacle for Pat Delaney, who, beyond his toils as a "garbage" salesman, is the circus chairman for the Shrine Club's Medina Temple in Chicago. In April, Rick produced "spot dates" in Nebraska, Arkansas, and Indiana.

And now he had arrived in Thunder Bay to begin the most difficult tour of his life. His route, a famous old tent-circus itiner-ary through north-central Canada, was at one time travelled by train, then on gravel roads, and is still considered one of the more arduous of North America's many recognized circus tours. For one thing it is long, with jumps as big as eight hundred kilometres. It is also isolated, meaning significant inconvenience and cost should vehicles break down on the stringy network of sometimes icy roads. Gas and food are expensive so far north, and, at any time of year other than high summer, the area can be tryingly cold, especially to performers more accustomed to the Gulf Coast of Florida and Texas than to the frozen muskeg of northern Ontario and Manitoba. On the other hand, the route is impres-sively scenic, taking in thousands of kilometres both of the open prairie, with its long views and wide skies, and of the northern boreal forest, with its rocks and lakes, and its impressive checklist of wildlife.

Beginning in Thunder Bay, on the north shore of Lake Superior, the tour would move west to Dryden, then on to Fort Frances and Kenora, would cross the Manitoba border, moving from forest to farm land, through Selkirk, Portage la Prairie, and Brandon, then north up the west side of Lake Manitoba to the Duck Mountains, into fifteen hundred kilometres of spruce forest as dense as any on earth – Dauphin, Swan River, The Pas, Flin Flon, and Thompson. Finally, it would travel eight hundred kilometres straight south for nine performances in the seventeen-thousand-seat Winnipeg Arena.

The backgrounds of the performers were, in many cases, as exotic as the landscape they would travel. While most of them now lived in the southern United States, they had come originally from Portugal, England, China, Mexico, and Cuba – from central India and from both coasts of Canada. A handful of trapeze flyers and daredevils who would be joining the show for the finale in Winnipeg had come from South Africa, Finland, and Switzerland. As is often the case in contemporary circus, the performers were together as a troupe for this run only, after which they would disperse like starlings – some to their homes in Chicago, Sarasota, or Dallas, others to Miami and Boston and Mexico City, where new engagements and new tours would begin. A few would stick with Ricky for his next date in Lincoln, Nebraska.

One thing that impressed me during the weeks to come was the degree to which circus performers – including those who have not worked together, or even seen one another, in months or even years – remain intricately, durably connected: by profession and spirit, but also by the survivalism and resourcefulness necessitated by their dwindling numbers. The world of the North American circus is one in which the main promoters of the industry, the Shriners, are a largely geriatric organization hastening with the best of intentions into the unknown; in which animal rights activists are (to quote Pat Delaney) "kicking the crap" out of even the most loving and benign of animal acts; and in which television and corporate uniformity have robbed at least one generation of children – a generation of potential circusgoers – of much of their appreciation of all but the most pallid and predictable entertainment. "Good circus expands a kid's imagination," trampolinist Paul Gadicke told me one day as we sat in a coffee shop in Brandon, Manitoba. "It invites a response that television stifles. And yet television is what shapes the kids' expectations for live performance. When I go out there and risk my neck doing a double twisting double, the kid in the audience has no way of differentiating that from what he's seen somebody do in some movie, performed entirely with camera tricks or animation. He can go to the circus and see an absolutely great flying act or acrobat, and say, 'I saw Batman do something way scarier than that.'"

Bobby Gibbs remarked to me one day that I had chosen to do a book on a traditional circus at exactly the right time. "Ten years from now," he predicted, "there ain't gonna be traditional circuses, because there ain't gonna be any animals in them, and circuses since time began have included animals. The activists are squeezin us to death."

More than one member of the Great Wallenda Circus told me there are, today, fewer than a thousand professional circus performers in North America (as compared to, say, a hundred thousand professional musicians), many of them from Europe or Latin America. And yet it is among this tiny, geographically and ethnically diffuse community that the institution still finds what the writer Edward Hoagland calls its "nationhood," its connectedness. "If you stay in it," sword balancer Jill Gonçalves told me, "you eventually meet and work with almost everybody. You may not see them for four or five years, but when you do, you just pick right up where you left off the last time you were on the same show."

Even performers who have never been on the same show, or even met, can find themselves connected. The Redpath and Luna families (the "Flying Redpaths" and former "Flying Lunas") had never worked together until they met in Winnipeg, but they had both, it turned out, worked at one time with the great Flying Gaonas on the Ringling Brothers show. Cyclist Brett Marshall had worked with Bobby Gibbs and Wilson Barnes, both of whom had worked with the ringmaster Bill Boren, who had worked with the Gonçalves family, who had worked with the Lunas, who, years ago in Mexico, had worked with the family of Chata Olvera, whose jobs on the Wallenda circus were to act as straight woman for her husband Paul Gadicke's trampoline act, to perform in the aerial ballet, and to do a ballet and juggling routine while hanging by her hair from the rafters. A few days into the tour, Gadicke and Brett Marshall discovered not only that they had both worked for Ringlings but that, during their respective years on the show, they had inhabited the same tiny living compartment, one of hundreds, on the Ringling accommodation train.

The routes and towns are themselves a kind of mortar or common reference among performers. A number of the performers on the Great Wallenda Circus were veterans of the route we were embarked on and remembered this restaurant, that roadside picnic grounds, this drafty motel. The animal truckers remembered every weigh scale on the highway, as well as a good many of the water faucets, feed outlets, strip joints, and beer stores – whatever was required to get them and their animals through the shivering days and nights. In Dauphin, Bobby Gibbs located the exact elm, with its faded rub scars, where he had anchored an elephant chain six years earlier.

For Rick, the route had more personal reverberations. The Winnipeg Arena had been among the earliest reassembly points for the Great Wallenda troupe after returning from Florida where the family had buried its dead during the winter of 1962. Joe Bauer, a one-time sway-pole performer, had been part of the same Shrine circus that had performed in the building that March, and recalled Karl Wallenda being "as nervous as hell when he came into Winnipeg" for a date that some members of the family had been reluctant to keep.

It meant more to Rick yet that, in 1982, at the Keystone Centre in Brandon, he and his wife had made their first appearance together on the wire. "She'd done individual bits before that," he told me, "but that's where we put her into the pyramid."

One day toward the end of the tour, Rick told me that, as he had been about to leave home in Sarasota a month earlier, he'd asked his prop men to go into the company truck and remove the cumbersome steel rigging that his grandfather had had built when the troupe left Ringling Brothers and formed its own circus in 1947. The tarnished old bones of the act had accompanied the family to Moscow, Berlin, and Tokyo, and had appeared in news photos around the world in 1962. It was the rigging on which Ricky had matriculated during the 1970s and which had been bequeathed to him, on his grandmother's orders, when Karl had gone down in 1978, in San Juan. It was the rigging from which he himself had fallen in Jacksonville in 1988, and then in Arnold's Park. "When we put it in the barn," he said, "it marked the first time since the poles were made, fifty years ago, that the Wallenda Circus had gone anywhere without it. It was definitely the end of something and the beginning of something else, and I've thought about it a lot."

But Rick was not thinking about it at one p.m. on April 30, as he addressed the tour's inaugural meeting in the west stands of the Fort William Gardens. Referring to notes he'd scribbled on the back of an envelope, he informed his cast and crew that he expected a family show free of sexual innuendo (an expectation that would, at best, be half met, considering the decisive brevity of much of the female costuming); that safety came first, and that despite losing a date in Selkirk to the flood, which was by this time making headlines across the continent, no one would lose any pay. He acknowledged that he had never before brought a circus into Canada and had never conducted the sort of old-time road tour that included overnight jumps from one town to the next, as this one did.

What Rick did not acknowledge was that, over the past few days, his planning and expectations for the tour had been unravelling as fast as he could ravel them back into manageability. His sister Rietta, an aerialist, had been scheduled to appear but was incapacitated with an eating disorder and had been unable to leave Florida. The owners of a dog act with whom he had thought he had an agreement to perform had disappeared without tracks. His lighting director, who doubled as the show's main clown, had been held up on the east coast, and now three tigers had been lost to the circus at the border. A replacement troupe of acrobats that included a recent Chinese immigrant was said to be on its way from Las Vegas but had not been heard from in two days and was unlikely to reach Thunder Bay for either of the first day's shows. A program printed a couple of weeks earlier and intended to be sold throughout the tour was looking more and more like the display list for another circus entirely.

There would be additional challenges to come – vile weather, transport breakdown, Shriner grievances – the sort of aggravations more or less expected by a contemporary circus owner on a lengthy tour in remote territory. What's more – as yet unperceived – a rival circus owned by John "Tarzan" Zerbini was making its way slowly across the continent toward Winnipeg, where, for five days at the end of May – the most important five days of the current tour – Zerbini would enact what Rick considered a "personal vendetta" by competing head to head with the Wallenda Circus for the attentions and dollars of flood-tired Manitobans.

But for now, Rick was as mercifully ignorant of Zerbini's agenda as he was of any of the other surprises that awaited him. Even had he known, he was at the moment far too preoccupied to burden himself with added concerns. Most pressingly, he had a show to produce – for a group of Shriners who would be watching and assessing every one of his merits and demerits relative to those of other circus owners who had worked the dates in the past, or who might work them in the future. Competition for the three thousand-odd annual North American Shrine dates is intense among the continent's roughly twenty-five significant circuses, one of which is always eager and ready should the current circus in any way disappoint or annoy the nobles of the local temple. What's more, Rick had sleep deprivation to deal with, as well as ongoing physical pain, not to mention a 2 p.m. interview with a broadcaster from Fox Television, who was preparing a documentary on the glory days of the Great Wallenda troupe and had come north from Los Angeles specifically to get Rick on videotape. It occurred to him almost as an afterthought that the show's aerial ballet, which was to go before the public in just over three hours, was yet to be costumed or choreographed. "Get it worked out as quickly as you can," he told his ballerinas, who had met for the first time at about noon that day.

"Some of you people have a lot more experience than I do on this sort of run," Rick said to the troupe as his meeting concluded. "Needless to say, I'd appreciate any help or advice you can give me along the way. In the meantime, let's be safe. Let's have some fun. Let's make some money."

"If we wanted to make money," hooted a rotund sceptic seated immediately in front of me, "why the hell would we be working in the circus? . . . How ya doin?" he said, turning to me. "I'm Bobby Gibbs. I got the elephant. You the guy who's writing the book?"

"That's the plan," I told him.

"Well, I can help ya," he said. "I've been in the circus fifty years. I'm like horseshit, I'm all over the place. I'll be out on the back lot. Come on out and shoot the crap any time ya want."

# 3

I T WOULD BE impossible to exaggerate the breadth of the appreciation I would develop for Bobby Gibbs over the weeks that followed. He is an unacknowledged artist and genius – not to mention a 370-pound affront to everything that is conformist and predictable and safe. During the time I spent with him, I would hear him called a bullshitter, a bully, a misanthrope, a troublemaker – all true assessments in their incomplete way, but none of which had any effect on me, except perhaps to strengthen the affection I felt for him almost from the minute we met. During our days together, he became not just a friend but a kind of hero, the reverse image of whose "bullshit" and "troublemaking" was his imagination and honesty and rage – his immense curiosity and, by no means least, his determination to make certain I understood not just the artifice of the circus but its terrifying risks and realities. As a response to my ignorance and need, he appointed himself my tutor and interpreter, becoming for me an endlessly expansive, endlessly entertaining reference work on the circus's arcane recesses and past.

In his "Circus Year in Review" for 1996, *Bandwagon* magazine's Fred Pfening referred to Bobby as a man "who loves the circus more than anyone else on the planet." When I located him behind the Fort William Gardens about an hour after we had met, he was manifesting that love by explaining to a trio of disinclined boys that if any of them should level even the mildest insult at an elephant or its trainer, the elephant would remember long after the trainer or the boy had forgotten, and would one day exact a terrible vengeance. "A few months ago," he announced to them, "an elephant of mine picked up my groom, that guy right over there, turned him over, and drove him into the mud half a dozen times. If you were to walk over to that elephant right now, and I gave the command, five minutes later we'd be washin you outta the pavement with a garden hose. *I've seen it happen loadsa times,*" he shouted at the boys' receding backs.

Bob was seated by the rear wheels of his tractor-trailer in an *al fresco* command centre consisting of six bales of hay, an open bag of feed grain, a pitch fork, a manure shovel, and a pair of Safeway grocery bags. The framework of his vinyl-upholstered chair had been reinforced with a thick wrap of duct tape and a liberal caking of the inevitable residue of the elephant business. As I seated myself on a bale of hay, he closed a jar of pickled garlic he'd been eating and drained a litre-sized carton of chocolate milk. "Whole class of kids came over here this morning to see the animals, and not one of 'em could tell me what the word Canada means. Not even the teacher," he said as he wiped his beard on a square of paper towelling. "So I went and looked it up. Ya know what it means?"

I admitted that I did not, and he snarled, "Land of Delusion. You Canadians are always deluding yourselves into believing that the good weather's coming. Tomorrow. Next week. A hundred miles up the highway. I've been coming up here since I was thirteen years old, and not once in all those years have I ever seen anything remotely like good weather. This is a climate for mastodons, not Asian elephants."

Fifty feet away, an aging female elephant was accepting edible honoraria – potatoes, apples, bananas, peanuts, melons – from an evolving gallery of curiosity seekers, many of whom had come earlier in the day and had been sent away by Bobby to bring back food. "If they wanta pet her, they gotta pay her," he said. "She ain't gonna dance if they won't sign her dance card. Besides, every buncha carrots they bring is one less bunch that I hafta cart from the supermarket. C'mon," he said, "I'll introduce ya to her."

As we walked the length of the truck, he explained that the elephant's daily diet included some fifty pounds of grain, up to two hundred of hay, forty gallons of water, plus any amount of fruit or vegetables that came her way. "Right now, she's got a cold," he said, "so I'm stuffin her fulla grapefruits and apples and stuff. This morning John, my groom, went on the bike and brought back a whole big box of overripe kiwis."

Bobby had medicated her the previous evening, he confided, with ten pounds of lemons, thirty pounds of cooking onions, and a kind of grain mash or porridge that included a quart of Canadian Club whiskey, because, as Bob put it, "She don't like the cheap stuff."

We watched as a woman in spike heels and a calf-length leather coat approached the elephant with a loaf of bread, unsure of the etiquette of handing it over, or of how close she could safely get. Before she had had a chance to decide, the nine-thousand-pound celebrity extended her trunk, plucked the loaf from the woman's hand, and, with approximately the effort a human being might expend eating a sesame seed, deposited it in her mouth, where it disappeared without apparent mastication.

"Wow!" smiled the woman. "What's her name?"

"Judy," said Bob. "If ya wanta pet her, give her a good firm pat on the shoulder. Or better still on the ass. She'd rather have it there than on her trunk." He stepped out of earshot and said,

"Five hundred times a day somebody comes up to her and touches her on the trunk, which is the same as you or me being plucked on the nose about forty times an hour by people we don't know." An elephant's trunk, he pointed out, is not just a breathing mechanism like the human nose but an all-purpose lifeline, incorporating arm, hand, and feeding and drinking utensils. "Some people think she drinks *through* it," he said. "It's not a straw. She sucks about five gallons of water into it, then shoots the water into her mouth, or over her back, or wherever she wants it. To compensate for aggravating her, I encourage people to bring her a fruit or vegetable, or I sell them a little cup of seed – they give it to her, so that she associates being touched on the face with good things."

He held out a hand to her, and when she put her trunk into it he drew it forward, gently laying bare the soft pink nostrils in its tip and the retractable anterior "finger," a muscular little mollusk, with which she can do everything from picking up a pea to turning on a water tap, to holding a flag, to removing a key from a lock. "In certain African tribes," Bobby said, "the word for trunk is the same as the word for hand." He gave Judy his thumb and she wrapped her trunk tip around it and hung on. "Once when we were in Cleveland," he said, "a blind guy maybe forty or forty-five came out on the floor with his mother at intermission, and the mother said to me, 'My son would like to touch the elephant – is that all right?' And I said, 'Sure, just take him out there.' And she said, 'He doesn't need me – he'll go on his own.' And this guy walked right out to where Judy was standing and put out his hand and gently started moving it across the side of her face. She don't miss much – she knew right away that something was different about him. She just stood there kinda lookin at him outta one eye, and then she very cautiously brought her trunk up and over and extended that little finger on her trunk, and brought it down so that it touched him lightly just below the eye. She was saying to him, 'I understand – it's your eyes.' There just happened to be a photographer from the Cleveland *Plain*

*Dealer* there, and he snapped a picture of her touching the guy's eye, and it appeared in the paper the next day, and ended up winning a national press award."

In a voice that he might have used to disclose family information of the most sensitive nature, Bobby revealed that, at the age of sixty, Judy herself is now blind. "She's got a bit of sight in one eye," he said. "But you can put a piece of white bread on the ground in front of her, and she won't see it – she'll *get* it, mind you, and put it in her mouth, but only by sensing it with her trunk." Elephants, he pointed out, "see" almost as much with their trunks, which are extraordinarily sensitive, as they do with their eyes. "They're so short-sighted that, in the wilds, they can't see water until they're almost on top of it. But they can sense it at a distance – kinda smell it through changes in their olfactory sensors. When they're moving through the jungle, they'll extend their trunks ahead of them, and they know what's coming without ever having to see it."

As we stood at her shoulder, Judy employed the bottom ten or twelve inches of her trunk in an endless sweeping and sifting of the ground in front of her, curling any loose debris and dirt into a pile, sniffing it for a stray peanut, sunflower seed, or cigarette butt (elephants love tobacco almost as much as they love alcohol), then lifting the pile with the tip of her trunk and tossing it back beneath her legs, before starting over. Occasionally, she slid the trunk into her mouth, apparently well down her throat, or curled it into a saxophone above her brow, tossing her head back as if to enjoy a laugh. "That's the 'trunk up' position," Bob explained. "Elephants are all trained to hold their trunks above their head when they're performing. *Trunk up, Judy!*" he yelled, and, on cue, she heaved her 150-pound snout into the show posture. "Whenever you see an image of an elephant on circus literature or a poster or something, it'll always have its trunk up. Any other way's bad luck."

I eventually learned that the only place the trunk is not depicted in the show position, but rather hanging or curled under, is in visual tributes to deceased elephants or elephant trainers, or in circus cemeteries such as Showman's Rest on Roosevelt Road in Chicago, where a nineteenth-century sculptured elephant stands grieving among the grave markers.

"Because Judy's blind," said Bob, "I don't get after her if she puts her trunk down in the ring. You watch when we do the spins, for instance. She'll set it on the steel swivel, just to locate the thing, before she puts her foot up. Then she'll fling it up. As far as I'm concerned, it's just the complete cat's ass that she's still going out there and doing it. She loves it. You watch her come down the track when we come in. She's still got that bounce in her step."

Bob took an orange from his pocket, prompting Judy, blind or not, to throw her trunk up and open her mouth, so that he could pitch it in. Her mouth, like any elephant's, is toothless except for four massive molars – upper and lower grindstones – set so far back in her jaw that they are invisible except when her mouth is open wide, and even then can be seen only by those who are virtually beneath her trunk. The tongue and interior of the cheeks are bright pink and are fleshy to a degree that suggests some ulterior sensory purpose. "She's got so many folds and pockets in there," said Bob, "she'll take some little piece of hardware you need – say, the clevis pin I use on her chain – and hide it so you'll never find it.

"Feel her ears," he said, and I took a handful of the cool ragged hide, perhaps a centimetre thick, that is the lower edge of her left ear. "That's how ya tell if she's cold. On a cool day like this one, she holds 'em tight to her head and closes up the arteries so that hardly any blood flows into 'em – that way she keeps the heat inside. On a hot day, she opens the arteries, some of them as big as a finger, so that the ear, in effect, becomes a radiator that she fans back and forth to cool the blood before it re-enters her body."

Back at the hay bales, Bob removed a ham and cheese sandwich from a Safeway bag, examined it fondly, and bit it in half. He was wearing red-framed sunglasses, commodious black jeans, and a beige quilted jacket, loosely cut, that fitted him like a tea cosy. Like the elephants he keeps, he is a formidable physical specimen, about six feet tall and, at the bulge, perhaps thirty inches wide. He has a luxurious beard and moustache and a vast, sorrowful face, slightly concave, that is, by turns, noble and kindly and vengeful. Even at their happiest, his eyes are a moody reminder of the exile that is both his banishment from the straight life and his refuge from decades of life on the edge. He is a nasal, Texas tenor, with powerful lungs, so that almost everything he says emerges as if intended to be heard through fog.

Even by the circus's freewheeling standards, Bob is an outsider of notable rank and eccentricity, Falstaffian not just in girth and tastes but in his contempt for authority and injustice and timidity. "With my attitude," he said to me one day half in jest, "about the only creatures I *can* hang out with are elephants and other elephant guys. They're all crazy enough to understand." He is particularly dismissive of political and social niceties, which, more than other targets of his scorn, embody for him the tiresome orthodoxies and attitudes that have kept him on the run for nearly half a century.

He is a self-described Christian and mischief-maker, and a storyteller of such range and persistence that his corpus of autobiographical tales adds up to nothing less than a kind of unholy scripture, a verbal codification of his values, actions, and ghastly sense of humour – all of this more or less befitting a man of distinct biblical presence and complexity. Within an hour of our meeting, he had told me half a dozen extravagant tales, ranging in content from his vain attempts to jettison elephant turds from the deck of an ocean liner in the South Pacific (an exercise that left his groom hanging from the rail above a riot of hungry sharks), to his Homeric battles with cops and border authorities, to his days with the London Palace Circus in Mexico, when he had presented both a bear act – *Señor Roberto con los orsos de Russio* – and a bullwhip and knife-throwing routine that he enacted in the guise of "a big fat Indian" named *Plumo Rojo*, or Rèd Feather. "I used to come in on a huge black and white horse, jump off hollering, and drive a tomahawk forty feet across the ring."

Over the years, Bob has owned sixteen animal acts, although these days it is enough for him to hire out through Clyde Brothers Johnson, and to work their animals for whatever circus happens to be hiring. "The only thing I never owned were tigers," he said. "I don't trust 'em – they're meat eaters, and I'm the biggest piece of meat around."

In Bob's younger days, it was not uncommon for him to travel a hundred thousand miles a year and, he said, "to stir up a hundred thousand piss pots of trouble."

In that respect, little has changed for Bob. Not once in the many hours I spent with him did I see him turn down even the slimmest opportunity to create a little chaos or instability, to get somebody's goat or point up some unacknowledged fallacy, cruelty, or hypocrisy. He took particular delight in goading bureaucrats, "experts," and officials – uptight store clerks and officious restaurant managers (some of whom, albeit, had been rendered uptight or officious by the presence of a yappy, 370-pound Texan in their establishments). Two weeks later, in Dauphin, Manitoba, I watched him trundle into the office of the manager of the local Wal-Mart, in a contrived rage, demanding the phone number of headquarters in Bentonville, Arkansas, so that he could notify Sam Walton (who is, in fact, dead) that he, Bobby Gibbs, had discovered in northern Manitoba a Wal-Mart franchise where the manager was so slack as to allow a line-up of twenty-three people to accumulate at a single checkout counter, while the other seven checkouts remained closed. "Are all Canadians such good cattle," he whined at the bespectacled young man behind the desk, "or is that just here in Dolphin?"

"I've got some girls out sick," grumbled the manager.

"You're gonna have some *customers* out sick in a few minutes if ya don't watch it! I've got three hundred dollars wortha merchandise here, and I'm not gonna wait twenty minutes to pay for it."

The manager, who by this time had risen from his desk, looked at Bob, as if at an escaped gorilla, and said, "Whaddaya expect me to do?"

"I expect ya to get your ass outta this office and open another till. The kid ya got out there's practically in tears."

When the manager had rung up Bob's purchases, he edged up to him, more or less belly to belly, and said, "You're not from around here, are ya?"

"No, I'm not," Bob glared.

"Well, I'll tell ya something," said the young man. "I'll be just as happy if you never come back,"

"By the looka things," Bob guffawed as he walked away, "you'd be just as happy if a lotta your customers never come back!"

Some of Bobby's capers stretched across hours or days, or even weeks. Through nearly a month on tour, for example, he sustained a relentless hectoring of the grand potentate of the Khartum Temple, a big, good-humoured guy named Bob Bridgewater, who travelled with the show and, to his credit, was able to laugh at his antagonist and even, it seemed, to appreciate his bizarre sense of humour. Bobby referred to him to his face as a "blowhard" and a "gas bag," and one evening when the potentate offered Judy a sliver of carrot swiped from a Shrine banquet, hollered at him, with no betrayal of jest, "What kind of a disgracefully pathetic offering is that to bring a gracious old elephant? That's an insult both to her and to me, and don't you ever come around her again with such a gawdam pathetic gift."

"Well, I have some mints, too," stammered the potentate, and he pulled from his pocket five or six wrapped candies, which he held toward Bobby.

"Well, for krissakes, give 'em to *her*, not to me!"

"Should I unwrap them?"

"Of course you should unwrap them – do ya think in nature they eat their candies wrapped?"

All of which, for Bob, was mere play relative to the contempt he could generate for genuine breaches of justice or compassion: for the way, say, in which greedy politicians invariably betrayed the trust that had been placed in them, or unscrupulous circus owners had at one time treated their performers or animals. "Oh, they were brutal," he said to me one afternoon. "Once on the way to Cuba a circus elephant acted up on a ship, wrecked some stuff, kicked a guy around, ended up killing him – they don't know their own strength. And they brought her up on deck and just knocked her into the ocean with this big deck boom, thinking she'd drown. But she didn't; she swam along behind the boat for miles, begging to get back on. Finally, they took mercy on her and shot her."

Nearly every day, Bob would express to me some grievous concern he was harbouring for this "old bugger," that "poor bastard," this pregnant teenager, that young man in Florida who had fallen from the trapeze and broken his neck. On at least two occasions, he described the fury he had felt over recent news that the Baptist hospital in Dallas had refused entry to a Mexican mother and her dying baby, "illegal aliens," because the pair had no health coverage or credit card. "For a few dollars' worth of drugs," he said, "those people, who I'm ashamed to call fellow Christians, could have saved that baby's life. But they chose to let it die." He had written letters to the hospital, the last of them telling the CEO that he hoped his "excuses for that baby's death would sound more convincing on the Judgement Day" than they sounded to Bobby Gibbs.

His empathy extended to all manner of outcasts and margin-dwellers, as well as to dogs and cats – and, in one notable case, to a pathetic, humpless camel that, during the mid-1960s, he had saved from an early grave at an exotic animal sale in Sedgwick,

Kansas. "In those days," he told me, "you could buy a good young circus camel for five thousand dollars. But that was more than I wanted to pay, so I said to the guy runnin the sale, 'Haven't ya got an older one, maybe a little cheaper?' The guy said, 'C'mon out back.' So we went outside, and he said, 'Ya can have that thing there for two thousand dollars,' and he pointed to this . . . well, it was like some mutated, fuzzy-lookin horse with a big fat lip and knobby knees. I said, 'What on God's good earth is it?' He said, 'It's a camel.' I said, 'Damned if it isn't!' Except instead of a hump, all it had was this big awful scar on its back – oh, it was ugly. I said, 'I'll give ya five hundred for it,' and we sawed it off at a thousand. And, I'll tell ya, that camel turned out to be the loveliest, sweetest, most beautiful camel anybody ever saw. Just like somebody's grandmother. Never bit anybody, never kicked, never even hissed. Anything you asked him to do, he always did his best. I named him Sudan after Lawrence of Arabia's camel and had a nice prosthetic hump made for him, like a big falsie, and had a beautiful spangled blanket made to cover it up, and a pretty halter with stones all over it. I took that camel all over North America. He performed in all the big Shrine dates for years – he was a big star. I wouldn't'a traded him for three camels with humps. When he died I buried him on my land in Mission, Texas, with Leroy the Llama and Skippy the Chimp – I loved them, too.

"Gawdammit!" Bob said suddenly. "What time is it? I gotta go to Zellers before the show and exchange a camera I bought yesterday. Have you got a vehicle?"

A functional Polaroid camera was vital to the sometimes lucrative photo sessions Bob conducted with Judy before the circus began, then again at intermission, and again when the show was over. For a fee of six dollars, up to four people at a time could have a Polaroid of themselves taken beside the elephant – a photo, as often as not, grainy and ill-lit, snapped usually by Bob himself, or at times by Brett Marshall, one of the BMX stunt cyclists, who over the years had worked a number of circuses with Bob and

Wilson and through a couple of seasons had shared winter quarters with them at Seagoville, Texas. From Bob's point of view, the profitability of this seeming cash cow was not what it might have been, in that nearly two dollars of each six-dollar take were consumed in film and camera costs, another two went to the local Shriners, and Bob split the remaining two with the Great Wallenda Circus. "I work for a dollar a picture," he grumbled. "And for that I'm supposta supply the equipment, harness the elephant, provide a paid groom to clean up the shit, kiss the customers' asses, be nice to their kids, spread the good news about the Shrine, represent Ricky, and put up with everybody's complaints." The complaints were kept to a modest howl largely because the photos took several minutes to develop, meaning that their owners had generally returned to their seats or moved on to, say, the hamburger or popcorn stands by the time the true value of their photos became apparent. Those who moved from the photo site to the "moonwalk" – an inflatable play enclosure, whose entry price was four dollars a child, for four or five minutes of use – were so stricken by this exorbitant new toll on their funds that they quickly abandoned any qualms over what they'd spent on photography. A few were persistent enough to return, often with photos so hazy that the line of yellowish smudges against the elephant's grey flank were all but unrecognizable as the faces of their children. When the protests came, Bob would take a look at the photos and say, "That one's gonna come up nice – it takes a while. If it doesn't, bring it back later." Only twice on the trip was a buyer cranky enough to demand a refund. "I don't *want* the thing!" a woman told Bob in Brandon. "You can hardly tell it's an elephant, let alone my kids. Give me my money."

Bob occupied the passenger seat of my van as if he had been inflated *in situ* to fill the available space. The ten-minute run to

Zellers covered the first of many miles I would travel with him over the next month, and as we wheeled along May Street and Memorial Avenue, he revealed, among other things, that he read a book a day, that he sent twenty letters a week (I have received as many as four from him in a single delivery), and that, as a personal mission, he had journeyed every inch of the route of the Lewis and Clark expedition sent west to the Pacific from St. Louis by Thomas Jefferson in 1804. He had once, he reported, consumed fifty White Castle hamburgers in a glutton contest in St. Paul, Minnesota. His musical cravings, he allowed, ran to gospel quartets and bandstand tuba, a taste he acquired from the writer and tuba player Daniel Pinkwater, who, for a number of months during the mid-1970s, worked as Bob's ring assistant and groom.

He also revealed that he had been born Robert Eugene Goldberg in 1939 in Cincinnati, where his father, a German Jew, ran a bakery and cake shop. "It wasn't a good time to be Jewish," he said, "So we changed our name when I was just a few months old."

For Bob's fifth birthday, his parents gave him a riding pony. "But a neighbour kid put a stick up its ass, and the pony kicked him in the head and did brain damage," he said. "The parents sued us, and we lost everything. We had to hit the road."

The road led eventually to a farm near Miller, Missouri, where on a fateful day in June 1950, young Bobby, now aged eleven, attended the local Shrine Circus, which that year had been contracted to the Gil Gray Circus from San Angelo, Texas. At a point in the matinee program, a tiny animal trainer named Dolly Jacobs (wife of the famed cat trainer Terrel Jacobs) marched three massive elephants into the building to the strains of "Enter the Gladiators," put them through a brisk routine, and marched them back out. "The hairs on the back of my neck stood right up like a possum," said Bob. "Here was this little lady in perfect control of nearly forty thousand pounds of elephant, and here I was struggling every day to get a buncha numbskulled cows to go into the right stalls and not to kick over the milk bucket. I said to myself, 'That's the life for me.' And I went straight onto the lot after the show and got a job helping with the ponies."

That night, as the circus loaded for Muskogee, Oklahoma, Bob led the last of the ponies onto the truck, but instead of heading home, as he was supposed to, he closed the tailgate behind him from the inside. When the horse grooms opened it the next morning, he came striding down the ramp with the first pony. "When my parents showed up, I told them, 'It ain't no use, because every time you take me, I'm gonna run. I'll never stay home again.' They said, 'Now, wait a minute – you don't have to run. We can work something out. We'll talk to these people.' They loved me very much, but they were broad-minded parents with six kids to feed on a farm that wasn't making much money. They went and talked to Ed Martin, who was in charge of the horses. And when they came back, my dad said, 'You can work summers with the circus, how's that? And you can keep goin to school in the winters.' So I went home with them, and when school ended that year, they drove me out to Colorado to join the show."

During his fourth summer of circus life, Bob met a sweet-tempered, four-ton teenager named Judy. She had come to America from India as a baby during the late 1930s and had learned her routines on the Cole Brothers railroad show. "She was probably trained by Smoky Jones, good friend of mine," said Bob. "Trained half the elephants in America. Used to be on Ringlings. Taught me a lot of what I know about elephants. You'd love talkin to him, except he can't talk no more; he had a stroke – sits there all day in a nursing home in South Carolina."

Judy briefly carried the colours of the combined circuses of George Cardin and Clyde Brothers Johnson, then during the early 1970s became the exclusive property of Clyde Brothers

Johnson in what her registration papers refer to as a "divorce settlement." Bob's relationship with her is not just the longest-lasting but one of the most intense and rewarding of his life. "I've worked lots of elephants," he said. "But me and Judy have been pretty much full-time partners for thirty-five of my forty-seven years on the circus. I reckon we've travelled more'n two million miles together. We've been on trucks, trains, airplanes, ships – been to Hawaii, Trinidad, Alaska, Mexico, fifty states, ten provinces. I'll bet I've shown her to ten million kids."

By this time we had arrived back at the circus lot, and as Bob spoke he walked toward Judy and said, "Isn't she a beautiful elephant? Way down deep, every kid she's ever met remembers her." He turned to me with an ecclesiastical look and explained that, as far as he was concerned, he had been put on earth to take care of Judy, and that he had done his best and she knew it. "In nature elephants are never alone," he said. "They live closely – always rubbin up against one another and massaging, and stuff. So, on a trip like this, where she don't have another elephant, I become her partner, and that's why you'll almost always see me sittin right here with her, watchin her like a mother. I know everything she eats, know what she passes, I check her ears, her mouth, her feet. I know more about her than practically any vet we could call if she got sick. I've had federal vets check her through at the border, and they don't even know whether she's African or Asian, or sometimes even male or female."

Bob cleaned a bit of drainage from an encysted surgical scar, perhaps three inches long, where Judy had had a tumour removed from the side of her face. "Ya know what?" he brightened. "You oughta travel with me and John in the elephant truck when we pull out. You don't even *need* a vehicle." I told him I'd be happy to when we reached Manitoba and headed north, but that I had already hatched a plan to dash home in the van after Fort Frances, so that I could pick up my son, Matt, and take him on the road with us for a couple of weeks. "All the better," said Bobby. "The *two* of ya can ride with us in Manitoba. Here, lemme show ya inside," and he led me up a set of detachable metal steps into the forty-four-foot semi trailer in which he and Judy slept, separated by a wall of three-quarter-inch plywood.

Bob's personal space at the front of the trailer contained a box-shaped bed (permanently unmade), several cupboards and shelves (permanently untidy), and a small colour television, which during my weeks with the circus was more-or-less permanently unplugged. The sole antidote to the elephant smell that permeated every molecule of vapour and solid matter encompassed by these cosiest of quarters was a faded "dusty rose" air freshener that hung by the cupboard, emitting perhaps a nanogram of freshness per gazillion parts of atmosphere per very long period of time. The space was so compact that any item in its extensive accumulation of clothes, papers, books, foodstuffs, and collectibles could conveniently be reached from the bed, which also served as the desk, card table, reading deck, picnic blanket, and chesterfield. One afternoon, during a heavy rain in Winnipeg, I sat with Bob on this all-purpose foundation, our knees tight to the cupboard on the front wall of the trailer, listening reverentially to a tape of The Speers gospel quartet. At the same time (with comparable reverence) we ate a late-afternoon banquet of barbecued chicken, coleslaw, French fries, Pepsi and lemon pie. When we had finished, Bob opened the tiny eye-level gate between his own quarters and Judy's, allowing Judy to put her trunk through to receive the remains of the French fries and coleslaw, as well as half the lemon pie, which she transferred so delicately to her mouth that not a crumb of it reached the bed.

Judy is a vegetarian of such resolute principle that one day in Brandon when my son Matt fed her an Egg McMuffin, she engulfed the thing and appeared to have swallowed it when she reached deep into her throat with her trunk, removed the tiny round of back bacon that is part of every McMuffin sandwich, and flung it aside, seemingly disgusted by a world in which honour among mammals had degenerated to a point where one would cook up and eat another, or, worse yet, serve it without notice to an unsuspecting third party.

There were no bathing facilities or toilet in the trailer, meaning that Bob and his groom, John McCoy, who slept in the truck cab, were more or less dependent on restaurant washrooms and on the dressing-room showers in the arenas where the circus set up. "In summer," John told me, "we take a couple of hundred feet of black hose, fill it, let it sit in the sun for a while till the water's nice and warm, and then shower under it in the back of the truck."

Nor was there any way of heating the trailer, although Judy's quarters were insulated with an inch of styrofoam between the thick inner plywood and the outer steel of the truck trailer. The metabolism of a nine-thousand-pound animal throws sufficient heat to keep the place toasty on a cold day, a truth that would gain considerable pertinence as the circus moved west and then north into the boreal forest. "If it's really cold," Bob told me, "I leave her poop in there overnight, and it helps keep the place warm."

Poop is an appreciable commodity in the life of an elephant handler, inasmuch as a mature pachyderm can produce upwards of two hundred pounds of it a day, in the form of two- or three-pound spheroids, visibly laden with half-digested hay and the undigestible selvage of the animal's diet: banana and orange skins, mango pits, corn cobs, or, on occasion among domesticated elephants, a plastic bread bag, cigarette pack, or French fry container consumed anywhere up to twenty-four hours earlier with its now-metabolized contents. Such prodigious input and output creates an ongoing need, particularly in the cities and towns, to find suitable disposal sites, often in the form of a works department dumpster or municipal garden if one happens to be at hand. John was invariably on the spot to shovel Judy's turds into the wheelbarrow within minutes if not seconds of when they dropped – as they did as many as twenty times a day – and I suspect that at least some of the highly fragrant feces got no further than the first discreet dropping spot behind a rural building or in a neighbouring woods or field.

Judy's quarters, behind Bob's, housed a constantly evolving inventory of hay bales, fruit boxes, and grain bags, as well as a fixed assortment of poop shovels, pitch forks, harnesses, ring props, chains, chairs, a wheelbarrow, and a five-speed black bicycle that Bob unloaded faithfully at every stop but, as far as I could see, never rode. Just inside the door hung an eight-inch-wide yoke made of industrial, reinforced canvas nearly half an inch thick and fitted with brass grommets about the circumference and weight of oarlocks. "Even at Judy's age," Bob told me, "if one of these trucks gets stuck, we can put this on her, and she has the strength to walk it out."

Her worth to her owners was not of course in her strength or pulling power but in her exotic presence and in her recognizability as an enduring symbol of the circus. "She may be old and blind," Bob told me on a number of occasions, "but we could get a hundred and thirty-five thousand dollars for her, no questions asked."

Not that the inherent worth of a live elephant can be meaningfully assessed in cash. It's simply that elephants – whether for circuses, zoos, or safari parks – are exceedingly difficult to come by in North America, and are getting more so as the years pass. "It's getting so bad," Bob told me, "some circuses'll paint a *picture* of an elephant on a truck, just to suggest one in their show." The reason for the shortage is that, during the late 1960s, the Commission on International Trade in Endangered Species designated both African and Asian elephants to be endangered, and outlawed their export from any country in which they occur naturally. Those that were already living in captivity outside their countries of origin – including three hundred or so then in the North American circus – were allowed to remain where they were but could no longer be owned strictly for purposes of entertainment. "From that point on," said Bob, "besides working them in the ring, owners had to use them either to propagate the species or to educate the public about endangered animals."

During the circus's second day in Thunder Bay, I watched Bob, in his role as an educator, receive sixty schoolchildren on the lot behind the Fort William Gardens and provide them with a twenty-minute object-lesson on the wonders of the Asian elephant. He is a compelling natural teacher, able to personalize virtually every trifle of dispensed information and to illustrate any point he chooses to make with graphic, sometimes shocking, anecdotes or analogies.

When a girl of perhaps ten asked about the use of tusks for ivory, Bob struck an august pose by Judy's shoulder and declared, "The elephant is a highly intelligent animal, dear, as sensitive in its own way as any human being. If you want to understand ivory poaching from the elephant's point of view, think about how you'd feel if a buncha crazy old fat guys like me came across this parking lot, grabbed you while your friends ran away, held you down and cut off your jaw because we wanted to make earrings out of a couple of your teeth. And then left you to die. How would you feel?"

"Bad," said the girl.

"You'd feel dead," said Bob. "And that's what happened to elephants. Ivory hunters killed hundreds of thousands of them for the specialized teeth that are their tusks. Nearly wiped them out. Now there are laws protecting them. If you get caught killing an elephant in some countries they cut you to bits and throw you to the hyenas – that's if you're lucky."

A boy said, "Are elephants afraid of mice?" to which Bob answered no, but that leeches and insects occasionally get into their trunks, lodge there, and cause tremendous pain – one reason why elephants will sometimes sleep with their trunks in their mouths. "In Africa," Bob said, "red ants get up in there and are so itchy that the elephant ends up beating its trunk against a tree or a rock until it injures it so badly it dies." He explained that there are hundreds of individual muscles involved in the trunk's movement, that the appendage is marvellously "dextrous," and recalled that one day at a truck stop in Iowa he inadvertently parked Judy and her partners beside a canvas-covered truck loaded with watermelons. "Elephants *love* watermelons," he enthused. "They reached through the side vents in the trailer – see those little windows," he said, pointing to the truck. "They lifted the tarp and brought the melons across one by one with their trunks. By the time I got back, they had thirty of them in there – big party. I beat it outta there fast."

As Bob spoke, Judy arched her back and dropped eight or ten good-sized loaves, provoking astonished laughter from the students. "Didn't you kids ever see an animal go to the bathroom?" Bob protested.

"Not *that* much," said a boy.

A minute later, a torrent of urine, perhaps five gallons of it, gushed from Judy's nether flaps, flooding the pavement and spreading so rapidly that it sent the kids tiptoeing for dry ground.

A boy asked if it is true that elephants never forget, and Bob, who himself has forgotten virtually nothing of nearly fifty years in the circus, told him about an elephant in Bombay that travelled daily with his keeper past a bakery, where every morning the baker gave the elephant a loaf of fresh bread. "One day when the owner was away," Bob said, "the guy who was keeping the bakery thought it would be funny if he gave the elephant a stone instead of a loaf. So he did that, and the elephant took the thing and just kinda looked at the guy outta one eye before he walked away."

Bob paused for effect, waved a cautionary finger, and said, "That elephant didn't see that guy again for more than four years. Then one day when she was walking through the city, she passed him on the street, and she reached out with her trunk, grabbed the guy by the waist, turned him upside down, and slammed him into the street headfirst. Dead. And that story was in the *New York Times* – I've got it in my papers at home."

Two hours later I was sitting in the front row of the arena as Bob paraded Judy in through the building's side doors, up an entrance ramp to what would have been ice level had there been ice, and out through a gate in the boards, onto the concrete floor. "*Now the attraction you've all been waiting for*," bruited Bill Boren as the two appeared, "*Judy, the ponderous pachyderm – under the capable guidance of Colonel Bobby Gibbs. Please welcome Judy the elephant!*"

The kids in the audience of perhaps two thousand raised a desultory cheer at the unlikely sight of Bob and Judy, and the orchestra pumped into the theme from the movie A *League of Their Own.*

Bill sometimes introduced Judy as "a ton of fun." But there was something in her blindness and years, and in Bob's own indisputable ripeness, that suggested, at least to me, something more along the lines of "a ton of melancholy," and I could never watch the act without feeling a pang or two of poignancy over their ages and impairments and enduring valences, not to mention the vague, childlike optimism that they always seemed to exude when they got all dressed up to perform. In the days to come, as they came down the track on their way into the ring, Bob would often gesture to me, seeming to acknowledge with a wink or shrug some obvious pathos in the situation, but, at the same time, reminding me (and perhaps himself) that, dammit, there *was* something fun and defiant and liberating in the campy unreality of it all – in what he and Judy had become, and in their impressive capacity to keep on becoming it.

Bob's performance wardrobe consisted of a pair of black dress trousers with a gold stripe and a 5XL red waiter's jacket trimmed with flairs of gold sequins on the wrists, lapels, and back. "It's hard to get wardrobe if you weigh three hundred and seventy pounds," he told me one day. "All I do is get a jacket from a restaurant supply dealer and get it decorated up. It'd cost a fortune to buy custom-made wardrobe for somebody big as me." He also owned a black waiter's coat and, during the act, affected a clip-on black tie, with a false knot – an accessory that, during photo sessions, he suspended by its plastic fastener from the pocket of his white short-sleeved shirt, where it could plainly be seen for the common ruse it was.

Judy had a somewhat more extensive show wardrobe, consisting of several tasselled headpieces, leather-backed, that she wore strapped onto her forehead, so that they covered much of her brow and the bony plain between her eyes. She had several pairs of front anklets to match her headgear, all of her accoutrements cut and stitched either by a Dallas costuming house or a traditional Amish harness-maker in rural Ohio. Every afternoon, before the matinee, Bob applied a coat of gold-coloured lacquer to her toenails, which are about the size and thickness of hockey pucks, though more lumpish, and which had generally shed most of their colour by the time the evening show was over.

Now, as they came into the floodlights, Bob prompted her immediately onto her "tub," a low, circular, stainless steel table that accommodated all four feet, if barely, and on which she proceeded to circle and then to dance, hopping from her left front and rear feet to her right, throwing the free feet out to the side in a jaunty jig, all the while staring out into the audience as if her thoughts and dance were happening in unconnected universes that just happened to be resident in the same willing body. She jigged first to a tune called "Merry-go-round Broke Down," which has always been played at the conclusion of Warner Brothers cartoons, and then to what Bobby and the band leader Larry Rothbard called "The Hoochy Koochy," a tune that a certain generation might associate with the lyrics "In the town of France, where the ladies wear no . . ." and so on.

She followed with a pinwheeling waltz around the perimeter of the ring, then stopped and, in a series of five-ton manoeuvres, settled first her right hip onto the floor, then her flank, and finally her shoulder and head, as the band played a few bars of Brahms's familiar lullaby.

Almost too soon, she pushed herself back onto her hind-quarters, threw her forelegs up in front of her, and sat as solid and pear-shaped as Buddha.

Unlike tigers, which respond to sight commands, such as the pointing of a bait stick or an arm, elephants, with their greater intelligence, take their cues largely from their handler's voice, and to a lesser degree from the touch of the bull hook, a two-foot hardwood shillelagh, one end of which bears a short blunt hook about the shape of a child's bent finger (the name derives not from any connection to cattle, but from the circus tradition of referring to all elephants, male and female, as "bulls"). The hook is the handler's fundamental tool – his "sceptre," as Bobby sometimes put it – and, in responsible hands, is used, say, to tap the inside of an ankle to get an elephant to dance, or to grasp a harness strap, or encourage trunk posture or general alacrity either in the ring or on the lot (there are stories, of course, about violent handlers and drunken grooms using the hooks to beat their elephants, or, at times, one another). The teaching of the tricks is arduous, and a move such as the hind-leg stand can involve days of repetitious command-giving, as well as a trunkful of medieval apparatus. "To get her to stand up," Bob explained to me, "someone, way back in the 1940s, would have attached ropes to her front legs and run the ropes through a block and tackle overhead. When her trainer gave the command to stand, she would have ignored it at first, because she didn't know any better, and they would have raised her front legs with the ropes. When this had happened a few times over a period of days, she would have heard the command and would have said to herself, 'My, this rope business is getting boring – why don't I just stand up on my own, so that we don't have to bother with the ropes?' And from that point on, she would have done the trick on command."

From her Buddhist sit-down, Judy proceeded into a hind-leg stand of the sort Bobby had described, then into a kind of goose-stepping circling of the ring. Then she placed her left front foot on a foot-high steel spindle that John had produced and began rotating around it, emulating, in ponderous slow motion with her rear feet, the crossover step that a defensive halfback might employ in keeping pace with a receiver coming off the line.

At a point when the audience suspected they had seen all they could justifiably expect from the sweet old maid, she quite delicately lowered her trunk and chin to the ground, driving off her enfeebled back legs, so that her ears flapped outward like Volkswagen doors and her massive back end and belly were propelled ten feet into the air – the equivalent, I imagined, of someone's arthritic 250-pound grandmother springing suddenly into a handstand. And there she perched on her front toes and trunk – two seconds, three seconds, four seconds – in what was certainly the *pièce de résistance* of her repertoire, before dropping again and tossing up her trunk in acknowledgement of the audience's cheers.

Her exit from the ring – her "blow off," to use the language of the trade – was "A *salute, ladies and gentlemen, to the longest undefended border in the world*" (a border so heavily defended against the free passage of elephants, ironically, that many circuses and animal owners have given up battling the red tape and expense that must be confronted to move their animals back and forth between the United States and Canada). Perhaps appropriately, the "salute" had more to do with procedure than proficiency and required only that Judy grasp the centre of a six-foot plastic flag staff placed horizontally in her mouth, so that the stars and stripes were suspended from one side of her jaw, the red maple leaf from the other. The band played the grand march from *Star Wars* as she padded around the ring with the colours, Bobby beside her, smiling and waving, the two of them buoyed at this point to have put another performance behind them.

And then they were gone from the arena, out into the sunlight and the more relaxed contrivances of life on the road.

# 4

THE PLACEMENT OF a circus's acts within its program may seem arbitrary to an audience, but veterans of the business know that, like most of what goes on in a performance, there is almost nothing arbitrary about it. A typical circus will open, for example, with its cat act – partly for the act's sensationalism, but, more practically, so that the time-consuming, and sometimes noisy, installation of the steel cat cage can be accomplished before the show. Such advance-work leaves only the cage's take-down to be camouflaged within a program that, once it starts, is, by show tradition, all but unstoppable.

Elephant acts, such as Judy's, by comparison, require little in the way of props or set-up and, in theory, could be scheduled anytime during the performance. But they are so intimately associated with the storied appeal of the circus – and are so impressive in their own right – that they are generally given honoured placement either at the end of the program or next to the end if the circus has some spectacle or thrill act with which to conclude. For years, Ringling Brothers and Barnum & Bailey, for example, has ended its performances with the Human Cannonball, an act that they are currently presenting as Ariana, the Human Arrow, but which, either way, entails a man or woman, sometimes more than one, slipping feet first into an immense air-powered cannon or catapult and being fired, at huge peril, the length of the arena into a net.

For lack of living artillery, the Great Wallenda Circus concluded with a pair of self-propelled cannonballs, in the form of BMX cyclists who whizzed into the arena as Judy was exiting and shot into a half-pipe ramp, constructed of ten-foot-high concave inclines facing one another across about thirty feet of open floor. Brett Marshall and Doug Pershuta are daredevils in their own right, and, as the band played "Enter the Dragon," they propelled themselves at such speed between the ramps that, as they reached the top of one or the other, they shot a good six or eight feet straight upwards beyond its lip, and, at the height of their wheeled leap, flipped themselves with extraordinary finesse, so that they came down front wheel first onto the ramp, building momentum on the downrun, peddling at top speed across the floor, up the other ramp, and repeating the takeoff, with perhaps minor variations in the flip. Kids in particular revelled in their act, flocked to them personally when the shows ended, and might have been puzzled, if not mortified, to know that each of them was interested in something as hopelessly uncool as the writing of fiction or poetry.

Doug, who lived in Chicago and made his living as a bicycle courier when he was not doing cycling demonstrations at truck rallies, circuses, and so forth, was never very specific in discussing his writing with me. But Brett, who had grown up in Springfield, Massachusetts, described to me in detail one day a story he'd written about an elderly widow who, as he put it, "had been married to this miserly department store owner who had mistreated his employees and, when he died, had bequeathed her the store, which she decided to take a hand in running." Unlike her

*BMX cyclist Brett Marshall with Kim Villeneuve, whom he met on the lot in Brandon, Manitoba – photographed here a year later in Grand Forks, North Dakota.*

husband, the widow was kind to the employees, as well as to a cat that would come down into the store from where it lived on the roof. "One day she went up there," Brett said, "and the roof was covered with all this neat vegetation – completely unexpected. That's how it ends. It's a weird story."

I did not always watch every act in a given performance, but that day in Thunder Bay, after Bobby and Judy's routine, I stood with Wilson Barnes and Connie in the exit ramp and watched the cyclists and then the ringmaster, Bill Boren, who closed each show with an ineffectual little musical contrivance called "Stardust, Spangles and Dreams." It was the sort of piece that might have been written by an ad agency for some sort of trade show or circus promo, and, during the days to come, I would find myself increasingly rankled not just by its glibness but because, in the dark cold arenas of the north, particularly at night, it often seemed to trigger for me some queasy intimation about aloneness and mortality that invariably sent me heavily, instead of happily, into the night.

As the crowd left the building that day, I walked with Wilson and Connie over to where the tigers were lined up in their cages in the passageway beneath the stands. Connie is Wilson's daughter by a former girlfriend who came to the United States from Tahiti and now works in a Dallas nightclub. Connie is black-haired and black-eyed, with a face about the size of a cottonwood leaf, and she was travelling in Canada with no documents other than a hand-scribbled note explaining that she had her mother's permission to be where she was. With his responsibilities for trucking and working the tigers, Wilson was pressed at times to provide the many levels of care that a three-year-old needs, but he was doing what he could, and was getting a fair bit of help, particularly from the itinerant teenage girls who worked the concession stands and who, with their touching profanity and poor tattoos, possessed as great a need to nurture and to belong as Connie did to be nurtured.

We stood for a while admiring the cats, which were entirely apathetic toward us, and to everything else that was going on around them. Writer Edward Hoagland compared the withering, ammonia-like odour around tiger cages to "rye bread spread with Roquefort cheese," a description I would modify only with the words "multiplied by ten." The smell was so pervasive that, one afternoon, after I'd left my van within a couple of metres of the loaded tiger trailer, I was forced to drive with the windows open for an hour or more in order to rid the upholstery of the stink.

Wilson's greatest fear for Connie, he told me, was that some day she would get too close to the tiger cages when he wasn't looking and would get savaged. For that reason, he was constantly instilling in her the greatest possible fear of the beasts that, twice daily, she saw him "playing with," apparently without consequences and to the great appreciation of hundreds, if not thousands, of onlookers. "I keep telling her they'll eat her," he said, "and yet she sees me go into the cage with them, smiling, and come out smiling ten minutes later."

When the arena had emptied, I walked Connie and her dad to their quarters in the tiger truck. Wilson is by no means fastidious about his housekeeping, but his living room is homier than Bob's, containing, for instance, a dark blue velveteen chesterfield that, during the day, is a catch-all for laundry and stray clothing, as well as chip bags and pop bottles, but in the evening becomes a pew from which the twenty-one-inch television can be watched and on which Connie eventually drifts off to sleep. The walls, too, are less stark than Bob's, and feature a striking poster of – what else? – a tiger, looking down on the scene through that benign and hypnotic mask that is perhaps the truest disclosure of the animal's paradoxical identity.

Wilson wears a tiger claw set in a gold bracket on a chain around his neck. It is a nasty-looking thing, greyish and opaque, and about the size of a large guitar pick, except thicker and with a barb. Wilson is quick to point out that it was neither extracted from a live tiger nor pillaged from a dead one, but that it simply fell out of one of his tiger's paws several years back, providing him an opportunity to make a piece of jewellery that he had wanted since he became a tiger trainer during the mid-1970s.

Wilson is a man of relatively few words, but he revealed in the moments before we parted that he had been upset by the animal-rights protest that had taken place in front of the arena earlier in the day. "When those people come up to me," he said, "it disturbs me so much that all I can do is ignore them, because I know if I get into it with them, I'll end up in trouble. They're ignorant," he said. "They know nothing about how I treat my animals, how much I love them, how much exercise they get, what they eat. And the worst of it is, they don't *wanta* know. They make it sound as if I'm the reason there are hardly any tigers left in the wilds – which is just stupid, because these tigers have never *been* in the wilds. We breed them. And people like us will keep *on* breeding them, so that tigers'll *never* be gone no matter what happens in the nature." Wilson reached into his jacket pocket, extracted and lit a cigarette. He exhaled his first pull and said, "Tigers'll be around a hell of a lot longer because of what I do than because of what they do. And they'll be a hell of a lot better treated."

"You oughta tell them that," I said.

"They wouldn't wanta hear it if I did."

As we talked, Bobby Gibbs came alongside the trailer and intoned that the trouble with "these animal-rights people" was that they were picking on the wrong guys. "Did you know," he said, "that, in labs right here in North America, scientists are keeping monkeys alive with their brains exposed and with electrodes implanted in their heads? Or that they're giving nuclear radiation to dogs to see what it does to their sex organs? Or that at these newfangled chicken factories, the last thing they do to the chicken before wringing its neck is break off its beak and put Krazy Glue up its ass, so it won't hurt the other chickens or contaminate the meat when they tear its head off? Half the seafaring countries in the world are catching dolphins in their tuna nets and letting them die there – the Japanese and Icelanders are still murdering whales! These are some of the most intelligent animals on the planet! I could give ya a hundred examples of the horrible stuff that's goin on. And here some snotty-nose teenager comes up to me on the lot, and I'm supposed to break down and repent because I've got a dear old elephant that, by the standards of the animal world, gets better food than you or I do, gets better medical care than ninety percent of the people in America, and is happier in the gawdam ring than she is anywhere on earth. I ain't like Wilson," he said. "I'll challenge these people anywhere, anytime. I can spot 'em a hundred feet away. They come up to ya all friendly, asking the elephant's name, can they pet her? can they feed her? and then finally the questions they've been pro-grammed like little robots to ask: can they see where she sleeps? what does she eat? does she always have to wear that chain? When they ask that, I tell 'em, 'She has to wear it if ya don't want her walking down the street crushing cars and tearing up every damn green thing in sight, including trees. That chain,' I tell 'em, 'is no more uncomfortable for her than those boots you're wearing are for you.' Then I tell 'em to get lost or I'll have the elephant catch them and make love to them."

When I called in at the Fort William Gardens the following morning at about ten o'clock, the animal and prop trucks were gone, but three or four mobile homes belonging to the performers were still on the lot. As I stepped from my vehicle, I spotted Paul Gadicke and Chata Olvera sitting in a neighbouring schoolyard, sharing a bolus cup of Tim Horton coffee. They had arranged to make the three-hour drive to Dryden with Brett Marshall, but Brett had been up late and was still asleep in the boxy fortification in which he lives, on the back of his five-ton truck. "Why don't you drive with me?" I offered, and twenty minutes later we were headed out Highway 102, which meets the Trans-Canada thirty kilometres to the west. For a stretch outside of Thunder Bay, the 102 parallels the mosquito-ridden, swamp-sodden mudway known as the Old Dawson Road, blazed by surveyors and axemen in 1871 when the new Dominion of Canada commissioned a road to link Prince Arthur's Landing (now part of Thunder Bay) in the east with Manitoba's Red River Settlement (now Winnipeg) in the west.

For Paul and Chata, the tour through northern Canada was considerably more than just a series of performances and a pile of take-home pay. It was a homecoming for Paul, who was born and raised in Vancouver and still carries Canadian citizenship. Until this tour, however, he had never made a circus appearance in his own country. For Chata, it was a first opportunity to see Canada's heartland. And as we wheeled through the spruce forests of northwestern Ontario, she was as keen to spot a bear, wolf, or moose as the average Canadian might be to see a parrot, iguana, or spoonbill in the Mexican hills. They had taken the gig, in part, as a kind of busman's holiday that would permit them to visit Paul's parents in Vancouver when the job ended a month hence. The only hitch was that they had flown instead of driving from Mexico City, which left them dependent on other people's vehicles to get around and to lug the heavy trampoline on which Paul performed. At the moment, the thing was somewhere out on the highway, squeezed into the prop truck with a more or less random muddle of sound equipment, light standards, ring mats, ring curbs, and wiring.

Despite the cosmopolitan origins of many of the performers on the tour, Paul and Chata were the only members of the troupe who did not live permanently in the United States – preferring Mexico, as Paul explained, because costs were low, circus opportunities extensive (there are four hundred circuses in Mexico, roughly fifteen times what there are in the U.S. and Canada combined), and because it allowed Chata to be close to her sister Flor, who led a semi-invalid existence in an apartment in Mexico City. As we approached the tiny community of Upsula, Chata described how, on a summer night in 1983, when she was twenty-four years old, she had received a phone call informing her that Flor had taken a thirty-foot fall while performing her aerial act in Munich, and was in hospital in the German capital, in a deep coma. "*Fue un numero nuevo . . .*" she called from the back seat, above the hum of the road, while Paul, who was in the passenger seat, kept his head cocked toward her, providing simultaneous English translation. "It was a new act," he said. "She dove off a platform with ropes attached to her ankles – she was supposed to get jerked to a halt just a few feet above the floor. But the straps had made her feet sore, so she slid them up a little on her legs, without taking into account that her ankles were ever-so-slightly wider a few inches up."

The result was that, instead of catching her when she hit the end of the ropes, the marginally expanded ankle straps allowed her feet to shoot through, and she slammed into the floor at unimpeded speed.

Within hours, Chata, who had been performing in Mexico City, had gathered every peso at her disposal and was on a flight to Munich, where for the next six weeks she spent twenty-four hours a day by the bed of her unconscious sister. When Flor regained consciousness, Paul reported, Chata spent eleven or twelve months with her, eighteen hours a day, watching the German physiotherapists who came for an hour or so each morning, then repeating what they'd done, hour after hour.

"*Tuve que enseñarle de nuevo a andar*," Chata called from the back seat. "She taught her how to walk again, how to eat, how to dress – how to brush her teeth, her hair, everything," said Paul.

Chata's circus pedigree was as long as anybody's on the Great Wallenda Circus. Her father had been a star on the "Washington" trapeze, able to perch on his head on the swinging bar without hanging on, while he posed and played his ukulele. Her sister America was the first female flyer in Mexico to do a successful triple somersault, while Flor was the first to do the double somersault in the layout position. Her nephew, Raul Jiminez, has, for nearly two decades, been considered the finest flyer in Europe, having "thrown" more than ten thousand triples without a miss, and her Italian-born brother-in-law, David Larible, is the best-known clown not only at Ringling Brothers and Barnum & Bailey but possibly in the world.

But of all these, Chata wanted me to understand, it was Flor who had been her mentor and inspiration. "*Desde que era niña me habían animado a volar*: From the time I was little, I'd been encouraged to be a flyer like my sisters. But I never liked the somersaults.

Flor wasn't bothered by them. She could do anything. Nothing scared her. She'd say to me, 'You've gotta do *something!*' Then one day, when she was seventeen and I was fifteen, she told me about this act she'd heard of – doing ballet while you hung by your hair. She'd tried it, but didn't feel comfortable with it. A few days later, they twisted up my hair, knotted it into a ring and attached me to a hook. And up I went. That was the beginning of the rest of my life."

The hair-hang is one of the strangest and, in its curious way, most affecting of acts. I had watched Chata do it during two of the four performances in Thunder Bay but had been so struck by its peculiarity that I had absorbed it not so much as the tidy little cameo of compressed action that it is, but as a kind of radical sample of so much of what is rare and unexpected and precarious about circus life. My first response was one of gaping surprise that such an act even existed, and I had laughed, not sighed, when the flying ballerina was swept into mid-air on a cable that seemed to rise straight out of the north pole of her cranium. She had swooped, she had posed, she had juggled – first rings, then clubs, then torches; she had spun like an egg-beater. But the part of her act that had most galvanized my attention was the endearing finesse with which she positioned her legs, the one bent at the knee and thrust forward, the other straight and thrust back and in constant motion to keep a juggler's ring spinning at the ankle, so that, seen at a distance, she resembled a sequinned tadpole or sperm swimming frantically for the stars.

Paul and Chata are a living rave to the principles of polar attraction. Where she is swarthy, dark-eyed, Latin, he is pink and Nordic, with hair the colour of Vencat curry powder. More significantly, where he grew up amid the fresh air and snow of the Canadian coastal range, living in an affluent suburban home, she was raised in a circus tent, in one of the largest, poorest, and most polluted cities in the world. But the circus makes such matches, and during the weeks I was with Paul and Chata they went

around for the most part like mutually adoring teenagers, cud-
dling and holding hands and exchanging meaningful glances and
grins. One night in northern Manitoba, unable to get a room,
they slept curled up in the prop truck, on a pile of folded ring
mats. Chata described their meeting in 1991 as "*un amor grande*"
– a Big Love that, between 1991 and 1994, when they got
married in Las Vegas, cost them more than thirty thousand
dollars in air fares and long-distance calls. "The amazing thing,"
Paul said, "was that, at first, I spoke no Spanish, and she spoke
no English. We'd write long unreadable letters to one another,
because who are you going to get to translate your love letters?
But I worked on my Spanish, and it wasn't long before I could
write her in a language she understood."

In the years prior to the *amor grande*, Paul had been a member
of Canada's national freestyle ski team – freestyle being a sport in
which daredevils on stubby skis shoot down an incline and off a
ramp into multiple mid-air somersaults and twists. The sport is
perilous, and Paul can name a half-dozen of his contemporaries
who, in perfecting or performing their chops, crashed onto the
hillside and, as he puts it, "snapped their necks or spines." In
1981, he injured his knee so severely that for months he was
unable to train, falling behind to the point that, when he *was* able
to get back on skis, he had lost his taste for the intensity of international competition and for the niggardly financial support
available to the sport in the days before it was incorporated into
the winter Olympics. "What I did instead," he told me, "was build
myself a huge steel and aluminum ramp. I covered it with plastic
snow – a sort of bristly carpet that you can ski on – and got myself
an airbag to land in. And for the next eight years, a few friends
and I travelled the continent, skiing at fairs, amusement parks,
mall openings, anywhere we could get the jobs."

Paul acknowledged that, in almost a decade of mall openings
and rural fairs, he never imagined that his one-time winter amusement would eventually take him not just to the circus – "at age

thirty, I'd been to the circus exactly once in my life" – but to what some would consider the pinnacle of the circus world.

But that is what happened.

In late 1989, a Las Vegas show agent sent a tape of the skiers to Ringling Brothers and Barnum & Bailey in Sarasota, Florida. "Ringlings always carries a novelty or two," said Paul, "and I guess we qualified – the ramp alone was an attraction." The inevitable call came, and a few months later the four skiers from British Columbia began a two-year contract with the Greatest Show on Earth.

"I don't think I really appreciated what had happened as much as I might have," Paul said as we sat in the Chinese restaurant in Ignace, about a hundred kilometres east of Dryden, scarfing down snow peas and fried shrimp. "Because it had come so easily for us, it was difficult to realize that some people spent their entire lives trying to get there."

Paul was emphatic in pointing out that Ringlings was not the sort of company everyone was cut out to work for. Indeed, during the weeks I spent with the Great Wallenda Circus, I would hear as many opinions of "Big Bertha" or "The Big One," as Ringlings is called, as there were people on the show who had opinions to offer: the pressure to conform was rampant, the sleeping train cockroach infested, the show the finest in the world. I would hear the company described as "conformists," "tightwads," and "commie fags" – and, again, "the finest in the world." Brett Marshall told me that his pay at Ringlings was exactly a quarter of the two thousand dollars a week he was making on the Great Wallenda Circus. However, what really stuck in his craw after four or five years away from the show was that Ringlings had tried (unsuccessfully) to get him to cut the long brown tresses that, as he put it, were "one of his best links" with kids – indisputably the most significant part of his audience.

"I call them McRinglings," said Bobby Gibbs. "I couldn't work for them. And they wouldn't want a shit disturber like me around,

*Paul Gadicke and Chata Olvera – "all the way from Mexico City," as ring-master Bill Boren liked to say.*

either." Bobby estimated that they paid their chorus girls perhaps three hundred dollars a week. "I'd be surprised if most of their clowns get even that much," said Ricky Wallenda, whose grand-father and his troupe had come to Ringlings as underpaid stars in 1928, and had realized too late that their combined salary of $350 a week was less than half what John Ringling was paying several of his individual performers. Typically, the Wallendas were housed with sixty-three others, some of them rowdies and drunks, in a single circus sleeping car.

"Like everybody else," Paul said, "I didn't think much of the accommodations. And the pay wasn't great, and you did what they said – I'd ski once down my ramp and head for the train. On the other hand, for two whole years, I never had to worry about the hassles of getting new contracts; never had to worry about travel – it was just get on the train and they'll feed ya and take ya where you're going. In those two years, I must've seen every state and city in the U.S. And of course the big thing is that, from that point forward, you have on your CV that you worked on the Ringling show. No matter how many cynics are out there, there isn't anybody in the circus world whose eye doesn't stop at the word Ringling when they spot it on your list of work credits."

When Paul's contract ran out at the end of the 1991 season, he took a three-month engagement with Mexico's famous Atayde (*a-ty-dee*) Circus. And that is where, within days of arriving, he met the bright-eyed sprite with whom he was now careering across northern Ontario in a green Dodge Caravan with a dent in the passenger-side door.

Somewhere west of Ignace, we stopped at a picnic grounds by a lake on the south side of the highway, and walked out along the frozen shore to stretch our limbs. "How much do you think it'd cost to buy a set of moose antlers?" asked Paul, explaining that the owner of a circus he and Chata had worked for in Mexico City would pay whatever was required to have a set in his living room.

I told him I'd never heard of anybody selling any, but that I'd often seen a grisly rack in the garage at my late father-in-law's in The Pas, Manitoba, where the circus would be performing in a couple of weeks. "We should look into it," I said without conviction. Paul told me Mexicans were fascinated by the big mammals of the north, and, on cue, a dozy-looking cow moose, clearly from Central Casting, appeared in a clearing along the shore, poking around disconsolately for a bit of fresh browse on the still-frozen ground. Chata gabbled excitedly, but at the moment she bolted for her camera, the moose looked up and loped into the woods.

A minute later, Paul bent over and gripped a good-sized balsam root that was protruding from the soil and eased himself into a flawless handstand – back arched, legs together, feet pointed. He was perhaps the best all-around athlete on the show, and certainly one of the gutsiest (at the age of thirty-five he taught himself to dive from an eighty-foot tower into eight feet of water). And he was a capable slapstick comedian. One of the more touching moments during my weeks with the show came a week later in Brandon, Manitoba, where a dozen or more mentally handi-capped men and women were seated mostly in wheelchairs along the edge of the arena floor, within ten or twelve feet of where Paul and Chata were to do the trampoline act Paul had turned to when he tired of lugging his ski show back and forth across the conti-nent. One woman, seated four feet in front of me, had shown no interest whatever in the tigers, acrobats, or aerialists, preferring to pick at the zipper of her jacket, or just stare into space. But a minute or so into the trampoline act, something about the move-ment or the brightness of the costumes caught her eye. She straightened in her chair and pushed her face forward, squinting and puzzling – at length raising a spectral finger and aiming it ever so slowly at Paul, who was by this time bounding halfway to the rafters. She laughed in sputtery little bursts, single at first, then in volleys, one after another – aha-aha-aha . . . aha-aha . . .

aha-aha-aha – on and on, continuing more or less to follow the act with her finger, until it ended and she was left in disarray, fussing and waving long after Paul and Chata had left the ring.

While I would not have admitted it around Paul, I have never been even remotely enthusiastic about trampolines, associating them perhaps with the tedium of high school gym class. The next day in Dryden, however, I paid particular attention to the act the two had developed, and for which they were now dressed in blue spandex suits, the backs of which bore large silver maple leaves. Paul believed that his recognizability as a Canadian in Mexico afforded their act a highly desirable international cachet. The pair had recently pumped four thousand dollars into new duds, stitched for them by an aunt of Chata who makes wardrobe for most of the major circuses in Mexico. It seemed a gesture of the most endearing and intimate affection that Paul had personally cut and sewed Chata's itsy bitsy performance bikinis – the itsiest in the show – and then spent a hundred hours stitching on one plastic sequin after another. Part of the act is, in fact, a paradigm of their life together – they dance, they kibitz, they flirt – while at other times she plays straight-pin to his pratfalling buffoon.

But while she plays to him, he plays largely to the audience, promising, with his gestures, miracles of athleticism that, at the moment of truth, go undelivered, because he has fallen on his face . . . or over the edge of the trampoline . . . or pranged his crotch into the elastics that hold the jumping surface in place. Of all his tricks, audiences responded best to one introduced as "*The highest back flip in history*" – in which he bounced three, four, five, six times, until he was perhaps twenty feet in the air. But as he came off the tramp on his sixth or seventh bounce, he cranked himself suddenly into a back somersault, transferring his immense upward thrust into such explosive centrifugal force that his shoes, a pair of soft white oxfords, loosely fastened, were catapulted from his feet quite literally at a hundred miles an hour, sixty, eighty, a hundred feet straight up, leaving his audience confused at first as to exactly what had happened, then laughing aloud and, in some cases, talking aloud about how on earth he had done it. The jewel of his act is a double twisting double in the layout position, and he blows it all off with a dozen rapid-action free flips – the human propeller – followed by a dozen front flips with a half twist, leaving his audience dizzy, himself not, as he leaps from the trampoline, slams his rhinestone fedora on his head, and then doffs it as he joins Chata in an exhausted bow to the crowd.

He told me as we approached Dryden that he hopes to perform till he is seventy-five years old, admitting that, at age thirty-eight, he has lost some of his athletic capabilities. However, he feels he has made up for the loss in improved rapport with the audience – in his capability, as he put it, "to tell a story without words."

"But I'm still learning," he said, adding that at times he felt inspired by his act. "Despite what they say about old dogs and new tricks, I learned the whole thing when I was thirty-six years old. And I'm still improving it where I can. The day I think it's perfect is the day I'll quit. Then it's boring." In the meantime, he explained, he talked about the act with everybody who might be able to give him some advice. "Even the guy who carts away the elephant poop can generally give ya some sort of perspective on what you're doing."

When we arrived in Dryden at about 2 p.m., the guy who carts away the elephant poop, John McCoy, was seated in a plastic lawn chair by Judy's trailer, drinking a two-litre carton of commercial iced tea.

"Where's Bobby?" I asked when we had said hello.

"He's on the phone in the building, looking for hay. Then he's taking a shower."

"Where does he get hay?" I asked.

"Anywhere he can. It ain't easy up here."

John explained that, at times, the hay situation got so bad – "in the mountains and places" – that Bob would get the ringmaster to ask the audience if anybody had any for sale. "Sometimes in the summer, we'll just stop on the highway and throw in a buncha bales from where they've been cutting along the right-of-way."

He said that when the supply of meat for the tigers ran low, Bobby or Wilson would often visit a slaughterhouse and pick up whatever was "dead and down," which is to say that it had died in the barn or field, as opposed to the slaughterhouse, and was unfit for human consumption. "They love cow lungs and stomachs," he told me, "except the lungs give 'em gas like ya wouldn't believe."

As we spoke, Judy was stretched out on her side on the boulevard, her stomach rising like a chest-high granite boulder on which half a dozen children might have played. I had spent the better part of three days in her presence, and still found myself marvelling at her mass. The prop boss Dave Connors had told me that, during the 1920s, a group of his ancestors had had a seven-piece orchestra that rode in circus parades on a single elephant's back.

In the outdoors, Judy slept almost exclusively on her side, as elephants do in nature. These days, unfortunately, she was spending every night in the trailer, where she slept standing up. If she was cold or restless, she would shift her weight in a slow, easy rhythm, hour after hour, so that the whole truck would rock like a boat at sea. For the most part, she had rocked, not slept, the previous night, and now she was making up for it.

A family of five pulled up in a car, emerged onto the boulevard, and advanced on Judy as if on a beachhead of thousand-dollar bills. John was immediately on his feet, imploring them with arm-waving and strained whispers to stay back and to allow her to snooze. The father came round to where we were talking and said, "We just wanta look at her – can we feed her?"

"I want her to get some sleep," said John. "Why dontcha come later – maybe bring some carrots, or something?" John has a brown beard, a reddish nose, and an ambiguous, liquid gaze. His permanently damaged lower back is the legacy of an encounter with an enraged circus elephant that, at some point over the past few months, had picked him up and slammed him onto the ground – an episode that he was decidedly reluctant to talk about. Like most animal grooms, he wore a khaki shirt and pants, in his case complemented by a peaked hat, bearing the symbol of an Arizona Indian reservation, and a gold-coloured San Francisco 49ers jacket. He is thirty-nine years old, and, until the spring of 1995, was the executive chef at the Radisson Hotel in Bismarck, North Dakota – a job he left because, as he put it, "Circus Gatti came to town and put an ad in the paper, and Bismarck was gettin boring." He had cooked, he said, in a variety of resorts and hotels. I remarked that it was quite a shift to have moved from gourmet food for hotel patrons to hay bales and elephant dung.

"Not that big," he said solemnly.

Bobby's twofold lament for John was that he enjoyed his beer too much and that he was unable to afford the sort of insurance that would have allowed him to deal with the plum-sized fibroid growth that disfigured his left cheek an inch or so below the eye. "It's the same thing the Elephant Man had," Bobby told me one day, with no apparent irony.

In the course of our conversation, John told me that elephants, for all their talents, cannot jump, and that a fall of even ten or twelve inches will shatter the bones in their legs. Nor can they sleep prostrate for more than four hours, because the weight of their intestines will collapse their lungs. "Elephants aren't half as tough as some people think," he said, looking askance at me to see if I was buying it. "The hide's three inches thick on her ass, just an inch or so other places, but it's so sensitive she can feel a mosquito anywhere on her body."

John's most compelling insights into Judy's anatomy concerned her teeth and tongue, the latter an instrument that, unlike the tongues of most mammals, is attached at both ends so that she cannot extend it to lick or to pick up food. In Judy's lifetime, he explained, she would have six sets of teeth, and there was always a new set ready to replace those that were "busted or worn down." An elephant, he said, will sometimes remove a wasted tooth whole with its trunk, or swallow it in fragments that are eliminated with its dung.

I asked John if he had ambitions to be a trainer or handler, and he shot back, "I'm already a handler."

"I meant, did you want to show her in the ring?" I said. "Maybe you can now."

"I could if I had to," he shrugged. Bobby had told me that, at first, John was so shy he'd been reluctant to go into the ring, even to remove the tub or bring in the spindle, but that he had developed a recent affection for the spotlight and, these days, would sometimes enter the ring fifteen or twenty seconds before his services were required.

I asked if he watched the other acts, and he said no, that he was bored by them. "Well, not really bored," he amended. "It's just that all the circuses do basically the same acts, except by different people. Well, that's not quite true," he said. "Sometimes you see a new act; I like the magic acts best." Which, it turned out, was not entirely true either. "I like the high wire best," he said, allowing that he was afraid of heights, which had sharpened his fascination for it. "The trouble with Canada," he said, "is that all the arenas are low, so you can't fit any high stuff into them."

I pointed out that Chata's hair hang and Liliana Luna's performance on the rings were both "high stuff," and that, according to Bob, three or four aerial acts were being added for the finale in Winnipeg.

"Bob," he said sonorously, "is extremely pissed off" – the explanation being that the elephant truck had been held up for hours at the weigh scale outside Thunder Bay the previous night. "He'll tell ya about it."

The prospect of a world-champion agitator like Bob being extremely pissed off was inspiring. But when he came around the corner of the trailer about ten minutes later, dewy from the shower, he seemed anything *but* pissed off. By this time Judy was on her feet, and the family of five had returned with a supply of cabbages that Judy was popping like speed balls, pausing every so often to grind them into coleslaw.

"*Ladies and Gentlemen,*" shouted Bobby from the top of the steps that led to his quarters. "*Allow me to demonstrate a true circus act, the best you'll see with the Wallenda Circus. A three-hundred-and-seventy-pound man is about to pass through a thirteen-inch door. Please hold your applause!*" At that he backed up to the door, which was less than half his width, and, with a flourish, thrust one leg back over the threshold into the trailer. "That's the first part!" he called, proceeding to work the other leg through, followed by his wriggling hips and stomach, and finally his shoulders and arms, the latter raised in a kind of steeple above his head.

What is not commonly perceived about the circus is that actual performance – the six or seven minutes that an act spends in the ring – is the smallest and most orderly part of a circus performer's life, and that when a performer or animal trainer thinks of life on the road, he thinks less about those six minutes (to which he has already committed hundreds, if not thousands, of hours of preparation) than he does about itinerary, vehicle maintenance, finances, domesticity, feed and care of the animals, child-rearing, home schooling – the long hours on the lot and in the trailer.

On a day off such as this one, the families tended to stay pretty much to themselves, do their grocery shopping, catch up on chores, confer with agents and banks – essentially attend to all the little business and family concerns that had been neglected during the days of driving and performance.

The single performers had time on their hands, so that, late that afternoon, I had a chance to talk at length with Chunyan Ho, a strapping little acrobat who had left China two years ago and was now performing in the Statues act with Evrardo Garza Sr. and Jr., whom he had met aboard a Caribbean cruise ship, where he and they had been stunting for affluent New Yorkers and Bostonians. The trio, whose act is a spectacular series of stacks, lifts, and contortions, unaided by gimmicks, had reached Thunder Bay a day late from Las Vegas in a palatial mobile home, in which Ho was contributing domestically by stirring up authentic Szechuan meals, using whatever ingredients he was able to locate in the produce bins and spice racks of the north. With his rela-tively light schedule, he had more than enough time in which to practise his juggling (four hours a day), as well as his Spanish and English, the latter now up to several hundred words – and to smoke, which he did often and with an uptown flair that did not quite mask his old-world Chinese gusto for tobacco. He was twenty-five, and had bitten on Western culture to the degree that he was almost never without his Pittsburgh Steelers cap (an ivy-leaguer turned backwards in the contemporary way), and his L.A. sunglasses, Colorado ski jacket, and calf-length Doc Martens. He wore a tiny hoop earring and one of those necklaces on which words can be built up in letter-shaped metal "beads." His said LUST, which suited him to more or less the degree that it would suit a Grey nun or kindergarten teacher. It intrigued me that he had grown up under a repressive Communist regime, but his English was not yet far enough advanced that he could describe in any detail what it had been like politically and socially for a Chinese student during the 1980s and '90s. When I asked about Tiananmen Square, all he could tell me was "Vehy bad. Vehy vehy bad," imparting a clue to his sensibilities if not to the texture of his life in Herbay Province, near Beijing. What he did tell me was that his father and grandfather had been circus acrobats, that he himself had started gymnastics at age six, that he had competed in international acrobatics competitions during his late teens, and had eventually joined the Chinese circus. "How did you get out of China?" I asked, to which he looked at me perplexed and said, "Go to aiipord – fie in airpane. Peepo can hleave China now."

Ho almost always carried a backpack full of juggling clubs, and, that night, at an impromptu barbecue that materialized among the animal and prop guys, I asked if he'd demonstrate his skills. Without hesitation, he sought out a little patch of free space away from the grill, emptied his pack, and zipped two, three, four, five clubs into the air, keeping them elegantly aloft, in a variety of juggling patterns, with the benefit of one eye – the other closed to avoid the smoke drifting from the cigarette lodged in the corner of his mouth.

The barbecue remains for me a sort of icon of *cuisine brute*, in that the menu consisted entirely of large hackings of nearly-raw meat, unseasoned except for a horrific curing of tar fumes that they absorbed when half the "stones" that had been used to build the barbecue pit turned out to be asphalt which melted mid-cooking, producing more smoke than the tire fires we had started as kids for the purpose of sending smoke signals to the other side of the galaxy.

As we gnawed on this unique combination of protein and pavement, Bobby announced to all and sundry, "We should get Wilson to show Charlie his whip tricks."

"Yeah," I said, "I'd like to see them."

"He can cut a cigarette right outta your mouth from ten feet away."

"He can cut a cigarette outta *your* mouth," I said.

"It don't hurt!" protested Bob.

"I don't smoke," I said.

"Wilson," Bob called. "Go get your whip. Show 'im how ya do it." Wilson, he elaborated, could line up "twenty raisins on a fence, two inches apart" and pick them off one at a time. "Ain't that true, Brett?" he said to Brett Marshall, who responded that it was true as long as Wilson didn't have to use a whip.

Wilson was eventually persuaded to get his bullwhip out of the tiger truck. "Here, gimme a cigarette," Bob said to John McCoy. And when John had handed him one he called, "Come on, Wilson, let's show 'em how it's done. Anybody ever trained a wild elephant ain't afraid to get a cigarette flicked out of his mouth." Bob walked onto the boulevard, wedged the cigarette between his lips, and thrust his face forward. "Show 'em what you're made outta, Wilson," he said. And Wilson, wearing the wide, serious grin that I had seen on him in the ring, stepped onto the boulevard, cracked the whip a couple of times to limber up, and stopped motionless about ten feet from where Bob stood. For several seconds he stared, then assumed a pose, left foot forward, right arm back and high, and brought the whip straight over the top. Bob removed the half cigarette from his mouth, tossed it to the pavement, and asked John for another one. "Here's yours," he said to me. "How ya gonna write about any of this if ya don't experience it?"

Knowing that Wilson had spent a fair portion of the afternoon in a fairly strenuous party mode (something he most certainly did not do before working the tigers) was anything but a comfort to me. On the other hand, the risk was in its own way seductive and, after a faint protest, I walked onto the grass, put the cigarette in my mouth, and showed Wilson a slightly distended profile.

It would be remotely literary to report that, these months later, I carry an inch-long scar on my lip, chin, or nostril. But, in fact, I barely carry the memory of the sound of the whip – would hardly have known that Wilson had done his job, except that, at the whip's crack, there was a brief burst of cheering from those standing around, and when I looked down my nose, there was half a cigarette where a second earlier there had been a whole one. "Next thing," said Bobby, coming toward me across the grass, "you'll be eatin that boneless meat called hamburger, you'll be talkin outta the side of your mouth, and askin the way to Swan Lake and Flim Flam. I *told* you it wouldn't hurt, didn't I?"

I asked Bob about his trucking hassles from the previous night and learned that they had begun with a dread Scale Open sign a few kilometres west of Thunder Bay, and had intensified when a Ministry of Transportation inspector had crawled under the trailer and emerged with news that the unit's brakes were deficient, and that he was declaring the truck officially out of service. "We went inside," said Bob, "and I told the guy I'd have to drive it back into town to get them tended to. He said, 'You ain't drivin that thing anywhere. I'm takin your plates off.'"

By the time the plates had been put back on – a process that included a dozen or more long-distance phone calls, the summoning of the local circus chairman and his wife, the involvement of a former police chief, the hiring of a towing unit, a lengthy visit to the brake shop, and a savagely protracted series of slurs between Bob and the trucking inspector – the delay had cost Bob $1,200 for the brake job, $200 for the tow, and $375 and $485 in driver and owner fines. Already on the trip, he had spent some $1,200 U.S. for the U-Haul that had been required to carry the tigers back to Seagoville and another $2,000 in fuel and upkeep, all of which pushed the cost of the trip so far close to $5,000 U.S., not counting wages.

For my broader benefit, Bob parlayed his fiscal despair into a primer on circus economics, explaining how show money concentrates and disperses, concentrates and disperses, beginning in this case with the Shriners, whose contract with Ricky called for a flat payment of some fifty thousand dollars a week, out of which Ricky paid his expenses, as well as the acts, technicians, and musicians, dispensing weekly pay envelopes that ranged from four hundred dollars, or so, for crew, as high as four or five thousand for families such as the Gonçalveses, who supplied perhaps a sixth of the program in the form of a sword-balancing act, a hula-hoop routine, and a rola-bola number (essentially, a man on a board on a roller) performed by forty-five-year-old Manuel, who had learned his chops in Portugal as a boy and had brought them to America during the early 1980s under the billing "the quickest balance" in show business. Ricky earned income from the moon-walk and the elephant photos, and had a cut of the concession receipts, while the Shriners kept all ticket proceeds beyond the weekly fifty thousand that went to Ricky, and had their own cut of the concessions, moonwalk, and photos. The drug trade notwithstanding, the circus is pretty much the last of the all-cash societies, and it was not uncommon to see Pat Delaney in the concessions room as each show ended, stuffing hundreds of five-, ten-, and twenty-dollar bills into his metal brief case. For his part, Ricky was never without the zippered vinyl tote – a most under-stated holster – in which he frequently carried as much as sixty or seventy thousand dollars. One night in Thompson, Manitoba, toward the end of the tour, he was rumoured to have backed a dresser up against the door of his hotel room, for fear that he would be ambushed and robbed, and to have switched hotels first thing the next day. Because the performers were paid in cash, they, too, accumulated fat piles of twenties, fifties, and hundred-dollar bills. Over the weeks, I asked several of them how they managed sums of cash that, in some cases, would have totalled upward of twenty thousand dollars. In the U.S., they would simply have deposited the money in branches of their banks. And even in Canada, some bothered to have the money transferred electronically, when such a service was available. But most just hung on to it – and when I asked, looked at me as if to say, I may be stupid enough to carry a lot of cash, but I'm certainly not so stupid as to reveal how and where I carry it.

The circus's imperative to gather any stray cash that can be gathered is so deeply ingrained that, the following afternoon, prior to the show, Ricky made a rogue pitch for the moonwalk and elephant photos – a job usually handled by Bill Boren, who had not yet shown up – when there were only four paying customers in the arena, including an elderly Native man and woman. By the time a few dozen had arrived, Bill's pitches were coming every three or four minutes – for food, for "garbage," for the moonwalk and photos. Even during the show they came, one in particular bruiting a variety of light-up swords, "rope lights," and wands, the hustle being that, at a certain point in the performance, the lights would go off, and children with their own lights would become "actual participants" in the circus. Pat Delaney had no illusions whatever about what he was selling, and explained to me one day that he priced what he called "all this junk" at whatever he felt the market would bear, noting that, in the big cities, where families were "accustomed to paying two hundred dollars for a night out," a plastic sword that sold for five dollars in Dryden might fetch "seven or eight, or even more," depending on how deep a gouge Pat felt the clientele would tolerate.

That same afternoon, as an act of solidarity with the Dryden Shrine club, a battalion of Winnipeg Shriners, including a Harley-riding honour guard, a team of mini-Mustang drivers, and at least four separate bands, descended on the town and on the circus, taking the floor for nearly half an hour before the show proper could begin. The change of format was decidedly unpopular with the performers and animal people, who saw it not through the eyes of the audience, most of whom enjoyed it completely, but as a delay that left them standing around, often in costume, until they could get to the rings. It bugged them further that the added length of the program shrank the ninety-minute break between performances to just under an hour – barely enough time for them to catch their breath, perhaps get a snack, deal with costuming, children, and so on, and get back out front.

The Shriners, it is far from an unkindness to point out, are a sort of well-oiled avatar of some benign alien force about half recognizable to the average earthling. How else can one explain an army of vintage lodge brothers in Persian palace wear, or in kilts, or play cars, or on Harley-Davidsons? An organization with an uncertain future they may be, but they are by no means fading without a good last blast on the trumpet. It insults reportage to have to say outright that, among them, are soulful, intelligent men, of varied politics and social perspectives. And yet if it is not said, the fact could easily fall prey to the apparently fatal determination of many of the club's members to present themselves as a tribe of rye-guzzling gizmo salesmen and good ol' boys, enamoured of carousing and of the goofy clubhouse regalia that is both their charm and a through-line on their lives as wacky wabbits. It further complicates their image – and is in fact a sublime kick in the teeth to the corporate greed that has pretty much taken over American health care – that, because of the Shrine, hundreds of thousands of children, many of them burn victims, are treated free of charge yearly in the club's twenty-two state-of-the-art hospitals. The collective expenses of those hospitals are more than a million dollars a day, most of which is raised by circus tours such as the one we were on.

Now, here they came down the track, some of them feeling very little pain, blowing bugles and trombones and pounding away on drums and cymbals and glockenspiels, the big ivory-coloured Harleys of the motorcycle brigade roaring and flashing and filling the place with exhaust, the twenty little Mustangs, each with a Shriner squeezed in, whirring and weaving among the bands. About the only thing missing that afternoon was the white convertible Cadillac – the "muffmobile," as Bobby called it – that would show up in Portage la Prairie and Brandon to carry the grand potentate waving around the arena.

During the show that afternoon, I did what I could to help Bob with Judy, who, when she had come out of the trailer at eight o'clock that morning, had been so incensed about the cold and about being cooped up for such long periods of time that, having reached the bottom of the ramp, she kept right on walking across the street to the landscaped banks of the Wabigoon River, where, in a temper tantrum, she wrapped her trunk around a six-inch diameter alder tree, wrenched it out of the ground, and flung it into the river. She ripped the limbs from a second tree and a third, before being persuaded by Bobby to return peaceably to the lot.

By show time, her spirits had improved, due to a mid-afternoon sleep and to a wake-up snack that included a dozen heads of wilted Boston lettuce and a fifty-pound bag of potatoes.

As the small matinee crowd left the arena, I stood by the orchestra pit chatting with Pat Delaney, whose concession sales for the performance had been a disaster, with little hope for improvement that evening. "What you've always gotta remember about blue-collar towns," he said, "is there's money in 'em, but that the people have paid for it with their lives, and they ain't gonna give it away – everything a blue-collar guy spends, he translates into hours in the salt mines." Pat presented me with an apple he had filched out of the boxes of B.C. Macintoshes that were always in the concessions room awaiting their glazing of red candy. "Every audience'll buy *something*," he said. "If you can't sell 'em the glo-visors and sword lights, you sell 'em colouring books, balloons, cheap stuff – we call it 'slum' – that's what we'll push tonight."

Forty minutes later, Bill Boren delivered his first cornucopian endorsement for the *"big bright souvenir colouring books with the clowns and elephants and circus tigers . . . WONDERFUL souvenirs that'll bring back all the FUN and EXCITEMENT of the circus every time they're opened for WEEKS and WEEKS to come . . . these FAB-ULOUS circus colouring books are just two dollars while the supply lasts . . . two dollars only. . . . Pick up a few, because they REALLY ARE that special item that'll give pleasure to the kids long after the circus is over . . ."* For the past ten minutes, Bill had been explaining to me the ringmaster's role in deflecting the audience's attention in case of an emergency and recalled now that, during a show in Terre Haute, Indiana, during the mid-1980s, when he was working with band leader Keith Killinger on Hugo Zachini's Olympic International Circus, he had "just completed the show's opening song and had introduced the cat act" when Killinger stepped from behind his music stand, staggered toward him, and fell dead at his feet. "Fortunately, Keith's sister, Wanda Darlington, was on the organ, and Keith's wife was right there, too" said Bill. "They were all old pros, and the moment they realized that Keith had bought the farm and there was nothing they could do, Wanda got up and started directing the orchestra, and Keith's wife went up and turned the music for her, right through until intermission. The band never missed a beat."

Outside, the temperature had dropped and it had begun to rain, and when Bob and Judy came in to begin their photo session they were as miserable as slough rats. As an act of mercy, I went to the van, drove to the Safeway, and bought Judy a five-pound bag of carrots and stopped at Robin's Donuts for an extra-large coffee for Bob. During the afternoon, he and I had discussed circus movies, and when I handed him his coffee, he asked me if I had ever heard of Julia Pastriani, explaining between gulps that she was a Mexican Digger Indian, a sideshow freak, famous for the long black hair that sprouted as thick as number-ten thread from every part of her body. "Oh, it was awful," he said. "She had these deformed little legs, overlapping teeth – never had any love. And this guy came along and told her he loved her, wanted to marry her, when really all he wanted was to get her away from the sideshow operator who owned her."

Bob reported that a movie had been made about Julia during the 1930s, and that she and her suitor "eventually got married" and had their own little show nicely up and running when she got sick and died. "He was makin such good money off her, he had her mounted in a glass case. He'd keep her in his hotel room at night.

Finally, she drove him crazy. The movie was just gruesome, make your skin crawl. I loved it."

As he spoke, an exceedingly skinny man and woman, with their heavily made-up teenaged daughter, each of them wearing a windbreaker bearing the insignia of a different National Hockey League team, approached and stood solemnly beside Judy while Bob clicked off a photo and handed it to them in exchange for six dollars in coins. "*That*," the woman said as they walked away, "is for the album."

The show had just started when Rick Wallenda, whom I had not yet talked to at any length, nabbed me in the corridor beneath the stands and told me that he was free for a while and would be happy to talk. We settled in a corner of the men's dressing room, where, at that moment, the Statues, including Chunyan Ho, were fidgeting by the sink, helping one another apply the gold-coloured gel that, by the time they had finished, would coat every inch of their skins not covered by their gold Speedo-style bathing suits.

In response to my prompting, Rick rummaged with good-humoured patience through his childhood. His earliest memories, he told me, were of driving "never-ending distances" with his mother, Carla, and infant brother, Mario, hauling the minuscule trailer in which the three of them lived while the 1950s version of the Great Wallenda Circus was on the road. Rick had been born on the road, in Chicago, the seventh generation of a circus dynasty that had begun in Bohemia during the Austro-Hungarian Empire. The earliest family performers were itinerant jugglers, acrobats, and musicians, the descendants of whom developed aerial skills and exhibited wild animals. An ancestral aunt of Rick's trained timber wolves and laughing hyenas, while another harnessed a team of seven sea lions that entertained nineteenth-century German villagers by hauling a chariot around the squares of their towns. Rick's great-grandfather had been a catcher in a flying act – and had remained one into his seventies, well into Rick's boyhood.

But it was the catcher's son, Karl, an intrepid young acrobat with a clownlike mein and remarkable balancing skills, who, in 1928, brought the family's four-person wire act out of the relative obscurity of outdoor performance in Europe into international prominence under the American big top. In those days, Karl worked with his future wife, Helen, his brother, Herman, and his friend, Joe Geiger. The troupe's first engagement in New York, in front of twenty-eight thousand fans a day, had barely begun when the union of Wallenda daring and Ringling hype transformed the four daredevils into circus celebrities.

Their departure from Ringlings twenty years later and the founding of the Great Wallenda Circus took them to new fame, in large part because they no longer had to compete for billing with other Ringling acts, and were free to assume both artistic and promotional control of their careers. In particular, the move gave the now-expanded troupe licence to mount its seven-person pyramid, a spectacularly risky turn that Ringlings had discouraged for fear of disaster.

By 1955, when Rick was born, the troupe included a dozen or more performers – mostly family. "There were always people coming and going," Rick told me that night in the Dryden arena. "My grandfather would bring them from Europe, pay their way over, give them accommodation, get them started in America, and at the same time teach them wire-walking, so that they could pay him back by working in the act."

Prep school for this evolving coterie of irregulars was the big backyard of the Wallenda's twenty-two-acre homestead in Sarasota, Florida, a tract of scrub grass, pine, and palmetto on which a number of family members had built houses and where practice rigging was always available in the form of a tightwire about two feet off the ground and another some ten feet up.

"I never had *any* lessons," said Rick. "It all just kinda rubbed off on me as a three- or four-year-old. My grandfather'd be teaching his protégés, and my cousins and I would be playing in the dirt, quietly absorbing the lessons to the point that they gradually became part of our consciousness. My grandfather and the rest of them would go away, and we'd get up there and try this stuff. And before we knew it, we were wire walkers – at least at the two-foot level."

It is the progression from the two-foot to the ten-foot level – and ultimately to the thirty- or forty-foot levels – that separates pretenders in the profession from those who will eventually hear the cheers and gasps of the crowd. But the final stages in the performer's preparation for the big top or arena have less to do with physical conditioning than with the conditioning of the psyche. "At the two-foot-level," said Rick, "if you're gonna fall, you simply touch the end of your pole to the ground. At the ten-foot level, you don't."

At the thirty-foot level, he added, "you're walking straight over the middle of your own grave."

The pole, Rick told me, is to the wire-walker what wings are to the aircraft or the tank to the scuba diver. "For the stacks and pyramids, all the sorts of things the Wallendas were doing at the time, it was absolutely essential for slowing down the balance – in a way, extending the arms. I'm not saying it's not possible to go out on the wire without one – I used to do it all the time; lots of walkers do it. But with weight on your shoulders you need it. Otherwise, you have no foundation."

The pole is a twenty-five-foot hollow steel tube, usually weighted at the ends and weighing between thirty and thirty-five pounds. "Thirty pounds doesn't sound like much," said Rick, "but try carrying it dead still for six or seven minutes in front of you, without shifting your grip, and you'll realize you've gotta be in shape – particularly with somebody else and *their* pole on your shoulders." The wire, Rick explained, is a five-eighths-inch steel cable, and the performance shoe a leather-soled slipper, preferably made of elk or deer skin.

Rick's own graduation from the two- to the ten-foot level came in 1962, at the age of seven. "The transition," he said, "is not about skills, it's about confidence. You have to have enough fear to respect the risk but at the same time be able to sublimate that fear so that you can get from one pedestal to the other. If you can't beat it down, you get nervous. If you suppress it too much, you get careless. My grandfather used to say he didn't want anybody on the wire who wasn't scared to be there."

Rick estimated that between the ages of seven and twelve, he made the crossing between pedestals two or three thousand times. "As I got a little older," he said, "I started learning the tricks – the bicycles, the chair, the headstands and stacks, and, finally, the pyramid."

As Rick talked, the Statues, now painted heel to forehead, moved into the centre of the dressing room and, on the grubby floor, began a series of warm-up drills so exacting and fluid as to constitute something of a circus in themselves. Evrardo Garza Jr., a trim eighteen-year-old, born in Mexico but raised in Houston and Las Vegas, pushed himself into a handstand, lifted a hand, and stood as if born to the position first on one hand, then on the other. I asked Rick if handstands had been part of his repertoire on the wire, and he said, "I can't even do one on the ground. My grandfather was the guy for handstands. At some point in every show, he'd do one on my Uncle Herman's shoulders, in the middle of the wire. They used to do it right before they mounted the pyramid. In fact, it was the last trick they completed the night the pyramid came down."

The circus, perhaps more than any other cultural construct, is about stories – millions of them, most of them the private preserve of animal trainers, ringmasters, band leaders, concessions men – all of them jackpot artists. But unlike stories from, say, the political or sports worlds – or the movies, or music, or crime – only a handful of the circus's tales have achieved anything even approaching the status of folklore. The arrival of Jumbo the elephant in America, in 1882, got almost as much coverage in the popular press as had the assassination of Abraham Lincoln seventeen years earlier. The death of Lillian Leitzel, the American queen of the air, in 1931, so moved New Yorkers that two daily papers made a lead story of her fatal fall; and, at a hockey game at Madison Square Garden the next night, fifteen thousand fans stood for a minute of silence in her honour. In 1982, the achievement of the "impossible" quadruple somersault by Mexican flyer Miguel Vasquez cut its own brisk swath through the popular media.

No story in the long history of the big top, however, surpasses the baneful notoriety of events that took place on the night of January 30, 1962, at the Coliseum on the Michigan State Fairgrounds in suburban Detroit. "The collapse of the pyramid," Rick told me that night in Dryden, "wasn't just the biggest accident in the history of the circus, it changed the way people *looked* at our kind of entertainment – the way the public looked at it, the way we ourselves looked at it. Suddenly, everything circus people had known for years about the risks, but that audiences had never really had to confront, was right out there in the open – people heaving their last breaths right there in the ring. I mean, even for us the vulnerability had been pretty much abstract most of the time – now it was this very ugly reality."

For Rick, who was seven at the time, and who on the night of the accident had been home with his grandmother in Sarasota, the specifics of the catastrophe had initially been little more than a kind of ghost story or sifting of rumours. "I don't really remember how much I was told," he said, "but it wasn't much. And the other kids and I weren't taken to the funeral or anything. I remember the crying and a certain amount of the agonizing and recrimination. But for the most part our sense of it was that, suddenly, people we had known weren't there any more, or if they *were* still there they weren't the same people – my Aunt Jenny, for example, lost her husband; and of course my Uncle Mario, who was basically just a kid, nineteen years old, was in a wheelchair and would be for the rest of his life."

It is easy to understand the elder Wallendas' concern for the sensibilities of their youngest, and tempting to speculate on the degree to which the details of the accident were suppressed out of concern for the family succession on the wire.

During the decades since, Rick has heard, read, and thought about the accident from every possible perspective. "I've definitely processed it," he smiled. But despite his openness about its effects and aftermath – and its impact on him personally – his answers to my questions about the specifics of what caused it were uncharacteristically curt. Asked, for example, if the troupe was perhaps rusty after a month or so off, he responded, "I wasn't there – I couldn't possibly say." Asked about what might have caused Dieter Schepp to drop his pole and to collapse, he said, "Dieter's the only one who could answer that, and he's dead."

The circus annals, decidedly more forthcoming, reveal that the Wallendas' arrival in the Motor City a couple of days prior to the accident had been anything but well-omened. For one thing, the troupe was tired from the long drive from Florida. The engagement was the first of the new season, and some of the Wallendas, including Karl's son Mario and daughter Jenny, were uneasy about the inclusion of a newcomer, named Dieter Schepp in the seven-person pyramid. Schepp had been raised in East Berlin but had escaped, and had been brought by Karl to America with his sister Jana, who had become an agile "top-mounter" and, like Dieter, was to make her first public appearances in Detroit.

Dieter had been far from an ideal student of the high wire. He was peevish about the training and discipline, complained constantly about sore shoulders and hands, and hated life in America. On top of everything, on the day the accident occurred, he had shown signs of illness, perhaps of the flu. But he had been reluctant to tell Karl, for fear of being taken off the prop crew, where he earned an extra hundred dollars a week – every dollar of which took him closer to his dream of abandoning the act, getting out of America, and returning to Germany.

During the afternoon, Karl himself had wondered openly about Dieter's participation that night. "Are you all right?" he is reported to have asked an hour or so before show time.

"I'm fine," Dieter told him.

"*Nicht nervus?*"

"*Nein,*" Dieter insisted.

Mario had complained quietly that he'd have felt much better if Mike McGuire, another Wallenda protégé who performed with the troupe, were to take Dieter's place in "the seven." But when the Wallendas stepped up the entrance ramp, ten strong, for the second-last display before intermission, it was Dieter, not Mike, who had been cast to lead the "big trick" onto the wire.

"*Ladies and gentlemen!*" the ringmaster cried as the spotlight picked up the troupe, prancing into the ring in their white silks, "*The Moslem Temple now proudly presents the GREAT WALLENNNNNDAS! Executing the most fan-TAS-tic exhibition of high-wire artistry in the ENTIRE HISTORY of the circus world!*"

Up the rigging they scrambled, putting an upward tilt on seven thousand transfixed faces.

The act began as it had for more than thirty years, with the men of the troupe mincing out onto the cable so that they were spaced from pedestal to pedestal, a distance of some fifty feet. At a command from Karl's nephew, Gunther, who acted as a kind of foreman, they stopped, each raised a knee, rested his pole on it, and released a hand to salute. Then, as circus chronicler Bill Ballantine once phrased it, the act "ground into its routine," a series of stacks and acrobatics, each of which evinced cheers and groans, and provoked its share of averted eyes. Dieter Schepp's first real responsibility came when he and Karl's son-in-law, Dick

Faughnan, walked to the middle of the wire, supporting between them a horizontal pole on which Karl performed a routine handstand. Next, to give the older men a breather, Gunther rode a bicycle, equipped with tracked wheels, from one pedestal to the other, and then Karl did his famous mid-wire handstand on his brother Herman's shoulders, a trick the two had been performing since they had begun working together as teenaged boys.

Edward Hoagland claims that, because of their purity and compactness, the best circus acts are difficult to capture in a medium as imprecise as words. Even the most exquisite wire tricks, however, unfold in painfully dilatory increments, of a sort that lend themselves quite well to the ofttimes painful dilatoriness of sentence-making. I have seen the "big trick" performed on two occasions and could perhaps offer a plausible version of it in words. Nevertheless, as a curiosity and something of a refresher, I asked Rick that night if he would describe the trick, as if to someone who had never seen it done.

"Imagine four guys spread out along the wire, all facing forward," he responded, holding up four spread fingers in front of his face to give the idea. "The front two are joined by a chest-high pole that fastens to their shoulders with a kind of yoke. The back two are joined by a similar pole. Now, imagine one guy standing on each of those poles, these upper guys also joined by a chest-level pole, on top of which a woman is sitting on a chair. All seven of them are carrying balancing poles. In all, the pyramid weighs about thirteen hundred pounds."

With the ringmaster's announcement of "the seven," the band slid into a tremulous rendition of Wagner's "Evening Star" and lowered their volume, so that the balancers could hear one another, and could be heard by the crowd. "At that point," Rick told me, "maybe nine of them would have been grouped at one end of the wire, some of them hanging right off the pedestal."

Dieter Schepp was the first of the "undermounters" to step out, wearing the front end of a shoulder pole. With meticulous care

*The Wallenda troupe, under Karl Wallenda, performing its famous seven-person pyramid during the 1950s. Karl can be seen here at the front of the second tier. His brother Herman is behind him; his nephew Gunther is at the back of the first tier.*

the pyramid formed behind him and inched forward, until Gunther, finally in harness in the rear position, gave the command to move – "easy out!"

And the bizarre organism, with its undulating tentacles, set off in lockstep on what would be its last and most famous journey. About halfway across, as always, the pyramid eased to a stop, and Jana Schepp, seated ten feet off the wire, rose in painstaking increments to a standing position on her chair, and then lowered herself with the same precision.

The first sign that something was wrong is said to have been a "whippish" tremor that rose upwards and backwards off the wire, through the connected bodies, when the pyramid was perhaps fifteen feet from its destination. Reports say that Dieter momentarily released his pole, tossing it slightly in an attempt to gain a more secure grip. "If that's what he did," said Rick, "it's a major major no-no." Certainly, the pole's importance had been drilled into Dieter day after day since his arrival in America. During the troupe's last workouts in Florida, Gunther had emphasized to him that he could not survive without it. So, when the others saw his pole leave his hands, clang off the wire, and drift into space, they knew as surely as he did what was coming next.

The pyramid is said to have collapsed silently, in what appeared to be slow motion, the bodies to have hit the dirt-covered floor nearly forty feet below with the sound an elephant makes when it smacks its trunk on the ground. Dieter, the reports say, hit headfirst, sending up a puff of dust and bouncing shoulder-high, followed immediately by Mario and Dick Faughnan. Above, Karl hit the wire with such force that his pelvis was broken and his abdominal muscles wrenched apart in a double hernia. Jana, on her way down, was able to grab Karl's back, where she clung, screaming for her life. Behind them, Herman hung from the wire, while Gunther, still on his feet and in possession of his pole, moved quickly forward, reached down and grabbed Jana's wrist. On the floor below, a dozen or so Shriners and crew grabbed a tumbling mat and, using it as a makeshift hand net, moved into position below the dangling topmounter.

"*Eins . . . zwei . . . drei,*" called Gunther, and, against her howled protests, he and Karl let Jana go, her downward force tearing the mat loose from its holders, so that she flipped onto the floor, striking her head with concussive violence.

Ron Morris's 1972 biography of Karl Wallenda describes Karl "trembling" on the pedestal, too stricken to move, as Herman and Gunther descended the rigging to where a priest and several Shrine doctors were already attending to the fallen. Dieter, it is said, lay just inside the curb of the centre ring, unconscious but still breathing, blood trickling from his mouth, while Dick Faughnan was on his back, as if in an untroubled sleep. Mario, according to a newspaper report, lay in a fetal self-hug.

"In what other business in the world," remarked Rick with a sardonic laugh, "would the partners and co-workers and friends go right on working under circumstances like that?"

But twenty minutes later, at just about the time Dick Faughnan was pronounced dead at the nearby Highland Park Hospital (Dieter Schepp would hang on until midnight), that is exactly what happened. The ten-piece band slashed into a brassy gallop, a half dozen clowns tumbled into the centre ring, and the Moslem Temple Circus surged back to life.

# 5

I F YOU TRAVEL the drunken highway that links the sizeable
towns of northwestern Ontario – Nipigon, Thunder Bay,
Dryden, Fort Frances, Kenora – at each of those towns, you'll find
a monumental pulp and paper mill, Baal among the Canaanites,
prevailing and unsightly, with its formidable stacks and effusions,
its chain-link fences, its pervasive agenda and rotten-egg smell. In
close proximity to that mill, you'll find thousands of tons of pulp
logs, mostly spruce and jack pine, cut in eight-foot lengths,
stacked holus-bolus like pick-up sticks, or as neat as a backyard
wood pile.

You might also find a lumber or "stud" mill, with its own chain
link and log piles. And invariably you'll find a river – the
Kaministiquia, the Wabigoon, the Rainy, the Winnipeg. At one
time these rivers were what historians referred to as "highways of
industry," which, hereabout, meant conduits for logs that were
piled on the ice in mid-winter, as far away as a hundred miles
upstream, and in spring were floated down river in massive drives
to the towns.

Today the logs come out of the wilderness either on rail cars or on the beds of trucks – huge, articulated flatbeds that rule the highways and roar into town at all hours, exploding the peace and making rubble of the municipal pavement.

The towns are connected by rail and air and radio, by telephone and e-mail. But when an inhabitant of the area thinks of the distance or route between his town and the next, he thinks not of airports or railways, much less of the "information highway," but of a *real* highway, a serpentine strip of blacktop which, when he climbs into his pickup or four-by-four, becomes both a means to an end (the next town) and an end in itself, with its implied freedoms and the rich evocations of its woods and waters and wildlife.

Highway 502 from Dryden south to Fort Frances is precisely such a highway, a capricious spider-line through some of the most remote territory in North America. On stretches of it, you can drive for thirty or forty kilometres without seeing so much as a road sign or cabin, let alone a store, garage, or restaurant.

For me, driving alone on the morning of May 3, 502 south was a rolling free-for-all of stimuli. I listened sporadically to the music of Tim Hardin and Annie Lennox, then, vaguely dissatisfied, turned to CBC radio, which, as the waters rose in Manitoba, had turned its attention pretty much exclusively to the destructive advances of the Red River. My thoughts, however, were not so much about flooding as about elephants, high wire, risk – all cadenced to the buzz of the tires, the hum of caffeine, and of course the primitive vitality of lakes and forests, Precambrian outcrops and cliffs as old as any on earth; a bear cub at roadside; ravens; a great grey owl; but mostly just trees and more trees, each bend another Kodachrome of highway and spruce as jagged as rickrack.

At one point, as I came over a hill, I could see in the distance the Lunas' silvery Airstream chugging along, bulletlike and purposeful, bearing Florida plates and an irrefutable measure of poignancy in the land of near-permafrost.

I passed them, waving, and within ten minutes came up behind the elephant truck, following closely enough that, after a minute or so, I could smell the elephant through the heating vents in my dash. Recalling what Bobby had told me about how the merest whiff of an elephant or tiger could send a horse into wide-nostrilled panic, I wondered what primitive terror or curiosity the smell must be loosing in, say, roadside rabbits and foxes, whose phylogenic memories could not have been stimulated comparably since the disappearance of the woolly mammoths ten thousand years ago. In the backwaters of my skull, I invented a bear emerging from her den, confused and dopey after months of hibernation, taking her first great whiff of spring and getting not just the essences of the North – of balsam, creek water, and birch sap – but of the Asian jungles and plains, of elephants and tigers; alarms shocking to the point of sending her whimpering back to her hideaway, protective of her brood.

Highway 502 ends near the Minnesota border, and the last thirty kilometres into Fort Frances must be travelled westward on Highway 11, through stands of white pine and a softer, less-dense forest than the spruce-heavy bush to the north. Within ten kilometres of Fort Frances along Rainy Lake, the wilderness gives way to fishing camps, cabins, real estate signs; motels, variety stores, bait shops; the occasional seaplane dragging its cruciform shadow across the roads and right-of-ways below. At the edge of town, a monstrous sign touts the area's annual international bass fishing championship.

In addition to pulp mills and log piles, towns such as Dryden and Fort Frances offer a Safeway, a doughnut shop, a strip mall, a couple of schools, and a couple of vehicle dealerships. Each has a library and hospital, a handful of churches, a decent hotel or two, and a couple of fleabags operated less in the interest of hostelry than in moving volumes of beer from the barrels beneath their bars into the bellies of the local mill workers.

And each town has an indoor ice rink, an arena, the *sine qua non* not just of winter recreation in these parts but of the cultural life of the community. From October to April, these rinks are occupied from six in the morning until well after midnight – sometimes by figure skaters or pleasure skaters but mostly by a panoply of able- or barely able-bodied hockey players: "mites" and "squirts," "midgets" and "juniors," "seniors" and "oldtimers," players just old enough to talk and those long-since retired from the mill. The best of them – the local kid who turned pro, the promising junior who died on the highway, the team that won the provincial championship – are remembered, if not canonized, in the heroes' gallery that invariably hangs in an arena's foyer or concession area.

The circus is a pretender in such spaces, a creature better suited to tents and humidity and lemonade-cravings, to the circus-educated towns of the American Midwest and South than to the phlegmatic mill towns of northwestern Ontario. And nowhere was this incompatibility more apparent than at the antique arena in Fort Frances, a cavernous old timber-pile, ill-lit, ill-heated, ill-adjusted in a dozen decipherable ways to the exotic conclave of tigers, acrobats, and aerialists that moved into its precincts and began to unload and set up at about ten-thirty that morning. Whereas Dryden's arena had hinted marginally at theatre or auditorium space, the Fort Frances arena was very much an ice rink, a winter place, and it was difficult to imagine even the hardiest women of the circus getting down to their Brazil-cuts and fishnets, or to imagine their men cracking a sweat later in the day as, in the frosty morning air, they went about their preparations in gloves, hats, and down jackets. Their limbs were stiff; their breath came in clouds; their faces showed the dreary forbearance that had settled on them as it became clear the spring temperatures were a long way yet from levels more amenable to the body and heart. The chatter among the Lunas and Gonçalveses and Garzas focused on the still-frozen lakes and streams they had seen by the dozens on the drive down, and on the snow that, in places, remained thick in the woods.

Somewhere between Thunder Bay and Fort Frances, Evrardo Garza Jr., had acquired a blue woollen toque bearing the insignia of the Toronto Maple Leafs, and this morning, perhaps for the first time in his life, he was wearing a hat out of necessity. John McCoy and Rick Robinson, the elephant and tiger grooms, had bundled on the full contents of their duffel bags beneath their work coveralls, and Bobby Gibbs told me as we entered the building that he had taken to sleeping in his quilted coat and an insulated beige cap, whose earflaps he was now wearing in the down position. For the most part, the Floridians, Mexicans, and Texans wore their winter clothes with glum rigidity, their shoulders knotted, clearly unaware that to keep moving, to stay loose, is half the battle of staying warm.

I chatted for a while with Bobby, then went out on the floor where Enrique Luna and his daughter, Liliana, were guying out her rigging, conferring in animated Spanish over a line that, it appeared, was going to have to be anchored where a twelve-inch steel girder came right down into the seats. I had known the family barely five days but already thought of them as friends, and had come to admire them immensely for their versatility, good humour, and humility. From the beginning I had been intrigued that they had once been a flying unit, trapeze artists – the *haute monde*, both literally and figuratively, of the circus. In the years before the formation of the family act, Enrique had flown with his brothers and sisters in the Atayde Circus, Mexico's equivalent of Ringling Brothers, and, in 1976, had moved to Ringlings to work as a catcher for Tito Gaona, who was at the time a kind of Michael Jordan among circus aerialists. It was with Atayde that Enrique

*The Luna family brings together two great circus traditions, from Mexico and Cuba. Left to right: Enrique, Rosa, Rolando, and Liliana.*

became the first Mexican to catch both the triple somersault and the so-called "three-and-a-half."

These days, however, he was doing a comedy act, a deceptively simple-looking low-wire routine that drew, in about equal parts, on the sweet Mexican sadness of his personality and the extraordinary balancing skills that he had learned as a boy in the family troupe in Mexico City. His wife, Rosa, had been born into the famous Torres Circus of pre-Revolutionary Havana, and carried beneath her pensive domesticity a streak of Cuban heat that seemed an ideal match for Enrique's tractable reserve. When the two met, on the Atayde show, she was making a living hanging by her hair, and might yet have been squinting down the barrel of a spotlight had she not felt that the births of Rolando and Genesis, aged nine and two, had taken more out of her (and, in her words, added more to her) than she could comfortably compensate for when strength and agility were all there was between her survival in the air and a thirty-foot fall. A few days later in Brandon, suffused by longing, she showed me a photo of herself in costume during the late 1980s, as trim and lithe as anyone half her age now on the show.

Rosa is a considerate, generous woman and was the first of the circus's female participants to show me any real hospitality, inviting me to join the family for a meal in the trailer one evening in Dryden, going so far as to give up her place at the tiny dining table, so that I could sit while she stood to eat. Partway through the meal, as we were discussing circus privation, she disappeared into the recesses of the trailer and reappeared with a goldfish bowl, half full of water, in which a good-sized goldfish was sculling. "We call heem circus fish," she smiled, explaining that, because of the rocking of the trailer on the road, he could have only a limited amount of water. "Leetle bit water," she laughed. "But he happy. He come with us everywhere. Like us, he survive."

Young Rolando did a top-spinning act and was an aspiring trick cyclist; but the troupe's heavy work these days had fallen to Liliana, an exuberant twenty-one-year-old with a deep, strong torso and a striking feline face. When the flying act dissolved in 1991, because her brother Ricky had left for Miami to become a TV Mousketeer, Liliana suffered a year of depression, then took to one of the most traditional pieces of aerial apparatus, the Roman rings, or Olympic rings as they are sometimes called. She works them not with the stubborn self-denial of the Olympians, however, but as a high-throttle swing that she will stand in, for instance, and pump to maximum height before firing her legs outwards in opposite directions, so that she comes rocketing through her foreswing, one foot in each ring, in a perfect version of the splits, her face transformed by a savage, joyful grin.

Another of her tricks is to "sit" in the rings, pump them to maximum height, then, at the apex of her back swing, throw her hands from the cables and fall rearward with a swoop, as if heading for the floor. This bold move invariably brings a gasp from the audience, followed by an appreciative exhalation as they realize that she is not in free fall but has caught the rings in the crooks of her knees. By this time she is sweeping through her fore-stroke, upside down, her hair and arms flying.

She looks, at such moments, as if she is having the time of her life. Which she is. "For some kids," she told me, "circus is just something they're doing until they're eighteen or so, or until something better comes along – then they're gonna move on, go to college, whatever. For me, it's a life, and my happiest moments occur out there on the rings."

Liliana has the X-factor – she is marked for stardom and knows it. But she is far too modest ever to talk about herself in those terms. She is more likely to talk about the hundreds of hours of practice required to perfect even the tiniest fragment of what she presents in a performance – or of the ever-present dangers of aerial work. She can name twelve aerialists – among them close friends and neighbours – who have fallen from their riggings over the past twelve months and suffered injuries that ranged from career-ending to merely gruesome. Liliana herself recently fell from her practice rigging in the backyard of the family home in Sarasota and crashed, uninjured, through the wall of her mother's Florida room.

Her ambition is to work for Ringling Brothers – to "do Ringlings," as she puts it – as her parents and both sets of grand-parents have done. And she has been promised by that circus's talent coordinator that she will get her chance. Her *dream*, however, is to work for the Canadian Cirque du Soleil, with its lavish staging and costumes and its avant-garde ideals. Her exotic Latin style would fit in well at La Cirque. As it is, she makes her entry in one of a number of hooded floor-length wraps, looking more like a member of some mystic Druid cult than a young athlete about to strut her stuff. She walks to the middle of the ring, and, as the orchestra swells and the ringmaster cries her name, raises her arms, seeming to say with that august gesture, *Greetings to you all! Let me entertain you!*

Liliana's dismount and finale take the form of a backward somersault onto what circus people call "the web" or "the Spanish web." From any distance, this apparatus appears to be nothing more than a linen-coloured rope about an inch and a half in diameter, suspended from the rafters, dangling loose to the floor. But it is in fact a tightly woven cotton hose, packed with pliant cord and as soft to the touch as old flannelette. When Liliana comes off the rings at the height of her foreswing, she throws her feet up in front of her, tucks her knees, and begins her somersault. At the point when she is directly upside down, back forward, her mother, Rosa, who is holding the web steady from below, moves it firmly into position against her inverted back and shoulder, so that she knows exactly where it is. As Liliana completes her spin and is for an instant suspended right side up, she grabs the lifeline in front of her and hangs on. "I go into it blind," she told me. "My only orientation is in being able to feel the web on my back." She is one of only three or four women in the world who have performed the trick – perhaps, in part, because at every presentation, the performer's highly torqued impact against the web sears away a two-inch-long oval of skin from the shoulder. Our month-long tour would transform the skin on Liliana's upper back into a raku glazing of welts, scabs, and calluses – these on top of the welts, scabs, and calluses already there from years of practice and performance. Nevertheless, she wants to be the first woman to do a double somersault to the web, an achievement that will require more torque, and result in greater impact and more severe lacerations.

And of course greater satisfaction.

"Is every performance painful?" I asked her one day as we chatted in the Airstream. Rosa, who was standing nearby, stepped toward me, hand raised, wanting to speak. In her inflected English, she uttered one of those simple-seeming observations that, considered in perspective, reverberate far beyond their initial significance or intent – in this case to the point where her comment has become for me a kind of mantra on the gist of circus life: "In the circus," she said, "anything that is any good is painful." Liliana performs without a net, and recalls that when she first mounted the rings, after years of working with a net in the flying act, she was overwhelmed by the realization, first, that "the ring curb looked so small away down there," and second, that there was "nothing down there but concrete."

Of all the people on the show, Liliana was the only one who ever made a point of asking me directly why I had chosen to travel with *this* show, with *these* people, at this particular time. "Why us?" she said, fixing me with her bright black eyes. "And why away up here?"

My answer could not have been very satisfying to her, because, really, I didn't feel I *had* chosen this particular circus, as much as it had chosen me, simply by appearing in town at a time when I had been thinking of writing about the circus and, by chance, had been free to go. "But why were you *thinking* about it?" she persisted, and listened intently as I explained that when my father returned from Europe at the end of World War Two, he brought with him from Italy an interest in clowning that he maintains to this day. One of my earliest memories was of an enormous, silky clown suit, cocoa-brown, that was always in the house but that I never remember my father wearing. *Somebody* wore it from time to time at community Christmas performances, school pageants, and so on, but I was not old enough to realize that, for an obvious reason, my dad was never with us at the time the strange brown figure with the red nose appeared, doing bits of magic and playing to his audience. At home, my dad *talked* about clowns – about Joseph Grimaldi and Emmett Kelly – and had great respect for anybody who could make people laugh.

I explained to Liliana that, for a time, when I was in elementary school, we had chased circuses to this town or that in southern Ontario, sometimes driving two or three hundred kilometres, round trip, to catch whatever little mud show happened to be on its way through. We saw big shows, too, with their elephants, wire acts, and flying troupes. Back home, we relived those acts, referred to them, elaborated on them, giving them a kind of codified longevity that, in some cases, has never died. For decades after we saw them, for instance, my mother and I made reference to a pair of daredevils at the CNE Grandstand who roller-skated on a tiny platform atop a one-hundred-foot-high pole (no net), the whole thing teetering back and forth as they spun themselves into a dizzying, terrifying blur. Thirty years after seeing them, my father would laugh aloud at the recollection of three or four clowns whose act was to move a grand piano into the second-floor window of a house. My older sister, Susan, on seeing Hugo Zachini fired out of a cannon during the Ringling show at Maple Leaf Gardens, in the months before I was born, is reputed to have screamed "Oh, do it again! Please, do it again!"

I attempted to explain to Liliana – however inadequately – that in a sense I was revisiting something that I'd always thought I'd like to know a little more about.

"That's neat," she smiled.

I told her I seemed to be attracted to the fringes, which gave her pause to think before she said, "I guess I am, too."

Unfortunately, that afternoon, Liliana was unable to perform her signature dismount, because of the low height at which she was obliged to rig her apparatus. "Same reason you can't have a flying act in these old arenas," Ricky Wallenda told me later. "People wanta *see* a flying act, but what can you do with twenty feet of clearance?" Rick acknowledged that he would like to see Liliana performing her somersault in every show. "That's why she's here," he said. "On the other hand, I'm not going to push her to do it if she's even the least bit uncomfortable with the conditions. She does other good stuff, and if I give her the benefit of the doubt here, she'll give me good performances when I need them later on."

The women of the circus are an undeniable draw, and the display that followed Liliana's featured the show's other nubile señorita, Daniella Gonçalves, a nineteen-year-old circus pro with lightning reflexes, a swell of black hair, and the stage cool of a Zen master. It is easy to find glowing things to say about the physical capacities of these superior young athletes, but what I found equally impressive were their inner reserves and capacities, which by and large seemed significantly to eclipse those of the average nineteen- or twenty-year-old. Like Liliana, Daniella has an agile, disciplined mind, honed on a dozen years of correspondence schooling and, more recently, by extensive reading in theoretical psychology. She speaks English, Spanish, and Portuguese, and has a working knowledge both of Italian (the language of the European circus) and of Bahasa Indonesia, which she learned on two working trips to Jakarta with the family. What's more, like so many circus kids, she has a practical knowledge of geography that, in her case, extends to England, Europe, the Caribbean, all of North America, and parts of the Far East. "The poverty in Jakarta is so horrible," I heard her tell Brett Marshall one day, "that after you've seen it, you never see America in the same way again."

In the ring, Daniella achieves with ice what Liliana achieves with fire – dancing into the lights in her fishnets and skimpies, wearing a five-mile gaze and exuding (as Faulkner once wrote of Rocket Richard) the "glittering, fatal, alien quality of snakes." Daniella's gizmo is, of all things, hula hoops, and her dad, Manuel, fires them at her, one after another, so that, before you know it, she has ten, fifteen, twenty of them spiralling and wheeling around her, on various parts of her body, and on various planes. Eventually the effect is that of a dizzying kinetic sculpture. In a micro-second, with a flick of her toe, she shoots a fallen hoop from the ring mat to her knees, to her hips – and then to anywhere else on her body, with little more than the twitch of an elbow, shoulder, or wrist. At times, she has as many as thirty hoops in play, her stomach muscles churning to keep them aloft. "People don't realize how heavy they are," she told me one day, taking one from her rack and showing me that they are indeed not the light plastic hoops of the late-fifties hula-hoop craze but made of aluminum (by her dad) bound in neon-coloured tape and weighing more than a pound and a half each. "Toward the end of the act, I'm working about fifty pounds of them," she said. It is an alluring performance, all offered from behind the invisible shield of her detachment and self-sufficiency.

Offstage, Daniella is friendly and unassuming. If, as we moved west and north, she seemed preoccupied at times, it was in part because she had a boyfriend, another circus kid from Sarasota, whose professional gig was the art of Risley or foot-juggling, which means that, in performance, he lies on his back, throws his feet in the air and uses them to juggle balls, poles, cubes, torches – anything that he can spin, flip, or toss. His name is Hanse, and each night, at whatever arena the Great Wallenda Circus happened to be in, Daniella spent twenty minutes on the pay phone talking with him in whatever city or outport his own circus commitments had taken him to. As of early May, the two had not seen one another since February, but hoped to rendezvous in Winnipeg in a couple of weeks. One night when Daniella got off a pay phone that I was waiting to use, I asked her if she was in love. She tilted her head demurely and said, "Sure," adding that, at some point in the future, she (hoops) and he (Risley) hoped to marry their persons and professions.

"Are you going to make a career of it, then?" I asked, and after a long moment's thought she said, "Actually, I've been struggling with that – right now, I don't really know." As much as she loves the centre ring, part of her suspects that, because of

the competition of television, pro sport, and other entertain-
ments, the North American circus is on a slippery slide, and may
not be able to sustain her (and hers) into the next millennium in
the way that it has sustained her parents. Even if it can, she knows
all too well the strictures of the circus life, having lived out of a
trailer, a suitcase, and a phone booth for most of her nineteen
years. Already, she has seen more than a half-million miles of highway (enough to take her twenty-odd times around the planet) and
has logged another quarter million in the air. Her friends, by and
large, have been reduced to entries in an address book, and come
to life only when the marathon grind of one show's tour happens
to intersect with the marathon of another's – or when she is
granted the rare treat of spending two or three weeks on the same
show as someone out of her past. The current tour, for example,
has revived an old acquaintanceship with Liliana Luna, with
whom Daniella last spent time as a six-year-old.

Because she has two younger sisters, aged eight and three,
Daniella has seen her mother Jill's life unfold under the full brunt
of parenthood and must surely see in Jill a foretelling of her own
future should she decide to carry on in the circus family tradition.
Like Rosa Luna, Jill Gonçalves goes around at times half whipped
by her responsibilities for, among other things, shopping,
cooking, cleaning, laundry, home-schooling, wardrobe (four
members of the family have a dozen or more costumes each, all
handmade and maintained), child care, and of course twice daily
performances. "You get up in the morning," Jill told me. "You do
some chores, get breakfast, do some schooling, go shopping, make
lunch, do a little more schooling, get ready for your afternoon performance, run back at intermission to put dinner on, go back into
the building for the finale, do a little more schooling, serve
dinner, get back into costume, do your evening performance, do
the finale, get the kids to bed. Then when you're completely
beat and you've got your props packed up, you drive a couple of

hundred miles to the next town in the middle of the night, and set your alarm so you can get up first thing in the morning and get your props up."

Jill told me that during the past three years, the family had been at home in Sarasota for no more than two or three weeks a year. "And those weeks," she said, "are even more hectic than being on the road, what with props and wardrobe to take care of, and months of undone home chores – an overgrown garden, you name it."

On an emotional level, Daniella would love to stay in the circus. On the other hand, she would like to try university, and has already passed the entrance requirements. "I've been told I really should go," she said, knowing that to commit herself to it full time would take her off the road and scupper her circus career as surely as a four- or five-year layoff would end the career of any professional athlete.

At about noon hour I spotted the circus's music director, Larry Rothbard, sitting at his electric piano in an overcoat, affecting a posture not unlike that of the late Glenn Gould. Larry has the tobacco appetite of a longshoreman, which he figures is healthier for him than the cocaine habit he developed during the late 1980s and which he kicked when he gave up playing what he calls "lounge lizard piano" in 1990. In the meantime, his love of cigarettes has instilled in him an (oft-verbalized) antipathy for smoke-free restaurants, so that when we chose a spot for a bump of caffeine during the mid-afternoon, it had to be one where, above all, he could freely incinerate four or five Lucky Strikes while we shot the breeze (fortunately, such a place is easy to find in northwestern Ontario, where tobacco is pretty much a match for food among nutritional preferences).

*Daniella and Talina Gonçalves, left and centre, with bandleader Larry Rothbard.*

I asked Larry if the cold affected the music, and he snorted and said, "It affects the musicians! I need an extra double-bourbon every night!"

When he is not out on circus gigs, Larry is the full-time organist and choir leader at the predominantly black Salem Lutheran Church at 74th Street and Calumet Avenue on Chicago's South Side, where he grew up. He knows what he calls "all the grand old hymns" – as well as hundreds of old blues numbers that he learned as a child studying piano under the émigré Russian blues legend Art Hodes. "Sometimes before or after a church service, instead of playing Bach or Mendelssohn or whoever, I'll play a little blues," he said. "I just tell the congregation it's all God's message." Versatility and quickness are paramount for a circus band leader, who must not only play but be able to focus simultaneously on the others in the orchestra pit and on whatever is happening in the rings. Larry and the band had nearly two hundred musical cues in the show, and had to switch, at times, from, say, ballad to polka to rumba within a matter of seconds. They played from a repertoire that included jazz, rock, blues, folk, Latin, marches, and classical, as well as a dozen or more movie and show tunes. The elephant act alone drew on compositions by the Beatles, Duke Ellington, Irving Berlin, Paul Simon, and Johannes Brahms.

No piece in the show gave Larry more satisfaction, however, than Canada's national anthem, which he first heard as a four-year-old attending a major league baseball game between the hometown Cubs and the newly created Montreal Expos. "I said, 'Mommy, what *is* that?' And I went home and learned it, and finally got to play it regularly when I was doing my Masters at the University of Wisconsin and moonlighting as the organ player for the local Junior hockey team, which often played Canadian teams. Up here, I get to play it twice a day."

Larry was under contract to the Great Wallenda Circus for thirty-five hundred dollars a week, and in turn held contracts with his trumpeter, Peter Bartels, and his drummer, Ronnie King, whom he paid as he saw fit. During the early 1990s, he had been told that circus musicians were not long for this world – exactly the point at which his work load began to increase. "Some producers think they can get away with taped music," he told me. "And maybe they can for a while, because a lot of people aren't very discriminating. But even those people, when they leave a performance where they haven't had the benefit of an orchestra, are going to be thinking that there was something missing, something fuzzy or unemphatic about the show. And they're gonna say to themselves, 'I guess the circus isn't as good as it used to be.' And even though they may not know why, they'll be right. And they won't be back."

Larry paused, lit a Lucky Strike, and exhaled. "The thing is, tape can't respond to what's going on in the rings the way live musicians can. And tape can't lead the show along if it gets sluggish the way live musicians can. With live music and live acts you've got two living organisms and an exchange of energy going on between them. With tape, you've got one living and one dead organism."

Bill Boren, the ringmaster, came into the restaurant and approached our table. We greeted one another, and he said, "You guys got this bug that's goin around?"

"Have you got it?" Larry said. "You're lookin kinda wiped."

"You don't know the half of it," he said.

"All I ever *did* know was about half of it," Larry deadpanned.

Bill smiled ruefully and sat down. "I'll have a coffee," he said to the waitress, then, turning to us, "Sometimes I get so gawdam lonely on the road, I feel like announcing to the crowd that if there's a lady out there looking for companionship, she oughta meet me after the show." Bill, who is sixty years old and whose wife died several years ago, is the epitome of the well-groomed nightclub entertainer – at least on the surface. His shave is flawless, his moustache a dart, his hair a sculpture in spun silver. He wears patent leather shoes and owns a dozen lurid tuxedos. He has worked in lounges, on stage, and in revues, and has made hundreds of radio and television appearances. His circus work alone puts him in front of two hundred thousand people a year.

"Maybe you'd get a dozen ladies," I said.

"Maybe you could get one for me," brightened Larry.

Bill sipped his coffee.

Larry smoked.

"I dunno," Bill said presently, "I guess I figure there must be *one* out there whose life is as lonesome as mine."

Perhaps predictably, the show that afternoon was a nightmare of blunders and bad timing. The arena's electrical heaters were turned on only at the last moment, so that, for the first twenty minutes, the crowd sat shivering and indifferent. During the tiger act, one of Wilson's cats got up from the laydown, returned to its seat, and vomited up a bellyful of semi-digested red meat. Wilson feeds each of the cats a daily ration of about twelve pounds of raw beef or horse meat that he stores in pre-packed sausage-like tubes in a pair of freezers in his living compartment in the tiger trailer. On most tours, the difficulty in feeding is that, while the meat is being thawed outside, it can become ever-so-slightly fricasseed by the sun or the pavement, rendering it inedible to the tigers, which will not eat meat that has been even minutely defiled by cooking. On this tour, however, Wilson couldn't *get* the meat thawed, and had to leave it out so long on the ground that, often, it had been considerably diminished by ravens by the time it was warm enough for the cats. While a Siberian tiger such as Seanna is genetically equipped to digest partially frozen meat, as her forebears have done for millennia in the Sikhote-Alin Mountains of eastern Siberia, the resident Bengals, with their jungle metabolism, would sometimes vomit it back up if it was too recently out of the freezer.

A minute later, with the cats in their pyramid, the floodlights flickered a sickly yellow, crackling as they did so, and then shut down, the arena's antique circuitry fatally overburdened by the combined demands of the heaters, floodlights, and spots. Ricky vaulted from his chair by the lighting board, lurched across the floor and out the main doors, in search of the switch box and controls. In the absence of the amplifiers and electric piano, the music was reduced to Pete Bartels's trumpet solo, while Wilson stood in near-total darkness, illuminated only by the exit signs, his back to the cage wall, more or less at the mercy of the tigers. As my eyes adjusted to the darkness, I could see the cats, dimly outlined on their seats, heads low in the stalking or defence mode, simultaneously ready to attack or to protect what was theirs. The power failure, Wilson told me later, was the second he had experienced in twenty-odd years of performing. "What saved me," he said, "is that the tigers are such loners, they're more concerned about getting hit by one another in a situation like that than they are about getting me. Still, if one of them has a mind to, that's the time they'll eat ya."

Under emergency power, a single spot came to life – an illuminated cylinder through the dark interior of the building – allowing Wilson to send the tigers from the ring and the Texans to dismantle the cage. Chata and Liliana did their web tandem so obscured and fragmented in the spotlight's tight grip that the effect of their performance was not so much aerial ballet as a succession of disembodied heads, arms, thighs, calves, and sequins, appearing briefly out of the darkness and then vanishing as the light wavered back and forth between them. Paul and Chata's trampoline act disintegrated into manic syncopation as the erratic spot scoured the space above the apparatus, up and down, attempting to locate Paul, who seemed always to be exploding upwards or plummeting through its beam in the opposite direction to which it was moving.

Enrique Luna's low-wire act, which was at the best of times a kind of abstract joke about itself and about stardom and glamour, was reduced to an abstraction of an abstraction – a joke impossible to understand about a subject impossible to see. He went about it, however, with his customary, admirable good will, the elegant "Sir Henry," staggering and pratfalling across the wire, first by himself and then in mock elegance with a life-sized rag doll in a red satin dress, whose feet and hands were attached to his own, so that the pair appeared to waltz – all of it thoroughly incomprehensible in the darkness.

In the attempt to restore power, Manuel Gonçalves, too, rushed off in the direction of the master electrical panel, neglecting in the process to move his wife Jill's prop rack from the wings out into the ring in preparation for her sword-balancing routine. The result was that, when *The lovely Natasha, exotic master of razor-sharp swords* appeared with a flourish in the platinum tunnel of the spot, there were no swords to master or balance, and she was left hollering for them, in escalating frustration, above the disco-like trumpet solo that was her introduction to the audience. She had all but turned to ice by the time Manuel emerged in cartoon haste from beneath the bleachers to deliver the hardware.

Jill's physique is a notable component of her presentation, and, at age forty-one, she does little to discourage interest in her strong, well-shaped lower limbs. Her one-piece costumes are cut high on the hips, and are only slightly more discreet astern than the tiniest circus bikinis, the backsides of which are not so much "worn" on the rear anatomy as engulfed by it. The costumes are designed, needless to say, for surroundings that are at least minimally heated, and on this day, with the audience in scarves and ski jackets, even the most ardent fancier of the female form might have speculated sympathetically about possible hypothermia.

Jill's stage is a low, chromed stand about the size of a dining-room table, in the centre of which stands a fifteen-foot ladder. Up she went, the rapier balanced in approximately the spot where the third eye of the mystic might shine, accentuating her act with a series of balletic postures and kicks. Before her second trip up, she placed the handle of a foot-long dagger in her teeth, balanced a sword from the dagger's tip, and lit a candle in the hilt of the sword.

At one time in the North American circus, the house lights were darkened only for the performances of the greatest stars. Nowadays, most acts are given the beneficial focus of the darkened house, a by-product of which is that clean-up and preparatory activities can be accomplished unseen on other parts of the arena floor while the acts proceed. As Jill reached the top of her ladder, however, the house lights came on, revealing the prop men scurrying about their chores, diffusing the crowd's attention, so that the balance of Jill's act and much of the rest

*Jill Gonçalves doing her sword-balancing routine in Flin Flon, Manitoba.*

of the afternoon's performance took on the unfocused feel of a rehearsal.

The Statues, which the program listed alternatively as "The Amazing Mayans" and "The Golden G Men," suffered particularly in this desultory atmosphere. Their brilliant sculptural gymnastics – an evolving flow of dramatically levered poses – had been voted the act of the decade during the 1980s in Las Vegas, had for years been a fixture at the Flamingo Hilton in that city, and was certainly among the most impressive acts in the Great Wallenda Circus. Its maximum effect, however, lay not in the typical bold strokes for which the circus is renowned but in its cumulative rhythm and power, and in the Promethean lifts that Evrardo Garza Sr., a one-time Mister Mexico, was able to effect with his son Evrardo Jr. and with Chunyan Ho. Unfortunately, the subtleties of the act could really only be appreciated either in an intimate seating arrangement, such as that of a one-ring circus tent, or under the act's own highly specialized lighting, neither of which was available that afternoon in the Fort Frances arena. In the cold, what's more, the sight of three nearly-naked men covered in metallic gold gel said as much about human frailty – in this case the hard cold shivers – as it did about the glories of physical culture or classical gymnastics.

Chata Olvera's hair-hang, equally ill-served by the circumstances, became a kind of gothic debunking, in that the mechanism for her flight into the rafters, normally shrouded in darkness, was glaringly revealed in the form of three powerful prop men hauling on the distant end of a rope strung through a pulley and attached to a ring through her knotted hair. If the resulting effect, with its clear hint of the gallows, was comic or even morbid, it also emphasized the baleful force that the lift line exerted on Chata's head and neck. At a signal from Paul, the prop hands simply dug in their heels and tractored backwards, lifting their quarry, it seemed to me, with no more sensitivity than they might have applied to hoisting a trophy tuna or a skid of newsprint. The day before, somebody had explained to me that, were it not for the application of an external anaesthetic that deadened the nerves of her scalp, Chata would have been unable to endure the pain of the lift. But when I pressed her on the secrets of her work she had laughed and assured me that there were *no secretos*, just hair and a ring and a hook – and years of practice. "Her advantage," Paul told me, "is that she's very light – about ninety-five pounds – and she has very dense hair. It doesn't hurt her at all. We just have to make sure we get every hair at the same tension and that we get the knot in properly." Chata's counterpart on another circus, a woman unknown to her, had failed recently to "get the knot in properly" and had fallen to her death when her hair unravelled suddenly in mid-lift.

Floodlighting was restored in time for the display of bicycle and unicycle tricks, but lapsed again halfway through the number, leaving a single spot playing ineffectually across Brett Marshall and Doug Pashuta in the outer rings and the unicyclist David Connors in the centre. Brett, who, like Doug, performs on a smallish, BMX bicycle, described to me later the sense of imminent peril created by the disappearance of the floodlights and, with them, what he called "the crucial security" of being able to see where he was headed as he rode. "In the little circle of the spotlight, you can't see more than a few inches ahead of your front wheel," he said, "so you have no idea where you are relative to the ring curb. Which isn't too bad, maybe, if you're just sitting on the bike, doing circles. But if you're up there in a handstand, one hand on the handlebars, the other on the seat, and suddenly you hit the curb, you're in trouble when you land – you could break your back, break your neck, anything."

❧

But it is unfair for me to go on about the performers on what was surely one of the worst afternoons of their careers. For most of them, even the cold and the wretched lighting could do little to disguise their inarguable talents and stamina.

During intermission, Rick initiated a spirited confab with his lighting director, Patty Alexander, whom he often referred to as his "rocket scientist" because she had trained and worked as an F-16 fighter jet mechanic during a four-year stint in the U.S. Air Force. Between the two of them, he was sure they could figure out some way of improving a situation that, at this point, could hardly get worse. Patty is an intensely energetic forty-one-year-old, with a spiked haircut, a mischievously boyish demeanour, and a *curriculum vitae* that includes acting, sales, magicianship, painting, fire-eating, marksmanship, ballroom dancing, and half a dozen branches of academic scholarship – and, of course, jet mechanics.

Like everyone else in the circus, she also has a story, which she tells with the same eddying enthusiasm that she applies to everything else about her life. Within ten minutes of meeting her during the early days of the tour, I learned, among other things, that as a teenager she had fled an unhappy home to live with Romanian gypsies in rural New Jersey; that, at the age of eighteen, she had given birth to a son, whom she has since raised to adulthood; and that, during the months of her pregnancy, she had embraced the intense, political feminism of the mid-1970s. "I just loved seeing these women with their well-founded ideas, speaking their minds, acting on their intelligence, just being complete people, which I wasn't at that time," she told me, proceeding to explain that, at a certain point in her young life, she had decided that, more than anything else, she wanted to be one of those women, was *determined* to be one of those women.

"Of course at that point, I didn't have the confidence to be one of those women," she said. "All through school I'd thought I was stupid – had been *told* I was stupid, because I didn't see things

*Matt Wilkins and Patty Alexander, the Great Wallenda Circus's clown, lighting director, and "rocket scientist" – on the floor of the arena in Swan River, Manitoba.*

the way other people did, including my teachers. Then I started reading – basically everything I could get my hands on. I just devoured books, and discovered, lo and behold, that my thoughts didn't *have* to be like everybody else's to be valid – that maybe I did have a brain after all." Patty went back to high school and on to college and university. "I aced an IQ test to get into the military," she said, "and gradually learned how to *do* things and how to *say* things. People's assumption is that I know how to work the lights because I studied physics or worked on fighter jets," she laughed. "It's a glamorous notion. But the reason I can work lights is that I worked them in my drama classes at Ocean County Community College in New Jersey."

Patty described the last dozen years of her life as "essentially a search for God" – a search that, in one way or another, had brought her as far as the circus. "Look at these people," she said to me one day. "They're heroes. They're resourceful. They're survivors. They're incredible risk-takers. I have such tremendous admiration for people with more guts than I have."

In addition to running the lights for the Great Wallenda Circus, Patty was its only professional clown, meaning that, half an hour before each show, she emerged from the catacombs in an elegantly farcical costume, the design of which combined the hallucinatory poetics of the Mad Hatter, the visual alarm system of the killer bee, and of course her own artful sense of play. She kibitzed with the audience, entertained the kids, did a little magic, posed for snapshots, generally made herself available and amenable. When the show started, she raced into the dressing room, scrubbed her make-up, whipped off her costume, and reappeared pronto to take up her duties as a rocket scientist.

By the time intermission ended, she and Ricky had restored the floodlights to about half power – not so bright as to blow out the circuit breakers, but bright enough that the house lights did not have to be on. At less than full power, however, the floods shone with a kind of radioactive pallor which lent to the skin of the performers, in particular the gringos, a lemony translucence that would not have been out of place in an episode of *The X-Files*. But it was better by far than single spots or house lights, and the second half proceeded in a jittery glow, so acceptable by comparison to the first half that, in retrospect, the latter came to be viewed as a kind of test for the character of the circus, or, as Bobby Gibbs put it, "some sort of cattle call for the Gong Show."

When Rick Wallenda entered the dressing room at the completion of the afternoon's performance he look haggard and pale, and urged anybody within earshot, as he had urged them on the floor of the arena, simply to "get the date over with, so that we can load the trucks and get outta here."

I had arranged earlier to meet him at the conclusion of the performance, and he now suggested that, instead of going for coffee as planned, I drive him to his room at the Rendezvous Hotel on the shores of Rainy Lake, where he could both chat and relax before cranking it back up for the evening performance. As we left the parking lot, he laid his head against the seat back and told me that, years ago in Fort Worth, the lights had gone out on the Wallendas while they were in the middle of their seven-person pyramid. "Actually," he said, "they were practising for their first remounting of it after the fall in Detroit. They couldn't see a thing. Couldn't move forward, couldn't move backward. Even the slightest jiggle would have thrown them off the wire. My grandfather just told everybody to hold perfectly still, not to panic and to breath slowly. And that's what they did. Seven, eight, nine seconds . . ." Rick's mother, Carla, who was watching the rehearsal from the floor of the arena, described the experience in a documentary film about the Wallendas made by Arts & Entertainment Television in 1996. "As the moments passed," she said, "I kept expecting to hear the sound of the poles and equipment hitting the floor, and then the bodies. When the lights came back on, and they were still up there, it was like awakening out of some terrible nightmare."

As we drove, Rick voiced his frustrations over the afternoon's performance and described how, from weariness and stress, the pain in his back and legs had worsened to a point where he was unable to escape or suppress it. So far, he said, he had limited his intake of analgesics to an occasional aspirin or two, but he was looking forward to a soak in the hotel hot tub and a good night's sleep before taking off for Kenora.

In the hotel room, he plopped into an easy chair, removed a pair of black athletic shoes, and said quietly, "Sometimes I think I've tried to do too much. A lot of people don't realize what I've been through since my accident."

I asked if he minded talking about what he'd been through, or about the accident itself, and having said he did not, he described at my request how, in early 1996, he had contracted to do his wire act above a small but popular recreation area called Arnold's Park in northeastern Iowa. On the morning he arrived at the site, he had set up his rigging, and when everything was accomplished except for the tightening of the turnbuckles and winches he had climbed one of the forty-foot poles to the takeoff pedestal to fine-tune his guy lines. "It's something you should never do unless everything is tight," he said matter-of-factly. "I knew that, but I figured I could get away with it, because I'd gotten away with it lots of times before. I loosened one bolt," he said, holding up a finger, "and I knew right away that I'd made a mistake, that it was all going down."

As the rigging collapsed, Rick jumped free of the pole and pedestal, so as not to get trapped beneath it or hit on the head. "My head had been hurt so badly in eighty-seven, in Jacksonville, I figured I wouldn't survive another head injury. On the other hand, I knew if I jumped my legs wouldn't survive."

Rick might actually have saved his legs *and* his life had he landed in the large children's play pit filled with sand, beneath the wire. "Wouldn't ya know it," he laughed. "I landed on the foot-high concrete curb around it."

I asked Ricky if he felt a landing on the sand would have saved his career, and he said, "Absolutely not. Even before my rigging hit the ground I knew that, in one way or another, my career was over, and that I was never getting back on the wire – I never *wanted* to get back on, and I was at peace with that."

I said, "You mean you were at peace as you were falling?"

"That's right," he said. "If I died, I knew where I was headed, and that everything would be fine. If I lived, I knew no matter how serious the injuries, things would somehow work out, because I'd established a relationship with God. I had no fear."

His forthright expression of faith caught me off guard, and in the brief silence that ensued he began to explain that there had been no such equanimity during or after his first fall in Jacksonville in 1987. "It was a very different time in my life," he said, explaining that during the 1970s he had been a practising Christian but had rejected God in 1982 and, at the time of the accident, had been mired in alcoholism, hostility, and spiritual emptiness. "That day in Jacksonville," he said, "I was doing a trick we called the leapfrog, where I'd come in behind my wife – my then-wife – who'd be crouched on the wire, and I'd jump over her, without touching her, and land out in front. Problem was, I didn't jump right and didn't hit the wire right when I landed."

I asked how it was possible, after doing the trick successfully thousands of times, suddenly not to "jump right" or "hit the wire right." Wasn't it pretty much instinct by this time?

"Sure it was," he said. "I was just too complacent. I was reckless. I wasn't centred when I took off. My feet were off to one side, but instead of stopping and adjusting, I just figured I'd compensate as I went up and over. What I didn't realize was that, because I was off to one side, I wasn't going to be *able* to compensate; I was only going to get farther off line."

Rick's feet hit the wire and glanced off, and he grabbed the wire with his hand behind his back. "But I couldn't hang on," he said. "And I can't really tell you what happened on the way down, whether I blacked out before I hit the floor, or whether the impact knocked me out. About all I could remember later was my realization that I wasn't going to be able to hang on and mentally saying goodbye to my wife and daughter. I was going headfirst; I was dead."

Out of (perhaps unseemly) curiosity, I asked Rick if, in the moment of reckoning, he had said anything to his wife, or she to him (it is a morbid bit of lore that, in the instant before the pyramid collapsed in Detroit, Rick's doomed cousin, Dieter Schepp, cried out to those above him, "*Ich kanns nicht mehr halten!*" – I can't hold it any longer).

"There was no verbal communication at all," said Rick. "I wasn't even aware of the reaction of the crowd."

As fate would have it, the cage for an upcoming cat act had been set up in the centre ring, directly below Rick and Debbie's rigging. "People tell me that when I was about two-thirds of the way down, I grabbed at the top of the cage and hit it with my wrist, which is probably what broke my arm. But by hitting it I also changed the angle at which I was falling. Instead of coming down headfirst, my body was now tilted, so that my head hit the concrete more on the side than directly on top. That's what saved me."

When Rick regained consciousness on the floor, a nurse who had come out of the audience and was at his side explained to him who he was, where he was, and what had happened, urging him all the while to lie still, and reassuring him that he was on his way to the hospital and that things would be all right. "Two of the things I remember," he said, "were trying to sit up and support myself with my arm and the arm just bending all over the place, and being terribly concerned that somebody call my grandmother and tell her what had happened, so that she wouldn't hear it on the news. Anything she knew about family accidents from the past would have led her to think the worst."

The toll on Rick's body included massive bruising and internal injuries, as well as severe fractures of the skull, jaw, arm, hip, and ribs. For his life as a whole, however, the most devastating effects of the accident were yet to come. "In retrospect," he told me, "I'd say it was the beginning of the end of my marriage."

From its start, the marriage had taken a course no one could have predicted. Rick had met Debbie in 1980 when, as a reporter for the Columbus *Suburban News*, she interviewed him while he was performing in Columbus, Ohio. "When we first went on the road together," he explained, "I thought she was going to do wardrobe, domestic stuff, and that maybe at some point we'd be able to get her to do the aerial ballet, or something. She'd been a cheerleader in high school, but she wasn't a particularly athletic person."

When Debbie made her first trip with the troupe in 1982, according to Rick, she barely had the strength to climb the ladder to the high-wire pedestal. But she was determined to be part of the act. "I started her by getting her to climb the ladder, up and down, to build up her strength," Rick said. "Then I got her to go up and down the webs, and taught her the aerial ballet routine."

In Sarasota that autumn, Debbie took her first walk on the high wire, and by January 1983 she was doing solo walks in the act. "By spring, she'd joined the pyramid," said Rick, "and by the end of that year she was doing everything my sister was doing."

Before long, she and Rick were doing a bold tandem, and Debbie was ambitious to break new ground. "She wanted," said Rick, "to be the first woman to do a leap to the wire from a 'two-high stack'" – in other words, from Rick's shoulders.

Then came Jacksonville and the trauma that, in Rick's words, "just totally blew her away. She knew we were in a dangerous occupation – of course she did; she was married to a Wallenda – but I don't think the worst possibilities had ever occurred to her. She wasn't *from the circus*. Put some of the girls in this show in the same position – say, Liliana or Chata – and they'll survive it, they've seen it, they were raised in the circus, they know what it's about. Debbie was a relatively protected kid from Grand Rapids, Michigan. It seemed to me that all she wanted to do after the accident was separate herself from it – and I guess from me, emotionally, because she knew that I wasn't going to give up performing, even though I did make a decision at that point to begin a transition to producing. I was thirty-two – that was the long-term goal."

The flu bug that was circulating among the performers had caught up with Rick in Dryden, and at this point he rose from his chair, went into the washroom, and gave his nose a loud, well-loaded honk. "I should be drinking more," he said as he emerged. "If you'll excuse me, I'm going to go get a pop from the machine." He left the room, came back a few seconds later, and asked me if I had a one-dollar coin.

When he returned, I asked him why, over the years, the family had so stubbornly refused to use any safety device, up to and including a net.

"You can't count on them," he shrugged. "You can get hurt just as badly with them as without them."

His answer, I suggested, had its conceptual base in the same fuzzy thinking used in the argument against seat belts (Pat Delaney had told me that Rick, so casual about his security on the wire, was, in fact, a zealot about seat belts and obsessive about reducing the risks of highway driving).

"Apples and oranges," he said.

I asked if a net wouldn't have saved lives in Detroit, and he said, "All seven of them might have gone down and been killed if they'd believed they'd be saved by a net." A net, he claimed, creates a false sense of security and would almost certainly have become a tacit cause for slippage in the family's meticulous performance standards. "If the net's not there," he said, "you have the best reason of all for staying on the wire."

What's more, of course, the absence of the net significantly magnifies the *appearance* of risk, which as anyone close to the Wallendas can tell you has always been as important to the presentation of the family act as the reality of risk. When Karl Wallenda appeared with his diminished troupe two days after the famous disaster in Detroit, one of the tricks he performed was a chair-stand on the shoulder bar above his brother, Herman, and nephew, Gunther. *The Detroit Free Press* said in its report on the event, "It looked for an agonizing moment as though tragedy might repeat itself when the chair swayed dangerously as Karl stood up, waving to the crowd. He fought for balance, got it, sat down, and rode to the safety of the platform." Circus writer Bill Ballantine wrote in turn, "Case-hardened circus hands coolly appraising the act's rebirth knew better; they recognized and admired the chair tremor as the 'selling' masterpiece of the maestro's long career."

"The Wallenda style of wire-walking was dramatic," Ricky allowed. "It was about danger and difficulty. If a trick doesn't look dangerous, as far as the audience is concerned, it isn't."

In the absence of nets or safety wires, the troupe's idea of a protective measure was to take a thermometer with them to their rigging in the uppermost part of the circus tent, where summer temperatures sometimes reached 130 degrees Fahrenheit, creating imminent danger of fainting or heat stroke. "That was my Uncle Herman," Rick smiled. "The idea was that they'd at least know if somebody was likely to pass out and would cut back on the most dangerous tricks."

Where most topics are concerned, Rick is an attentive and imaginative conversationalist, inclined to introduce bits of wordplay or irony to his discussions, or to track suddenly into new territory or call up a literary or biblical reference. But when he is detailing or interpreting family history, a listener might occasionally get the impression that he is working from a text that he has perhaps referred to one too many times and would just as soon abandon. Perhaps for that reason, he seemed relieved rather than cornered when I asked if, given his spiritual perspective, he had been able to see anything of the workings of God in the disasters that had befallen him. "Oh, boy, you wanta hear some theology," he brightened, proceeding to explain that, while his grandfather had been "a fatalist" who believed that the affairs of humanity were played out as if to some careful precoding, he, Ricky, believed that people's free will and choices dictated their fates against the larger backdrop of God's plan. "There was an evangelist named Charles Finney before the Civil War," he told me, "and he taught what he called 'the incipiency of the will' – that human beings had been given the power to choose or to reject God, and that the world was in such a mess because most people had rejected Him. That's kinda my philosophy. I believe in a God of love, so it's very difficult to think that, even during the decade when I rejected Him and turned to alcohol and secularism, he caused all these awful things to happen to me. That's not love. But I do believe He's *used* these things, and is still using them, to get my attention and teach me that there are other possibilities for my life."

Rick reported that, in the aftermath of his accident in Jacksonville, he had been taken to a Baptist hospital, where Christian visitors came to his room to evangelize as he convalesced. "I threw them out," he said. "My cousin Tino called me up. He and I weren't on good terms at the time, because he's a Christian and I'd walked away from God. I loved attacking his faith. Nevertheless, he had the guts to call and tell me God was trying to communicate something to me. And, predictably, I guess, I made a very nasty response; my vocabulary had degenerated pretty severely at that point. The fact is, the spirit was stirring, and now that I've responded to it, I believe God is using my brother's death, my accidents, my wife's leaving, to teach me and direct me."

Rick reflected briefly and said, "My wife's departure was the worst thing I faced by far. I was a tough, macho sort of guy, the Marlboro Man – nothing was going to reach or affect me. When Debbie left, all my defences collapsed – all the armour I was wearing to disguise who I was inside. Within two weeks I was suicidal. That's when I went and got Christian counselling. Nineteen ninety-three. I quit drinking, started praying, got my hostilities under control, my vocabulary. I gradually started healing."

For a few moments, we sat in silence.

"Suicide fantasies aren't a good thing for a guy who walks the wire," I said (knowing even as I spoke that I would have to think long and hard to come up with a more facile or obvious comment).

Rick (who was probably thinking much the same thing) said, "I don't think I'd have done it on the wire."

After another silence, I asked whether he could still get out there and take a few steps if he had to. His laugh was both wistful and dismissive. "You should see my feet," he said.

I asked if I could, and he took off his socks, revealing heels that resembled well-baked dinner rolls to which someone had taken a two-by-four. "The calcaneus, the heel bone, was completely powdered when I fell," he said. "When the surgeon got in there, there was no bone left to attach together. They just kinda pushed it all back in and sewed it up."

By his own assessment, Rick has broken every major bone he possesses, except the ones in his neck. "And I'm not going to break those," he told me, "because I'm not a wire walker any more. I have a new job."

He could, he suggested, make a wire walker out of *me*. "Actually, out of anybody who can ride a bicycle," he said. "In theory, I could get Bobby Gibbs up there. Whether you can do it in a show or not depends on whether you have the guts to do it up high – the lack of brains, as I like to put it. If you're stupid enough, we can make a wire walker out of you."

Despite the stress, Rick was by no means dissatisfied with the circus's overall progress on the tour. In fact, he was immensely pleased at having moved the show overnight from Dryden, a feat common enough among travelling circuses, including enormous operations such as Carson and Barnes, but nonetheless an accomplishment for a fledgling producer.

The success of the move, however, owed less to Ricky than to a laconic and soft-spoken circus veteran named David Connors, who had spent his childhood as an animal keeper on the Carson and Barnes Circus and possessed a greater range of show talents than perhaps anyone else connected to the Great Wallenda Circus. Not only could he juggle and ride unicycles, as he did daily in the show, he could walk the wire, do rola-bola and trampoline, and presented what circus people refer to as a "comedy car" act – a routine in which one or more clowns, usually of the tramp variety, meet a series of carefully planned misadventures as they nurse a customized jalopy onto (and off) the arena floor.

But on this show, as well as others these days, David was best recognized as an outstanding prop and rigging man, a guy who could take a show down in short order, truck it to the next town, and put it back up. He and his three assistants, all from Gainesville, Texas, had worked for Ricky off and on through the mid-1990s and were said by Wilson Barnes to be the best crew he had worked with in two decades in the business. "It doesn't matter how good your acts are if you can't get your circus from one town to the next," said Rick. Out of respect for his prop crew's efforts, he compensated even the least experienced of them at a rate of nearly four hundred dollars U.S. a week, about twice the pay they'd have made on some other North American shows.

*David Connors, seen here warming up on the lot in Thunder Bay, Ontario.*

What fascinated me as much as anything about Ricky and David as I got to know them was the almost uncanny number of common valences that defined their otherwise quite different lives. It would have been difficult, however, for either of them to see, much less admit to, these, given their respective backgrounds, one at the patrician end of the circus's human spectrum, the other at the end where everything a person owns eventually smells like elephants or tigers or horse manure. Even on the current tour, while Ricky slept (alone) in the best hotels he could locate, David spread his sleeping bag (alone) in the bed of his half-ton truck. Trappings aside, each was forty-two years old and could claim seven generations of ancestry in the circus. Each was single, with two children. Each, I believe, was lonely. Each, what's more, had experienced childhood displacement that had reverberated, at times unhappily, throughout his adult life. Ricky, who was raised in part by his grandmother, was the offspring of a liaison between Carla Wallenda and an Italian acrobat named Eugenio Bogino. David was the son of a long-time circus journeyman and a French-Canadian mother, who, having raised him to the age of three, handed over full custody for both David and his brother to a middle-aged uncle and aunt – she, a Cherokee Indian – who for years had husbanded truckloads of domesticated animals on the immense Carson and Barnes tent circus. "They were hard people, and they kicked the crap out of the boys," said Bobby Gibbs, whose years at Carson and Barnes overlapped with David's. "They didn't even feed them right. It's a wonder David turned out to be the guy he is."

The brothers' childhood responsibilities encompassed twenty-seven horses, twenty ponies, dozens of monkeys, dogs, and miscellaneous domestic animals. "Our job," said David, "was to feed them, water them, clean their cages, brush them, wash their tails, harness them, saddle them for the pony rides, get 'em all ready for the show, then take everything off afterwards, all this twice a day. I was doing this from the time I was a tiny boy till I was eighteen. And by that time, I'd had enough; I wasn't going for the gold shovel award."

Of all the similarities between David's life and Ricky's, perhaps the most striking was that, during the early 1990s, David, like his boss, had experienced the loss of a partner – a loss that compelled him, as it had Rick, to take refuge in Christianity. David's wife, Belinda Jean, or "Sissy," had come from a family of Oklahoma concession operators. But by the time she met David in 1976 she had branched into performing and was doing simple presentation turns such as riding the elephants, styling for the animal acts, or appearing in production numbers. "Then we started doing unicycles together. A unicycle doesn't look like much," David laughed, "but it don't eat, and it don't shit. And at that point in my life, that was enough to make it attractive."

It is a sweet point of trivia that Sissy was a champion bird mimic, able to imitate with a ten-cent bird whistle the song of any winged creature from a sparrow to a finch to a bluebird. "She'd wet one of these little whistles that she and Dave used to sell at intermission and put it in her mouth and start makin sounds," said Bobby Gibbs, "and people'd just flock up around her and reach for their money to buy one. She and Dave could sell two or three hundred dollars worth of them a day."

Along the way, Sissy gave birth to two daughters, now aged nine and thirteen, and developed an aerial act on a piece of apparatus called the loop-the-loop – in effect, a mid-air swing or trapeze, but with rigid steel rods instead of ropes or cables, the whole device just big enough that a person can stand in it and pump it to the point where it arcs up and over its own axle, into a spectacular succession of revolutions. "You work it holding a pair of hand loops, with your feet in special shoes that key into the swing, so you can't fall out," explained David. "Sissy just loved it. She'd kick it back and forth till it was almost over the top, then just hold it up there, then go backwards, hold it again, then forward. Then round and round. It was exciting."

On April 15, 1991, in Marquette, Michigan, Sissy was winding down her performance when she did what she had been doing for years – confidently removed her feet from the locking devices while the swing was still in operation. "On the upswing," said David, "she somehow lost her grip on the hand loops, fell out backwards, and down she came."

"She was a big girl," said Bobby Gibbs. "The impact popped her head right open. Killed her dead. David was there on the floor – just wasn't close enough to do anything about it."

For a year after the accident, David continued to travel with the circus. "Then I kinda crashed," he told me. "I went home to Gainesville – I own the house my step-parents raised us in – and for the next couple'a years I pretty much just lay there thinking about it all.

"Then one day, I woke up and said, Where is everybody? Where are my friends? And the answer was, they're out there on the circus, havin fun, doin what they do, while I'm sittin here brooding and lookin at my gear. The circus is a family in itself," he said. "If it's in your blood, it's extremely hard to ignore. So I got on the phone, got some dates booked for myself and the girls – they do circus, too – and away we went."

As I had done with Ricky Wallenda, I asked David how an experienced performer like Sissy, so comfortable on her apparatus, so familiar with its vectors and whims, could have failed so decisively in her operation of the thing. "A lot of people felt she was *too* comfortable," he said, "that she'd gotten lackadaisical about her safety. For myself, I suspect she was tired or wasn't feeling well and wouldn't admit it. People don't realize how exhausting circus can be – the travel, the set-ups, the performances. I did six hundred and ninety performances one year, on three hundred and forty-five dates – every one of them in a different place. You work dizzy, you work hurt, you work half-asleep. Half the time, I can't even remember what state or province I'm in, let alone what town."

But David, like Ricky, is a survivor. And that night in Fort Frances – perhaps dizzy, perhaps hurt, perhaps half-asleep – he was out on the floor, as always, fulfilling his roles both as prop boss and performer, alternating his visible identity between the rumpled black tux that is his floor-director's attire and the blue sequinned sausage-suit that he wore as a unicyclist during the first half of the show and, later, as the fire juggler El Flamo, or, as Bill Boren sometimes called him, the Human Cigar.

Afterwards, as his crew tore the show down, I watched David, now in jeans and a sweatshirt, clamber into the rafters, and step with the confidence of a steelrigger across a six-inch-wide beam, thirty feet above the floor, loosening turnbuckles, releasing clamps, undoing guy lines – no hands, no safety belt – until at a crossing of beams in the highest part of the arena, he tripped on a junction plate and, from a sick angle, grabbed a two-inch strut, steadying himself casually when he might well have been heading for the floor.

"It ain't over till the fat lady sings!" he hollered down, laughing. "And I don't hang around with fat ladies."

He proceeded across the beam, aware that I had sharpened my focus on him, and a few seconds later yelled, "What do they call the white stuff in chicken shit, Charlie?"

"I dunno," I shouted up.

"They call that chicken shit, too!"

# 6

J UDY'S BEDTIME SNACK that night consisted of a dozen-odd kilos of candy floss, half a bale of hay, and several bunches of overripe bananas. With the sixty-year-old showgirl more or less cosy in her quarters, Bobby and I drove to the Red Dog Inn, where I was staying, hoping to catch a televised documentary on elephants that I had seen advertised earlier in the day. Bob has a scholar's thirst for any new scrap of information on pachyderms, and, according to Wilson, keeps such a vast collection of books, clippings, and videotapes on the subject – as well as on hundreds of other circus matters of interest to him – that open space in the mobile home in which he and his wife, Rosa, live in Seagoville has been reduced to a labyrinth of passageways among the stacks. "I've got some rare stuff," he told me one day, citing, for example, an early film of Thomas Edison electrocuting an elephant in New Jersey, in a demonstration of the power and efficiency of his electric chair. "Ooh, it's awful," he winced. "Edison wanted to show that, if you could murder an elephant with this fabulous new invention of his, you could sure as hell kill a human being. Poor elephant's standing there, shaking and smoking. They did horrible things back then. When they wanted to execute an elephant they'd stake her legs to the ground and loop a long steel cable around her neck. Then they'd hitch a team of horses to either end of the cable and they'd pull in opposite directions until she strangled. Later they staked them to the railway track and used train engines to pull the cable."

I asked what circumstances might lead to the execution of an elephant, and Bob said, "Killin people. Not just one or two – they can work around that. A buncha people. Some of those elephants would kill five people over a period of years. Then they were considered too dangerous."

The route from the arena to the hotel took us through the commercial heart of Fort Frances, past the bridge that leads to International Falls, Minnesota, and around the mammoth Boise Cascade pulp mill. Earlier in the day, Bob had persuaded Bill Boren to drive him across the Rainy River to International Falls, where at a U.S. Post Office he had placed fifteen thousand dollars in cash and ten bottles of 222s – ASA and codeine – in a postal express pack and shipped it to his boss, Donny Johnson, back in Seagoville. "Ever since Donny got hammered by Congo, he's needed them two-twenty-twos," Bob told me as we stopped to pick up coffee at Robin's Donuts. "You can't get 'em without a prescription in the States."

Johnson, who owns Clyde Brothers Johnson, is a long-retired trapeze star who, according to a former employee, has "a bit of a case of Howard Hughes-itis" and spends eighteen hours a day alone, watching television with the blinds drawn in his mobile home. I asked who, or what, Congo was, and Bob explained that during the early 1990s the company had been given a middle-aged African elephant that, over the years, had been owned (and given away) by several American circuses. "I never liked the deal," he said. "An elephant's worth a hundred and thirty-five thousand dollars and we get one free. I said to Donny, 'Dontcha think just maybe somethin's a little strange here?'"

In the end Johnson paid heavily for the elephantine gift, taking a near-fatal beating from Congo as he attempted to water her one evening when Bobby and the others were out on tour. "Rosa saved his life," said Bob. "I'd warned her to stay away from Congo and to keep an eye on Donny when he went to the barn. Sure enough, when Rosa went up there one night, he was lyin by the stall, nuthin but his hair movin in the breeze. Congo'd caught him with her tusk, threw him in the air, wrecked his leg, then stomped hell out of him. Every time he tried to roll away, she pulled him back in with her trunk. At first Rosa thought he was dead, then she heard him whisperin he was alive but that he was busted up bad and couldn't move or Congo'd finish him off. 'Course Rosa's tough as scrap iron. She picked up the pitchfork and moved Congo back until she was well away from Donny, then hauled Donny forward till the elephant moved back in – pitchforked her again and pulled Donny forward some more. It took her twenty minutes to get him outta there. When I got back I had my big Asian, Betty, kick the crap outta Congo – broke her tusks right off. Not too many elephants tougher than Betty. In the end, Donny wouldn't even go to the hospital. Survived a year of intense pain on two-twenty-twos."

Bob went on to describe Betty's occasionally murderous dealings with human beings, including his groom, John McCoy, who, after a few bottles of beer one day the previous winter, made a passing attempt at "working" the elephant on the acreage at Seagoville. "I looked out the window, and I thought, Betty's got a piece'a canvas or something. She was just throwing this thing back over her head, way up in the air. She'd slap it into the mud, then pick it up and throw it down again. Then I realized it was John, and I went runnin out there. It was a good thing it was muddy and he was wasn't resisting too much, or he'd be dead. Betty won't hurt Rosa or me 'cause she likes us, respects us, but she doesn't like any of my grooms. I musta gone through fifteen of them last year. They'd be there a few days, they'd get too close, and they'd go sailing."

At the hotel room, we discovered that we had missed the elephant program because of a misunderstanding about our recent transition from the Eastern to the Central time zone. I suggested that we go out for Chinese food, to which Bob responded that he'd had a Chinese meal in International Falls at noon, one of the worst he'd ever eaten. I suggested pizza, and he said, "I prefer Chinese – only, first, I gotta call Rosa," and, telephone in hand, he settled into an easy chair from which he would not rise for the better part of the next three hours. He punched in his well-memorized calling-card number, pulled a candy from his jacket, and waited. "We got no damn buzzer in the barn," he said, pressing the receiver so deep into his jowls and beard that it all but disappeared. Eventually, he slapped it into its cradle and said, "They could drop the big one on Dallas, and Rosa wouldn't know it because she was out there in the barn shovellin bull turds!"

Bob's discourse is not so much conversation as improvisational monologue, all but impervious to interruption; and when a second call to Rosa produced no response, he offered up an encyclopedic treatise on the many and extravagant deceptions he had pulled during his decades as a circus animal trainer. He explained, for example, that he had once owned six white mules which he presented to the public as zebras by painting on stripes with Miss Clairol "satiny black" hair dye. "Depending on how much sun they got, their stripes would turn brown after a while, and I'd hafta paint them on again. The Shriners'd say, 'Hey, the stripes are fadin on the zebras,' and I'd tell them these were Siberian zebras, very rare, and that in summer they turned white because they lived on Arctic ice floes, and they needed the camouflage so the polar bears wouldn't spot them and eat them."

He further described how, during the early 1980s, he had built a side-show act around a pair of forty-pound nutrias, vegetarian

bayou rodents with webbed feet, sharp teeth, and the dispositions of bunnies. As he laid forth the details of the hoax, he
segued suddenly into a facsimile of the spiel with which he had
once conned circusgoers into laying down a dollar for the privi-
lege of seeing the world's largest and most deadly sewer rats –
*"live on the inside, not dead, stuffed or mummified – feet the size of
your hand, tail like a broomstick, jaws like those of a pitbull. These
are the ones that ate our boys in Vietnam – they crawl outta the
sewers, hide in the toilets, eat the noses off babies in their cradles.
You've read about 'em in the* National Enquirer, *my friends, but
unless you've lived in the slums of Hanoi you've never seen 'em live
on the inside, not dead, stuffed or mummified . . .*

"Oh, we'd get priests, grandmothers, bikers, guys in eight-
hundred-dollar business suits. I'd go to the supermarket and buy
dog bones and throw 'em in there with the nutrias, so they'd look
like meat eaters. I'd put rotten tomatoes in and tell the people
they were blood clots. And of course the nutrias'd be lappin away
at them when the people went in."

At a more raffish point yet in his career, Bob had displayed a
cabyragora, a fifty-pound tropical lizard, which died on tour in
North Dakota during the late 1970s. "We were making such good
money on him," he said, "that as soon as he died I sprayed him
with shellac, put a nice nest of straw under him, and kept on
showin him. He'd never moved around much anyway, and with
the lights down people couldn't tell he wasn't breathin. But after
two days in the heat, he started to decompose. *Stink!* Oh, it was
bad. I'd rush in there after we'd cleared the people out and spray
deodorizer all around. When I was giving the spiel, I'd hear people
inside go '*Aaarrrgghh*, that stinks!' And I'd holler, 'Not only is he
vicious, he stinks!' On the fourth day, it was so bad I started
burning incense in the tent. I couldn't even go in there without a
towel around my face.

"That night, a guy said, 'That thing ain't moved since I saw
him this afternoon. You sure it's alive?' So I started goin in

between shows and movin him with a stick. Oh, it was awful. His eyes were turning white; bugs were crawling in and out of his nostrils. The next morning I went to move his legs around, and one of them fell off, so I nestled it back into place. Finally, that afternoon, a guy came out and wanted his money back. I said, 'Why, sir?' And he said, 'It's dead.' And I said, 'I *very* much take offence to that, sir.' He said, 'Get your fat ass in there. I'll show ya offence.' So we went in, and he said, 'You mean to tell me that thing's alive?' I said, 'They hibernate.' He said, 'Hibernate, my ass. Lemme show ya something.' And he takes out a nail clipper and holds a nickel in it and heats it red hot with his lighter. Then he drops it into the case, right on the lizard's back, and the thing don't move an eyelid. I said, 'I believe I owe you an apology, sir – he's passed away. Here's your quarter. Now, get outta here.' My partner Gary Henry says, 'We gotta get ridda that thing.' We couldn't even drive down the highway without all the windows open. I got six extra days out of him before he died, I mean after he died. But I didn't wanta waste him, so I got one'a them plastic-lined boxes they put chicken parts in, and took a big scoop shovel and put him in the box, and we took him to a mall and left him in front of a K-Mart store." Until this point, Bob had related the story with a Sunday school reserve, but the mere mention of the word K-Mart seemed to detonate something deeply heretical within him, causing him to shriek with satisfied laughter. "The papers got hold of it," he wailed. "You shoulda seen the headlines: 'MONSTER MYSTERY LIZARD FOUND IN FRONT OF K-MART STORE.'"

I said, "I guess we better go if we're going," and he said, "Not till I reach Rosa. She's out in that barn feedin tigers, and I don't trust them." Rosa is Bob's wife of thirty-five years and, in the vastly uncertain world of the circus, is his moral and emotional anchor. Like many of those around her, her life has been deeply affected not only by the pleasures of the circus but by its sometimes harsh impositions. Born during the early 1940s into a family of Mexican circus performers, she was present in the tent on the night her father, a well-known clown named Pipino, was kicked to death by a five-ton Asian elephant as he helped ready the animal for its turn in the ring. Her mother carried on in the circus, raising six children on the earnings from an "iron jaw" act, in which she did a variety of spins and manoeuvres while hanging by her teeth in the highest part of the tent.

Bob and Rosa met in 1962 on the Hamid-Morton Circus, where Rosa, newly arrived from Mexico, was working as a trapeze artist with the Flying Padillas, and Bob was showing bears, monkeys, and miniature Zebu cattle. "In those days," said Bob, "I had lots of animals, but no money. I'd make peanut butter sandwiches for myself and for Mickey the monkey, and we'd sit there on the hay bales and eat them. Rosa used to see me and ask her friend in Spanish what kind of a slob slept in a truck with a buncha animals and shared his lunch with a monkey. I liked her girlfriend – that's who I wanted to go out with. I used to say to my friend Gary Henry, 'Ain't that Rosa a witch? Boy, she's bad-tempered.' And he'd say, 'You watch what you say or you'll end up married to her.'"

During their salad days Rosa was as much a part of Bob's acts as he was: riding elephants and horses, working bears, ponies, dogs; providing cheesecake and femininity to turns that were otherwise long on testosterone. And, always, she had her own dramatic routines, including the iron jaw, the hair hang, the slide for life, the single trapeze and, of course, the flying trapeze, which had been her ticket out of Mexico. "We'd get on a circus," said Bob, "and we'd be doin so much of the show, the producer would get panicky. If we ever broke down, or got hurt or something, he'd hafta cancel the date."

And like all circus performers, they did break down, they did get hurt – bitten or kicked or thrown by animals; tossed or dropped by improperly installed rigging. "Once I bought a nice black and white horse," Bob told me. "Rosa was gonna ride it

*Rosa Gibbs, Bobby's wife, with a friend in West Bend, Indiana, in 1968. Rosa is renowned for the respect she elicits from even the biggest and unruliest of elephants.*

bareback in an Indian costume in the parade at Circus World in Baraboo [Wisconsin]. Turned out the horse had never seen an elephant till that moment. It flipped out – bucked Rosa off, busted her pelvis."

On another occasion, in Malden, Massachusetts, she missed a "heel catch" on the trapeze – a dramatic move in which the sitting performer drops backwards off a stationary (or in some cases swinging) trapeze bar, spreading her legs and angling her feet outward at just the right moment to catch the ropes as her heels hit the bar on the way down. "The problem," Bob explained, "was that we had an unfamiliar aluminum rigging, and it flexed some when her feet hit the bar. The ropes went slack for a fraction of a second, and she shot on through and crashed onto the concrete – broke her spine. I was in the ring with her, but I couldn't get under her in time to soften her fall. With the stuff Rosa's done, it's a wonder she's alive. Once at the fairgrounds in Lincoln, Nebraska, a bear of mine was killin her sister, had bitten through her abdomen into her intestines, wouldn't let go. I'd staked the bear in a field, and Rosa's sister'd gone out to pet her. Rosa went runnin out there and beat the bear off with her fists, saved her sister's life. Even elephants know Rosa's the law. They don't mess with her."

If Bob was more concerned than usual about Rosa that night in Fort Frances, it was because, for the past week, she had borne the uneasy responsibility of taking care of the tigers that Bob and Wilson had sent home from Minnesota before coming into Canada. "Every night when I know she's out in the barn, I get fidgety," said Bob. "If one of them cats catches hold of her, she's gone, 'cause there's nobody out there to help her."

In all probability, Rosa would have been sitting in the hotel with us, or at least been on the tour, had Clyde Brothers' other elephant, Betty, not yielded an inconclusive tuberculosis test a few days before departure and been confined to the farm until the results from a further test could be confirmed. The testing of all

American elephants had been mandated by the federal Department of Agriculture after an elephant owned by John Cunio, the Illinois printing magnate, had come down with the disease a few months earlier. "We *know* she doesn't have TB," Bob protested, hastening to explain that the test for the disease requires a vet to put a small scratch in the tissue of the elephant's rectum and then to check it for swelling after seventy-two hours. "If it's swollen up hard, they've got it. Betty had a little scab, no swelling at all; I felt it. But she's an enormous animal, balky as hell, and when the vet tried to get up in there to feel it, she kicked him, and he said, 'If I can't feel it, I can't call it a clean test. I'm gonna have to turn it over to the federal inspector.' I said, 'Come on – my test's okay, Rosa's is okay, Judy's is fine. If Betty had it, we'd all have it.' But, no, he wanted a blood test, a stool test, a tongue swab. Betty won't be free for eight weeks now, maybe longer. In this business, we could be bankrupt by then."

On the current tour, the consequences of bringing one elephant instead of a pair, as promised, were a significantly reduced workload – fewer hay bales, less manure, less grooming – and a weekly reduction of a thousand dollars in the twelve-thousand-per-week fee that Rick Wallenda had contracted to pay Clyde Brothers Johnson for the combined elephant and tiger acts. It also meant a loss of ancillary revenue, in that Judy does not "do rides," as Bob puts it, whereas Betty is well accustomed to having the riding harness or howdah on her back and to carrying up to eight people at a time, as many as twenty times during an intermission, two shows a day, at up to four or five dollars per person. "Actually, Rick did us a helluva favour," Bob said. "He coulda wrung us for another thousand at least when Wilson showed up with five tigers instead of eight. But he chose to accept that there was nothing we could do about it and clearly hadn't intended it."

The less obvious consequence of Betty's absence was that Judy was without her working and living partner for the first time in nearly twenty years and was grieving the loss, at times intensely, although not in ways that any but those close to her would recognize. "You watch her at night," said Bob. "She'll take that manure shovel in the truck and, because its got Betty's smell on it, she'll wrap it all up in her trunk, cuddle it, cry over it." Bob admitted to shedding a tear himself as he left Seagoville with only Judy on board. "I knew it was gonna be hard for them," he said. "I took her outta the barn as if we were only going for a few minutes. If she'd known what was happening, I couldn't'a moved her with a bulldozer. Right now, she doesn't know if she'll ever see Betty again."

Betty's response to the separation was to trash the interior of the barn, destroy the water hoses, and smash the locks from the gates. The separation anxieties of both elephants had been heightened in 1995 when their long-time partner, Mary, died of old age on tour, in Granby, Quebec. "Elephants'll mourn for days," said Bob. "They won't leave their dead behind, but of course we couldn't take a dead elephant with us, so I gave her remains to the zoo in Granby, and they're gonna dig her up and mount her skeleton at some point in the future. Betty was so upset about it all that, if she'd had the chance, she'd have killed the guy who came to pick up Mary's body in the truck."

An elephant's maximum lifespan, Bob explained, is just under seventy years, and, under most circumstances, they will continue to perform happily until the day they die. "Usually, as they get older they either go blind, like Judy, or their trunks seize up, or both. Mary had very little mobility left in her trunk. She came off the truck that morning, walked down the ramp, and fell over dead, as if somebody'd shot her. It shook me bad. You spend fifteen, twenty years with an elephant, you're on close terms. You have the shock of them dying, and before ya can come to terms with that, you've got a ten-thousand-pound carcass to deal with. A class of little school kids were standing right there watching when she went down. I thought the teacher'd have a fit and hustle them outta there. Instead, she just started explaining to the kids in a calm voice that death was natural, and all living things die, and not to worry about it. And they all went back to school and drew pictures of their impression of Mary's death. They brought them to me. It was great. Instead of avoiding the issue, that teacher made a lesson out of it that those kids'll never forget. I said to her, 'I've gotta thank you, Ma'am. You not only helped those kids but you helped *me* deal with this.' I think I was just about as torn by it as Judy and Betty were."

In elaborating on elephant sensitivity, Bob described how, in 1992, when he took his elephants into Dillon, Montana, with the King Royal Circus, Judy had wandered repeatedly into a field near the big top and focused her attention on a particular patch of high-grass range. "I couldn't figure it out," he said, "until I walked out there in the evening and found this little weed-covered plaque saying that in 1942 a circus elephant had been hit by lightning and killed during a show there at the fairgrounds, and that she had been buried at this site." Bob fixed me with a squint and said, "Fifty years! And five *hundred* years from now, some elephant'll *still* be able to tell there's an elephant down there."

When a fourth call failed to reach Rosa, Bob decided to call Donny Johnson, whose mobile home sits on the same acreage that Bobby, Rosa, and Wilson inhabit at Seagoville. He poked in the numbers, and the mystery was over – Rosa, after feeding Betty and the tigers, had gone to visit Donny. "Gawdammit!" Bob shouted into the phone. "I thought them tigers musta ate ya. . . . Yeah, yeah, yeah. . . . You what? . . . Oh, yeah? . . . It's stinkin cold up here. It's horrible. I'm never comin back to Canada. These people are crazy. Judy's so cold I hafta leave her in the truck mosta the time. They been puttin heaters on in the buildings! . . . Oh, dammit, no, it's not as bad as Quebec . . . Oh yeah? Seventy-five? Send some'a that up here, will ya? . . . Tell

Donny I sent him some two-twenty-twos with the money. . . . Yeah, I did. . . . Hey, I told ya it was the mother that killed little JonBenet, didn't I? Either her or the father."

While Bob warmed to his call, I left the room and wandered the hotel in search of food. When I returned without a morsel, Bob was staring, as if comatose, into the carpet a few feet in front of him. "We shoulda gone for a meal," he said.

I remembered that I had some strawberries and dried apricots in the van and went out and got them. "Elephant food," Bob muttered as I laid them on the table beside him. But in no time, he had chewed up a dozen or more apricots and had taken out his jackknife and was daintily hulling the berries (it was the same knife I had seen him use to clean his fingernails, scratch his back, and scale the rust off a length of steel rod). I asked him if he thought the people on the show were comfortable having me along, and he said, "They're coughin up their stories to ya, aren't they?"

"You are," I said.

"Ya got Dave Connors's story – I never thought he'd talk to ya. Ya got Ricky's. Those are hard stories to tell. There's a lotta pain there." He said that, thirty years after the fact, there were parts of his own remarkable story that he could still not comfortably tell. Most notable among them were the deaths of his parents ten days apart in 1969, a catastrophe that so thoroughly wasted him that, had it not been for the comfort provided by Jehovah's Witnesses in the hospital where his dad died – "the same hospital where Kennedy died" – he would, in his words, have gone crazy.

"I was thirty years old," he said. "I was just getting used to my dad being gone when my mom went. Oh, I tell ya, it was the end of my world. Even though I left home young, I was very close to my mom and dad. I called them every Sunday from wherever I was. I always went home in the winter. They loved me. Always encouraged me." Bob dipped two fingers into his shirt pocket and plucked out a newspaper clipping bearing a deeply devotional memorial verse that he had harvested from the obituary page of the Thunder Bay *Chronicle-Journal* that afternoon. "I read stuff like this," he said, passing it to me, "and even after all these years, it still makes me think about them."

In practical terms, the death of Bob's parents transformed him from renegade son to self-appointed guardian and personnel manager for five younger brothers and sisters, two of whom were still in school, two barely graduated. "I had to do something for them," he said, "and since the circus was the only thing I knew, I decided to put 'em all in the circus."

Within weeks, Bob's brother Buck was on the road with a "liberty" pony act (a "liberty" act being one in which the animals work without riders). "I gave Casey the elephants and pony ride on the King show, and my youngest brother, Bingo, came with me, working as a groom, because he wasn't old enough to drive."

For his sister Pat, who is now a federal judge in Roanoke, Texas, Bob created a knife-throwing act that required her to don fishnet tights and a spangled bikini and stand at attention while, from twenty feet away, he pitched hunting daggers that thudded into a board behind her within inches of her head and torso. "Roseanne and I did bullwhips," he explained. "Just like Wilson. She'd hold a candle, say, and I'd flick it out, or I'd cut cigarettes out of her mouth." What ended the act was Bob's attempt to copy an old Whiplash Larue trick, in which the famous show cowboy removed the cap from a bottle of 7-Up with a flick of his scourge. "We went outside to practice this new trick," he explained, "and I had her hold out the bottle, and I hit it, and, dammit, the lid never come off. I said, 'Shake it up a bit, maybe it needs help.' And I hit it again. Still nuthin. 'Okay,' I told her, 'hold it tight.' I was really gonna hit it. The problem is, the more power you put into a whip, the less control you have. Well, dammit if I didn't slice open her hand this time – those little thongs at the end of the whip'll just peel the flesh right off the bone. Had to rush her to the hospital – oh, she was upset, kept howlin that she'd never forgive me.

"Later I saw Whiplash. I told him I tried to steal his trick, asked him what the gimmick was. He said, 'The first thing ya do is open the bottle, drink the pop, and fill the bottle with water. Then you put the lid back on, very lightly.' I didn't hafta hear any more. I said, 'I've got a deal for ya, Whiplash – I'll give ya a hundred dollars right now if you'll promise never to tell my sister how that trick is done.'

"All my brothers and sisters have done great. They're in business or with airlines, whatever. And here's me still in the circus," he laughed. "Every time I see one of them, they say the same thing – when are ya gonna quit? We'll put ya in business. Whaddaya wanta do? And I tell 'em I'm *doin* what I wanta do. I've travelled the world, read ten thousand books, and so far I haven't found anything interests me half as much as what I'm doing right now and hope to be doing on the day I drop dead."

During the weeks I spent with Bob, and in many subsequent phone calls and letters, speculation on what he'd be doing on "the day he dropped dead" was a recurring magnet for his thoughts – as was the decline he had begun to perceive in the quality of his career.

What Bob does *not* want to be doing on the day he dies is atrophying in a nursing home – "distrophying," as he sometimes calls it – or lying in a hospital bed with "tubes and bottles and stuff" hanging from his anatomy. "Nobody wants to damn well go downhill," he said. "Look at me! A fat old guy with an old blind elephant. People who don't know about Judy must sit out there thinking, *Jesus, is that the best the guy can do?* I've had some great acts in my day, worked some good elephants. I'll tell ya one thing, I wouldn't want Buckles Woodcock to see me out here doing this, although he'd understand. The act's better, of course, when

Betty's in the ring, too. Then Judy knows what to do, because she can smell and hear Betty, and she just kinda follows her around. Without her, she gets lost. I have to lead her, support her act."

Bob's idea of the fitting conclusion to a circus career is most pointedly embodied in the horrific, if romanticized, death of Karl Wallenda in San Juan, Puerto Rico, in 1978. "What a way to go," he said to me, "dying during his act. He never had to go through any of this slowing down, losing it. He *said* he wanted to retire – even announced at one point that he was never going to walk the wire again. But he couldn't stick with it. His daughter Carla, Ricky's mother, would take his shoes up onto the pedestal when the family was performing, and the ringmaster would announce to the crowd that the great patriarch of the Wallenda family was standing beneath this rigging – *Would you like to see him walk the wire one more time?* And of course the crowd'd go nuts, and the old dog would get up there and walk out in his street clothes. This was all in the last couple of years before he died."

Earlier that day, I had asked Ricky if what I had heard about his grandfather was true, that he had expressed a desire to die on the wire. "I know he didn't want to go gradually," Rick said. "That was probably his greatest fear." To dispel any notion of suicide, Rick explained that when Karl had gone to San Juan to walk between the towers of the Condado Holiday Inn, he had not accounted for the strength of the wind off the ocean, particularly as it was funnelled into an updraft between the two buildings. "The wire wasn't guyed out properly," Ricky said. "And he may have been tired, who knows? But he didn't go off deliberately, if that's what people think. With the wind, it was all just a little more than he could handle at the age of seventy-three."

Film of the catastrophe shows a virtual gale tearing at the foliage on the palms in the vicinity of the hotel. Nevertheless, for the first twenty or thirty feet of the walk, Karl moves with the mantle and confidence of a teenager, protected in the lee of the building. It is only as he emerges into the full strength of the wind, and the wire begins to shimmy, then undulate, that he slows, then stops, uncertain, and begins to grope for stability, aging in front of our eyes, until, clearly aware that nothing can be done to salvage what is still merely a disgrace, and unable to turn back, he squats, an addled and frightened old man, refusing to let go of his balance pole, which, as he has always stressed to his protégés, is the walker's breastplate and ordnance and prayer shawl. By refusing to let it go, however, he can not grasp the wire, and, as it bucks a last time, off he goes, tracked by the camera, a hundred and twenty feet onto the hood of a taxi in the parking lot below.

"I still say it was a great conclusion to his legend," said Bob. "Don't you think Clyde Beatty woulda preferred to get killed by a cat than to die of cancer in a hospital bed? In fact, if you'd offered him the chance of going into the ring knowing that a tiger was gonna hit him and kill him instantly, he'd'a gone, rather than die in a hospital."

Bob described to me how, during her late seventies, Mabel Stark, the great female cat trainer, had taken a permanent position at Jungle Land in Thousand Oaks, California, and how she had gone early each morning to the park, had entered the ring with the cats, and had provoked them intentionally, hoping one of them might "hit" her once and for all. "The park got wind of it," said Bob, "and they changed the locks on the gate. They figured if she got killed they'd lose their insurance. The day she found out, she went home and tied a plastic dry-cleaning bag over her head and suffocated herself. You gotta wanta die to go that way, knowing that you could puncture the bag with your finger.

"There's no life for most of these circus people once they're done," he said. "No income, no pension to speak of, no excitement compared to what they're used to. It ain't like workin in an office, where people are glad to get outta there. They're all like me – doin it because they love it."

I asked Bob if he thought he could stay out another ten years, and he said he had to. "Problem is, in ten years there aren't gonna be many elephant acts left. The animal-rights people are gonna put us outta business – finish off what the endangered-species guys have started. Forty years ago, I never thought I'd live to see it. My problem," he said, "is that I was born about fifty years too late. I missed the golden age. Oh, I woulda loved it in the days when they carried seven hundred draft horses, fifty camels, seventy or eighty elephants."

For several seconds he fell silent, either unable or unwilling to voice the deepest of his reflections on what might have been. "Damn thing about those days," he brightened, "is I probably wouldn't'a gone far anyway. They had guys back then who were *really talented* around elephants. You shoulda seen the stuff they could do. A guy like me would probably have been a groom or something. I mean, I've done all right, but I've always had somebody helping me, encouraging me – Smoky Jones, Johnny Herriot, Buckles Woodcock. I've never worked a big herd. We had twenty-three elephants when I was with Dory Miller at Carson and Barnes, but I wasn't the head guy. The biggest act I ever worked alone was five."

Again Bob fell silent, rubbing his face, then folding his hands calmly across his stomach. "When I go," he rallied. "I wanta get whomped on the back of the head by some big bull, and put outta my misery with a well-aimed kick. People'll say, 'Look'a that Gibbs – killed by the elephants he loved.' What a story. Trouble is, Judy ain't gonna do it for me. Betty ain't either. I've just been too damn good to them – I'm too nice a guy."

Sometime after midnight, Bob, in a deepening funk, reported that he had done some "real bad shit" in his day. "You wouldn't believe some of the shit I've done," he said. Out of exhaustion, I had been on the verge of suggesting that I drive him to his truck. Instead, I wrenched myself upright, put a filter of grounds in the coffee maker, and went into the bathroom for a carafe of water.

"What sorta shit?" I said, as I came out.

"Evil shit," he said. "Stuff I'm ashamed of," and he told me about an enormous Canadian brown bear that he had owned during the 1960s – a bear with an antagonistic temperament but capable of an impressive array of athletic stunts, including a tight-wire routine, handstands, and walking on his forepaws around the ring. "The cue for the handstand was you tapped him on the back feet, and up he'd go. The trouble was he had two of the biggest balls you'd ever seen on a bear, and one day in Pennsylvania, when I cued his back feet, I hit him in the nuts by mistake – oh, he turned on me, woulda eaten me on the spot if he hadn't had his muzzle on. From that day on that big brown bugger hated my guts – every chance he got he gave me a hard time; and after a while I didn't like him much either."

That I should record Bob's story in its entirety, as well as the one that follows, is a deliberate testimonial not just to the story's shock value or to Bob's storytelling capabilities, both of which are undeniable, but to his admirable determination that I understand even the cruellest realities of who he was and of what his life in the circus had been about.

During Bob's days as a trainer, he was assisted in the ring not only by Rosa, who he says saved his life on at least five occasions, but by a groom named Steve "Hogjaws" Patton, well-remembered by Bob for his commitment to the act and to the animals. "One day in upstate New York, I was workin a bear named Bubbles while Hogjaws and Rosa held the others. And when nobody was lookin, this big one, Pierre, took his claw and somehow pulled his muzzle over to the side, so his snout was free. Suddenly, Steve says to me, 'Hey, this bear's got his muzzle off! I ain't holdin him!' And I didn't blame him – if that bear bites ya, he can kill ya. See, a bear has the ability to lock his teeth closed, so you'll never get away.

"I was only about halfway through the act, and I must have been overconfident, because I thought, *I'll just put the muzzle back on him,* when what I shoulda done was take all of them outta the ring, right to the truck, because Pierre's lethally armed now, and I'm nothin. If he gets his teeth into my groin or stomach I'm dead. And of course all this time he's buildin up confidence, right up there on his seat as tall as I am.

"I said to Hogjaws, 'You hold Bubbles.' And I went over to Pierre and undid the buckle on his muzzle, because you have to get it back over his face. I always rewarded them with a cube of sugar when they put their noses in the muzzles. So I put the sugar there for him, and said, 'Come on, Pierre, let's go, buddy, put your head in there.' But now he don't want that muzzle back on. They have those little pig eyes, you don't know what they're thinking. But he was weavin, that's a bad sign, although not as bad as hummin. The thing is, you're so used to working them you get complacent; you become careless. I rapped him – I said, 'C'mon, let's go.' And the instant I did that, he dropped his head and put his teeth right through the soft part of my leg at the back, just missed the bone, and he held me.

"Funny thing was, there was no pain; it felt like I was in a vice. If he'd'a jerked back, he'd either've ripped my leg apart or put me on the ground, then he'd've killed me. So I went, 'Uh, uh, uh. . . . Okay there. . . . Daddy's boy now. . . . Easy, Pierre.' And he released me, and I gave him the sugar. Then he started that hummin shit, and I said to Rosa, 'Let's get them outta here.' So we put them all out in their cages.

"Up to that point, I didn't feel nuthin. Then Rosa said, 'Damn! Look at your pants!' Then I noticed that my boot was all squishy from the blood. I took it off, and my flesh was all torn up.

"When we got to the emergency room, the first thing the doctor wanted to do was sew it up, but I knew damn well if he did that I was finished, because bear teeth are all germ-covered – the wounds get infected. They don't even sew up dog bites any more. So I said, 'Nah, nah, nah – you're not gonna sew it up.' And the guy goes, 'What are you, some kinda doctor or something?' And I said, 'No, I just don't want ya to sew it up. I've been around animals all my life; I know what these wounds'll do. I just want you to treat it.' The guy says, 'If you're so smart, you treat it yourself.'

"So we left, and every day I'd get a bucket of hot Epsom salts, and I'd put my leg down in it. Then the leg started itchin. Rosa thought this was a good sign. Then it got real red. We got in the car one day, turned the heater on – and, *damn*, when the heat hit my leg, it stunk like latrine gas or somethin. Rosa said, 'That ain't right.' So I went to another doctor, and the guy said, 'Holy shit!' and he told me they were gonna hafta amputate my leg; I had gangrene – that's what that itchiness and smell was; it was all rotted in there.

"*Dammit*, I thought, I can't be a one-legged elephant guy. Oh, I was sweatin. I said, 'You gotta try to save it, Doc.'

"He said, 'I'll do my best.'

"'Rosa,' I said, 'you're gonna hafta go on to Denver and come back and get me.' And that's what she did. Hogjaws drove the truck, and Rosa worked the elephants.

"In Herkimer, New York, they packed my leg in ice and put me on pure oxygen. The hole went right through the leg. When we got to the operating room the doctor said, 'We hafta clean all this up, Mr. Gibbs, and I'm afraid we can't give you a whole lotta tranquillizing, because we hafta be able to tell the dead flesh from the good flesh – with the dead flesh you'll have no feeling, but with the live flesh you will.' So they laid me down, and they run this thing like a bottlebrush through the hole in my leg, back and forth, and the shit that came outta there smelled so horrible and disgusting the nurses had to cover their faces to stay in the room. 'Now,' he said, 'I'm gonna pour some liquid in there. First it's gonna be cold. Then it's gonna be hot. But it'll eat up all that dead flesh.' And he was right, it was cold. But he didn't tell me the

*Bobby Gibbs with Bubbles the bear in 1970, at Circus World Museum in Baraboo, Wisconsin.*

whole story, 'cause all of a sudden it was so painful I went half crazy – I was screaming. They had to hold me down. Right then, I *hated* that bear. The only good thing was that all that dead flesh was burned right outta there."

At this point in his story, Bob leaned forward, straining over his corpulence, and tugged at the leg of the black trousers in which, three hours earlier, he had appeared as a swashbuckling elephant trainer in the centre ring of the Fort Frances Arena. By turning sideways and reaching from behind, he pushed down his sock, then thrust his leg into the lamplight. The ankle that rose from his black leather walking shoe was as thick as a fence post and blotchy pink in colour, except for a four-inch girdle of disfiguring red scar tissue a few inches above the ankle bone.

He let the pant leg drop and said, "A couple'a days later I went back to the circus, and I woulda been okay, except that every time I got near big Pierre he'd start yackin at me, teasin me, messin me around. One day, suddenly, I just flipped – right over the edge. It was ugly. I said, 'You wanta cause me more pain, I'll show you what pain is.' This, ya hafta understand, was thirty years ago, a bad part of my life – a part that I'm not at all proud of. I was very impetuous, very temperamental. I went and got a twenty-two short rifle and put short little bullets in it. He came up to me at the bars ready to kill me – he already thought he'd got ridda me when I didn't come back in New York. I stuck the barrel into his cage – he tried to bite the end off it, and I fired, *pop*, right down his throat. I said, 'Go to hell, bear!' And then I just went berserk; I emptied a whole box of shells into him.

"Rosa came out, and, boy, she was steamed. She said, 'I don't like this – I oughta whack you with this elephant hook.' And she meant it. She said, 'You make sure that bear's dead, then you put that gun away, or you may not see me around here again.' I took another shell and popped him in the ear, and later that afternoon took him to a taxidermist and said, 'I wanta make a rug out of him, so that every day I can wipe my dirty feet on him.' But when the guy got the skin off, he phoned up and said, 'That hide ain't worth shit – it's fulla holes! You can't make a rug out of it.'

"Rosa and me almost got divorced over this. Oh, she was hot. She said, 'That's the cruellest, ugliest thing I've ever seen.' I said, 'That damn bear caused me ten times as much pain as I ever caused him. He wanted to kill me, and one day he would have. Who would you rather have dead, him or me?' She said, 'He was doing what nature intended him to do. What you did is just anger and craziness – and you better get hold of yourself.'"

Bob took a fluttering sip of coffee and checked his watch. His bulk was a capacity load for the light-framed easy chair beneath him – so much so that when he shifted his weight, the chair shifted with him, leaping sideways a centimetre or two, back or forth across the carpet. "I'm very sorry for that stuff now," he said solemnly. "I shouldn't'a done it. It was probably the most irresponsible thing I ever did. If you're workin with animals, you need patience, cause they'll try ya every chance they get: elephants, tigers, monkeys. Chimps'll get ya any way they can. They don't just bite, they sit around and think up devious tricks. If ya put your thumbs in your pockets, for instance, they'll grab your fingers and pull down so hard it'll tear your thumbs loose. Or they'll take their leash while you're talking, and wrap it around your hand a couple of times, just smilin away while you're not payin attention. Then suddenly they'll give it a yank and just about take your hand off. Or they'll come up to kiss you, all sweet and nice, and, instead, give ya a good sharp bite on the nose or lips. They hafta try you every day, they wanta be boss. And the worst thing about my chimps was they all loved Rosa – male chimps imprint sexually on human females. Every time Rosa'd yell at me, they'd take her side – I swear they wanted to kill me."

During Bob's forty-eight years with the circus, the animal that, in *fact*, came closest to killing him was a five-ton Asian elephant named Sherma that had already killed two men when Bob acquired her in the late spring of 1972. "I'd worked her for four years back in the sixties," he told me. "Then John Cunio had her for five years. But when she killed one of his guys, he was gonna shoot her. I said, 'God, no, don't shoot her. I'll take her and retrain her and sell her to the Mexicans.' See, in those days the Mexicans would take any elephant they could get – the circuses down there love 'em but have a hard time acquiring them. But of course Mexicans couldn't work her in English, so I had to teach her Spanish."

To accomplish this, Bob took the homicidal elephant to the fifty-acre Circus World Museum, in Baraboo, Wisconsin, where off and on for two decades during the seventies and eighties he spent his summers showing everything from elephants to camels to miniature Brahma cattle in the daily big-top performances on the site. "Every day between shows I'd take Sherma into the ring and go through the tricks with her in English and Spanish. At this point, I'd never been hurt bad by an elephant in my life. I mean I'd been knocked down – that don't mean nuthin. An elephant'll kick ya around a bit – you just gotta take that. But one comin to kill ya is different. A great elephant trainer named Smoky Jones told me once that elephants are like gangsters; always look 'em in the eye.

"I guess I was getting complacent, because one day after Hogjaws and me had been workin Sherma I turned my back on her, and in the very same instant, *boom*, she had her mouth and trunk around me – picked me up like a rag doll, ran through the menagerie tent, and just flung me. From that point it was just one blow after another – she stomped my ribs, my legs, my stomach, my shoulders. Blood was pourin out my mouth and ears. Every time that big front foot came down, I thought, *this is it, I'm dead.* But because I'm so fat, I kept rolling with the punches. And I *woulda* been dead if Rosa hadn't appeared with a pitchfork and driven it three inches into Sherma's back leg. Sherma spun round, yanked out the fork with her trunk, and let it go like a spear; it sailed forty feet across the tent, just missed Hogjaws. Then Sherma, who was real scared of Rosa, ran right out the front door into the park where there were hundreds of people around."

So severe were Bob's injuries that he would spend two weeks in an iron lung in Baraboo while his crushed ribs and internal organs healed. "In the meantime, that elephant was my responsibility," he said. "If she hurt anybody, it was my fault. So, even though I could hardly breathe, I had Hogjaws and Rosa put me in a wheelchair and get me my twelve-gauge shotgun; I was gonna blast Sherma's eyes out so she couldn't kill anybody. Either that, or I had to get a chain on her. I told Hogjaws to go get Lydia, my big female fighter. See, in every group of elephants, you train one police elephant, and that elephant's job is to punish the others on command, to kick the stuffing out of them if they kill somebody or tear down the tent or something. In India they call them *kunkes*. Lydia was a bully, and Sherma was deathly afraid of her."

One of the displays at the Circus World Museum is a number of early circus train cars, most of them once owned by Ringling Brothers, whose circus wintered on the Baraboo site from 1884 to 1918, when they moved their quarters to Sarasota. "Sherma went out and stood alongside them rail cars," said Bob. "We put a thirty-foot chain around Lydia's neck, and I said to Hogjaws, 'You push the wheelchair.' And he said, 'I ain't goin out there. She'll kill me.' And I said, 'Not if I shoot her eyes out she won't. Just get me close to her, and you run and hide.' You gotta understand that, even though I had liability insurance, if anything had happened I woulda been in court for years."

As Hogjaws pushed his boss across the gravel roadway that led from the menagerie tent to the train car exhibit, an announcement came over the PA system imploring everyone in the park to take immediate cover in the nearest building. "Of course, when the people heard that," said Bob, "they were more curious than ever about what was going on. They wanted to see the elephant kill somebody – long as it wasn't them. Sherma saw me comin, and, boy, she was agitated, bouncin her head up and down like they do when they're cranked up – she wanted to finish me off. Then, suddenly, she seen Lydia comin, and right away, she started makin that chirpin sound they make when they give up.

"I told Lydia to go get her, and within seconds she had Sherma up against one'a them rail cars, pounding her so hard with her front foot that they nearly knocked over the car. Lydia outweighed her by half a ton.

"'Sherma's quit!' I said. 'Hold her, Lydia.' And we were able to get in there and get the two of them chained together. 'Way ya go, Lydia,' I said, and she dragged Sherma back to the pen.

"When I got there I was just crazy – just like with big Pierre. I was busted up so bad, in so much pain, all I wanted was to have Hogjaws shoot that elephant, put her away for good. I offered him a thousand bucks if he'd do it. But Rosa wasn't havin none'a that. She's always been more level-headed than I am. I said, 'Dammit, Rosa, this time you're wrong; we gotta shoot her.' And right then, Chappy Fox, the guy who started Circus World, arrived at the tent and said, 'Don't do this, Bobby – we can't have this on the property.' See, Circus World is owned by the State of Wisconsin Historical Society. I said, 'Oh, man, Chappy, this sonofabitch oughta die.' He said, 'Forget it. Just get her outta here as soon as possible.'

"While I was in the hospital I got holda some guys in West Palm Beach – we offered her to them free, and when they came up to get her I warned them to watch out, she'd killed two guys – I woulda been the third. They said, 'Doan worry, meester, we know howta train thees elefan.' Within a month, she'd killed one of them. Lion Country Safari ended up putting her to sleep."

Bob leaned as far as he could to his left, shoved a thick right hand into his front pocket, and pulled out a minutely folded piece of paper that, judging by its appearance, might have been secreted on his person since he left Missouri as an eleven-year-old. He opened it, passed it to me, and said, "Remember I told ya about the list of bad elephants? That's it."

The document was, in effect, a warning to elephant and circus owners about the diminishing standards for elephant discipline and care. "The guys who put it together are all old-time elephant trainers," said Bob, "and they did it because they care about preserving what's left of the elephant business on this continent, and about protecting people who care about and attend circuses. If these bad elephants are allowed to stay in the business there's eventually gonna be a big public stink over it, and it'll kill it for all of us. We got enough trouble as it is with the animal-rights people. See what it says there at the top? The owners of dangerous elephants are being urged to get rid of them, to take a loss of revenue now, or else accept that, ten years from now, there won't *be* any revenue, because we'll all be out of business."

The list, some of it barely legible after what had obviously been multiple photocopyings, noted twenty-nine elephant "incidents" that had taken place between 1980 and 1994 – fourteen "serious injuries" and fifteen deaths of handlers or circus and zoo spectators. It named the circus or elephant owners responsible for the incidents, although not the elephants themselves. "They *could* have named the elephant," said Bob, "but it's easy enough for an owner to change the elephant's name – the elephant ain't gonna tell. It used to happen a lot. It's the owner, not the elephant, that's gotta be named and held responsible."

I noted with surprise that the majority of the deaths had occurred in zoos and nature parks, not circuses, and asked Bob if things were worse now than in the days when he started. "Sure they are," he said. "At one time, no circus ran elephants without a proper elephant trainer. Often the trainer owned the elephants, and that meant he was accountable. Of course, competent trainers cost money. Now, to save a buck, some circuses'll buy their own elephants, and the owner'll get his girlfriend or somebody to work them, whether they know anything about elephants or not. Of course, there are still lots'a damn *good* people in the business, too."

I asked what an owner might be expected to do with a delinquent elephant, assuming he'd be reluctant to dispose of it if he'd paid a hundred thousand U.S. for it.

"If that elephant kills somebody, a hundred thousand might turn out to be a pretty small loss," he said. "But nobody's askin anybody to dispose of them. A bunch of them right now are in the Ringling breeding program in Florida. It doesn't matter how many guys ya killed if all ya hafta do is make babies."

The document estimated that some thirty-eight of the more than four hundred elephants now on display in North American circuses, zoos, and animal parks posed sufficient danger to spectators that they should be allowed no direct contact with the public – no rides, no petting, no photos or feeding.

"It's not that elephants are temperamental by nature," said Bob. "There's a great range of personalities within the elephant world. They're very complex animals – some are surly, some defensive, a few are downright nuts, just like in the human world. A lot, too, are just loving and gentle and can be trusted completely – like Judy. She couldn't do wrong if she tried. Then again, even *she* gets frustrated sometimes, like the other day when she tore up them trees along the riverbank in Dryden. She'd been in the truck all day, and she was cold. I just let her work out her frustrations. She can't be a saint twenty-four hours a day. But even at her worst, I wouldn't hesitate to set a child right up on her back – or let a child feed her. She's never hurt nobody, and never will."

Bob noted that, on the other hand, if Betty were along on tour, he wouldn't let a soul within yards of her, except when she was giving rides. "When I'm with her and she's working, anybody in the world is perfectly safe around her – kids can feed her, can pet her, they can come right up behind her, and she's no danger whatever to them. It's when she's in her own space, not in the ring, not workin, and I'm not around, that she'll get testy – particularly if somebody she doesn't respect tries to tell her what to do, which as far as she's concerned is just a nuisance to her. For her, the easiest way to get somebody to stop aggravating her is to kill them, get ridda them, the way you or I would kill a mosquito. That's what happened with John. As far as she was concerned, he was in her face. She respects me, because I'm responsible for her. I love her, and she returns that love. When I was little, my mother and father loved me dearly, and they made the rules. With my dad, it was: As long as your feet are under my table I'm in charge. If you can live with that, fine. If you can't, saddle up. And I could, and did. But I wasn't gonna listen to just anybody who came around my parents' house. And it's the same with

*Legendary circus trio: Judy, Bobby, and Betty.*

elephants. They wanta hear it from the people they respect – in Betty's case, Rosa and me."

Bob is a lifelong abstainer and takes robust delight in the fact that elephants are especially antagonistic toward drinkers, particularly those with fresh evidence of consumption on their breath. "They've learned from experience to associate alcohol with unpredictable treatment, sometimes harsh treatment," he said. "A lotta grooms who'd normally be too scared to work an elephant will get a sense of false courage when they're liquored up, and that's when they'll go out and think they're gonna bring that elephant under their control. I've seen Betty whack lotsa drinkers. That's why these Shrine dates can be tricky. A lot of the Shriners party while the circus is in town – you've seen their little party rooms in the arenas – and they'll come up to Betty with booze on their breath and grab her ear or something, and she'll whomp them." Bob recalled with delight how, in 1995, a well-oiled Shriner approached Betty in Winnipeg and blew into her trunk. "She whacked him so hard his fez flew off."

Paradoxically, elephants will *drink* alcohol and enjoy it – in the wilds, as well as in captivity. Herds of African elephants have been known to trek hundreds of miles to gorge on fermenting fruit – and then terrorize local villagers who can do nothing more than watch the drunken interlopers destroy their crops and sometimes their homes. A handbill advertising the first elephant to arrive in America, in 1796, noted that the animal drank "all sorts of spiri-tous liquors" and on some days as many as "30 bottles of porter, drawing the corks with his trunk." The legendary Jumbo, brought to America from England in 1882 by P.T. Barnum, is reputed to have enjoyed a quart of whisky a day, and often to have shared a pint of beer with his keeper, Matthew Scott. Several times I saw Judy savour a paper cup of liquor or a can of Labatt's Blue, taking the unopened beer in her mouth, aiming its pull tab in the direction of her throat, and crushing out its contents between her molars. She was equally fond of Orange Crush or 7-Up and dis-posed of the cans by pulling them from her mouth with the tip of her trunk and zinging them over her shoulder.

I asked Bob if there was any way, short of Prozac, to change the behaviour of a delinquent elephant, and he told me that in India the worst are sent to remote camps in the hope that they can be rehabilitated under a new mahout. "There's always somebody wants the challenge of turning them around. The boss says, 'Who'll work this black-assed killer?' and some young cowboy says, 'I will.' Some of those Hindu guys have got 'Living with a Killer' tattooed right on their arms and chests. They know if they make a mistake they're gonna die – just like high-wire guys. What nobody's gonna tell ya is that a few of the worst of those ele-phants, the ones nobody could do anything with, probably ended up in our zoos and circuses."

❀

Bob's elaborate disquisitions on elephants invariably returned to a single salient point that impressed him as sharply after nearly fifty years in the business as it had on the day he began – the point being that, where elephants were concerned, not even the most experienced handler in the world could take his safety entirely for granted. Bob's personal fix on the notion shifted from Sherma to Congo to Betty and, for a moment that night in the hotel, took in an unnamed elephant that, in France, in 1996, chased circus owner Danny Ranz from the ring, out of the tent, into a parking lot, where it turned over Ranz's mobile home, beneath which he was hiding, and kicked him to death.

"Look at Axel!" Bob exclaimed, referring to Axel Gautier, who for twenty-seven years was a respected elephant man at Ringling Brothers and Barnum & Bailey, at times in charge of as many as seventy-seven elephants. "When Axel decided to retire a few years back, Ringlings asked him if he'd go run their breeding farm in Florida, and they'd get Ted Svertesky, who was running the farm at the time, to come run the show elephants. So Axel goes down there to take over and walks into the compound the first morning. Ted says, 'Good to see ya, Axel. Make yourself at home. I've got a few things to do – I'll be with ya before long.' Axel gets out his video camera and wanders into the area where they keep the dangerous elephants, the ones that have ended up there because they can't be trusted anywhere else. One of them was originally named Daffodil, but her name had been changed to Reba – she killed a guy on a show up here in Canada. I guess Axel thought the warnings about her didn't apply to him. He started taping, and before he knew what hit him, she lowered the boom. Twenty-seven years on the circus, and in one moment of careless-ness, he lost his life.

"And that's how I got hit by Sherma. I was thoroughly convinced that that elephant liked me – that I was the guy who could ride the horse that couldn't be rode – even though she'd killed two guys."

Circus people from Mexico and Latin America have perhaps seen more "bad" elephants than anyone else; and each day as Bob brought Judy into the building, whether to perform or for photo-taking, Rosa Luna, who worked one of the spotlights, would pick up two-year-old Genesis and either protect her bodily as the elephant passed or set her behind the boards. The Lunas, Rolando told me, had been on tour with the George Cardin Circus in Atlantic Canada when one of Cardin's elephants threw a tantrum in a small-town arena and pitched a row of steel chairs into the audience.

"Never screw with an animal that weighs five tons," Pat Delaney told me on the morning I met him in Thunder Bay. "That's the first rule of life in the circus. Same with the tigers. You might see a guy reach in and pet one of them on the leg, or take something out of the cage. And you think you can do it, not realizing that the tiger knows that guy, and isn't gonna be spooked by him. Joe Blow tries it, and his next stop is either the emergency ward or the embalming room."

As we left the hotel room that night, Bob said, "Wilson coulda been on the slab in a heartbeat, with the lights out this afternoon. Even with them on, any one of them cats would kill him in a second if he made a mistake. There's no such thing as a foolproof wild animal. That's part of the deal. And in their hearts the audience knows it. Which is why it's all so exciting."

# 7

BOBBY GIBBS'S BATTLE with Sherma was by no means the only significant antipathy he experienced during his days at Circus World Museum in Baraboo. But judging by his employment on the Great Wallenda Circus and his warm relationship with its owner, no one would have guessed that he had once been part of a fiendish "practical joke" – in effect, an act of protracted social discrimination – that, at the time, all but assured he would never again be on amicable terms with Ricky Wallenda.

"What we did to that man was shameful," he told me as I drove him to his truck that night in Fort Frances. "I don't even know why he speaks to me today."

The spirit of what Bob and his animal cronies did at Baraboo was not unprecedented in the circus world, which, historically, has imposed upon its families and employees a level of policing and discipline – a commitment to internal order – that was frequently vengeful and, at times, cruel or even criminal. During the late nineteenth and early twentieth centuries, for example, a male circus employee who attempted to court a female member of a performing troupe without the approval of the woman's family or guardians was subject to penalties that ranged from banishment from the show, to severe beatings, to forms of corporal punishment so decisive that, in some cases, they amounted to manslaughter or murder. The lower the young man was in the circus's hierarchical order, the more severe the punishments were likely to be. Regardless of the role or intent of the young women involved, young men guilty of moral violations against them were commonly carried to the roofs of tall buildings and thrown into alleys below, or were "red-lighted" from speeding trains – that is, thrown out or, in severe cases, dropped into the spaces between their cars.

Well into the middle years of the twentieth century, the circus's punitive measures remained disproportionately harsh for the offences that provoked them. Some circuses, for example, prescribed immediate dismissal for violations as seemingly insignificant as wearing performance wardrobe outside the tent or arena, for missing an entry cue, or for any breach in the enactment of duties around the animals.

Arrogance and conceit have always been among the circus's most harshly judged offences, which is perhaps why, over the years, many of the most talented performers have tended to go (more or less voluntarily) unrecognized, their identities buried beneath nicknames, stage names, or clown make-up – or beneath the names of the troupes with which they performed. "Producers hire *acts*," Pat Delaney told me one day. "The stars are in heaven."

While today's penalties for arrogance or egotism are far less obvious than were the extravagant punishments of the past, they can be every bit as brutal in their way. Which did not bode well for Ricky Wallenda when he signed on at Circus World Museum as their star attraction for the summer of 1987, just months before his accident in Jacksonville. By his own admission he was at the time "an obnoxious, self-centred alcoholic, emotionally distant and insensitive to just about everything and everyone" around him.

"He was an overbearing no-good prick, with an ego the size of Wisconsin," said Bobby Gibbs.

As fate would have it, Ricky's tenure at Circus World came at a time when Bobby, too, was working there for the summer. By equally exacting fate, the nadir of Rick's life as an overbearing circus star corresponded to the pinnacle of Bob's as a grossly nettlesome provocateur with the diplomatic standards of Congo the elephant.

"There are very few names that matter in the circus," Bob told me that night as we sat in the van outside the arena. "Ringling, Emmett Kelly, Clyde Beatty, and of course Wallenda. That's why they hired Ricky. I mean, he was good, but there are lots of good people in the circus. In reality, his name's what they were payin him for; they had his picture on advertising billboards all over the state. Some of the best and most knowledgeable animal trainers in the world were there. Buckles Woodcock is the dean of elephant guys in America. Jimmy Hall had the best bear act anywhere. I was in charge of all the rest of the animals. Rosa did the trapeze, the slide for life, the daily parade. But even though our acts were good, our name wasn't Wallenda, so really we didn't mean shit. And that woulda been okay. All any animal guy wants to do is show his animals, get outta the ring, and have a good time. But Ricky in them days could get under your skin – he had staritis; they told him he was great, and he believed it."

I remarked that Rick's possession of the name seemed far from an out-and-out blessing.

"Of course!" Bob squawked. "D'ya think he'd be all hobbled up if it wasn't for that name? D'ya think he'd'a been alcoholic – or have lost his family? Mind ya, he's done okay by it, too – he's made a lotta money on it. Then again, he mighta made a helluva lot more if his name was John Henry."

Bob explained that, as the various acts had settled in that summer, the animal trainers had made something of a ritual of gathering for coffee and doughnuts on the lawn behind the big top, when they had finished their morning chores. "We had a picnic table out there," he said, "and after a while, as a bit of joke, we started calling ourselves the Breakfast Club – it was nothing really, just me, Jimmy Hall, Buckles Woodcock, the grooms, sittin around telling lies. Along comes Ricky one morning and says, 'What's goin on? Mind if I sit down?' And as a joke, one of us says to him, 'Well, Rick, we'd like to have you sit down, but, on the other hand, these sessions are restricted to animal guys, so I'm afraid we can't invite you to join us.'

"What you have to understand," explained Bob, "is that animal guys tend to have a strange sense of humour, often a very sarcastic, even vicious, sense of humour. The work is hard and isolating, and if you stay in it long enough, you begin to develop your own little society and boundaries. The Breakfast Club was a joke! But when people started gettin their hackles up over it, that just made the joke all the sweeter for us, and before long, we had a rope up around the table, and we had T-shirts and caps printed up. When people from the office would come down, we'd yell at them, 'Hey, get out from behind that rope! We didn't invite you in!' And they'd slink away, apologizing. Or we'd say, as a joke, 'You can come in, sir, but you can't bring the child. No children allowed.'"

"Anyway, here comes Ricky one morning in the middle of July, and he says, 'Hey, guys, it's a long summer.' I said, 'Good to see ya, Rick – whaddaya need?' He said, 'I don't need anything; I just thought maybe I'd come over and jackpot with ya.' I said, 'Well, we don't have much to say about the high wire, and you don't know a damn thing about animals, and, well, it is kind of a private club, ya know.' Finally, he was so hot, he went to the director and said, 'They're not gonna let me in their club!' and the guy said, 'Well, I run the museum, and they won't let me in!'

"One day some kids came along, including Ricky's daughter, Aerial, and there was a circus wagon there. I said to them, 'You be lions, kids, and we'll put ya in the wagon.' They get in, they're roaring away, until they realize they don't know how to get out, and they start to cry. I said to Buckles's groom, Chico, 'Go tend to them wild animals, will ya?' And just then Ricky's wife came over the hill – she was real straight, a news-reporter type, didn't care for our kind – and, *ooooeeee*, she was hot when she seen them kids. She called us everything but white men. Later, Ricky came over. He was hot, too – he said, 'That's it, guys – I don't need your Breakfast Club.'

"But, dammit, a couple'a weeks later, if he ain't back at the table, this time with a nice German coffee cake he'd had his wife bake! He said, 'I figure it's time we made up, fellas – how be I bring the cake in the morning from now on; you won't even have to buy doughnuts anymore?' I said to him, 'First, Rick, I'd appreciate it if you'd stay behind the rope, and, second, there's something you don't seem to understand here. And it's that you're the Flying Wallenda guy, you're the glamour guy; we're just animal guys, and this is an animal guys' club.' In those days, you've gotta understand, Rick was the kinda guy ya love to bring down. Oh, we were awful. We used to sit watching him and his wife practise, and make loud criticisms of every little thing they did.

"Eventually, Greg Parkinson, the director, came down and said, 'You guys are without a doubt the worst guys I've ever had to do business with.' He said, 'I'm sick of the way you're carrying on, and I don't wanta hear one more damn word about you and the Wallendas. Is that understood?' I said, 'I think I get the point, Greg.' 'And if you must know,' he said, 'I'm paying them more than I'm paying you because they're *worth* more to me than you.' He was all steamed up. I thought he was gonna fire us. But he didn't, and we pretty much laid off at that point."

Bob and I sat silent for a few seconds, looking out through the windshield at the elephant trailer, which was rocking gently in the dim light from the street lamps. The sky had cleared, and a bright quarter moon hung like a flaying knife just above the horizon.

"I just love Ricky," Bob said quietly, and he described how, during the mid-1980s, Ricky and Debbie had begun sending out a Wallenda newsletter. "She'd write it," he said, "and Ricky would add some sort of postscript, usually quite bitter stuff about the competition – how the Wallendas were gonna kick ass, and so on. Then a couple of years ago, he sent out a letter that was entirely different than anything that had ever come before. He described how he'd lost his wife and family and grandmother, how everything had fallen apart for him, and how he'd found God and had quit drinking, and only realized too late that he'd been on the wrong path, and would never get back what he'd lost. . . .

"When a man bears his soul like that, if you don't feel for him, you don't have much humanity. I'll tell ya, I respected him for what he'd done, and if you ask Ricky, he'll tell ya that the first person to write him and express support and admiration was me, even after all I'd put him through. You think I didn't feel badly for what I did to that man? I felt terrible. Here he was, the son of a guy who died of alcoholism, practically an alcoholic himself, with all sortsa problems, just craving acceptance – and look'a the way I treated him. I was ashamed, and I told him in my letter. I asked for his forgiveness. I said, You're twice the man you were, and you're twice the man I am."

Bob shifted to look at me, and said, "There's one gawdam reason I'm sittin here tonight. And you wanta know what it is?"

"What is it?" I said.

"It's because Ricky Wallenda was big enough to forgive me for what I done to him. By rights, he should never have spoken to me again. And when we saw one another for the first time after I wrote him, I held his hand and we prayed. I'll get down on my knees with him anytime he wants. When he paid me in Dryden the other night, I told him again how much I admired him. Losin his family was a disaster, and he knows it was his fault. And now he's makin up for it."

# 8

I LEFT FORT FRANCES under a welcome blue sky on the morning of May 5 and drove the four hundred kilometres back to Thunder Bay to pick up my nine-year-old son, Matthew, who was jittery to get going and who inspired the westward trip the next day with an almost feverish sense of anticipation. "Will we be staying right with the animals and stuff?" he asked me at one point. "Are we sort of like part of the show?"

By seven that evening, we were in Winnipeg, a city eerily transformed by the Red River roaring through at street level instead of at the bottom of the thirty-foot-deep trough that it usually occupies, and by sandbags stacked by the hundreds of thousands throughout dozens of neighbourhoods in the vicinity of both the Red and the Assiniboine rivers. On the way into the city on the Trans-Canada, we crossed the Red River Floodway, normally a vast near-empty diversion ditch but now brimming to within inches of the highway, its current moving at intimidating speed, carrying everything from trees to furniture to fence-posts. Everywhere to the south, fields and towns were drowning in chest-deep swill.

We ate a late-evening dinner at Da Mama Mia's, a one-time bivouac of mine, and spent the night at the apartment of my old friend Jake Macdonald, who had been covering the flood for *Maclean's* magazine and gave us a dramatic play-by-play of the building of the forty-mile-long Brunkild dike across Winnipeg's southern boundary. Its last-minute construction had brought together hundreds of bulldozers and earth-moving machines and thousands of men and women, who, in some cases, had worked for days without sleep to divert the tide and salvage the city.

I swapped circus stories for flood stories, and in the morning, Matt and I drove west onto the prairie, expecting to meet the circus in Brandon, two hundred kilometres away. Halfway there, we stopped in Portage la Prairie, where the circus had played the previous day, and where there was a chance some of the performers might still be around.

From the top of a railway overpass, I glanced at the town's new arena and was happily surprised to see a pair of familiar profiles by the back door, but with no truck in sight.

Bobby seemed as glad to see us as we were to see him, and disclosed immediately that he had blown the engine of his truck on the highway north of Fort Frances, incurring yet another run of unimaginable expenses. At the moment, the truck was in Winnipeg and was likely to cost ten or twelve thousand U.S. to repair. During the two days I'd been gone, Wilson had hauled the tigers and then doubled back to pull the elephant trailer. In fact, he was expected on the scene any minute, having taken the tigers to Brandon that morning.

"Donny won't even talk to me," Bob mourned, "won't even talk to me," and he launched into regrets that, before coming to Manitoba, he had not thought to have T-shirts printed with the message I SURVIVED THE FLOOD OF 97. "Coulda sold fifty of them last night. All anybody can talk about around here is that flood. Ah, well, life goes on. Come on, Matt," he chirped, "if you're gonna join the circus ya gotta know how to feed and water

*Matt and Bobby, with Judy and Betty, during our visit in May 1998.*

an elephant. She won't hurt ya. Here," he said, handing him a bucket. "Go over to that tap and get some water. Then ya can drag a couple'a forkfuls of this hay over to her."

Matt took to even the smallest responsibilities toward Judy as if he had been handed the keys to some vast and tantalizing kingdom.

"How about I ride with you?" Bobby said to me when Wilson returned. And off we went, Bob in the passenger seat, Matt behind, straining to catch every lurid word that, for fifty kilometres westward from Portage la Prairie, poured out of Bob in a kind of random dispatch from the loony bin. Story after story after story – some of them so preposterous and indelible Matt would be reciting them in detail six months later: Bob under the curse of the Caribbean voodoo queen; Bob and the mad barracuda; Bob and the revenge of the rhinoceros; Bob and George Plimpton's soiled underwear; Bob driving a forty-horse hitch through the Lincoln Tunnel. As with many of Bobby's stories, most of these evolved to some slim moral point – none more so than the one about the time in Missouri, where, at his friend Dave Hale's exotic animal sale, Bob had seen a lion bite three fingers off a careless woman, who in the process of ripping her hand free sent her Rolex watch flying four or five metres across the ground to Bob's feet. "She and her husband ran off to the hospital," Bob yelled into the back seat. "I picked up the watch, and then, dammit, if I didn't find one of her fingers right there at the edge of the cage." The crux of the story was that when Bob phoned the hospital, the husband expressed no interest in getting his wife's finger back but was determined to get the Rolex. "I said to myself, I'll show that heartless bastard, and I took the finger and pierced it and put a string through it and put it around my neck. And I started tellin everybody who came along what I called the Terrible Parable of the Ugly Bugger who cared more about his wife's watch than he did about his wife."

I caught a glimpse of Matt in the rear-view, staring bug-eyed ahead, clearly receiving every utterance as an article of gravest import and fact.

Like most of all of Bob's stories, this one did not so much end as divide, spawning one or two further stories that would themselves divide, claiming bits of one another and transforming them, so that, say, the Russian quick-change artist in the Las Vegas anecdote was reinvented as the Bulgarian teeter-board king, or the finger-eating lioness of Cape Girardeau became a cage of lions on a fiery parking lot in the centre of Port-of-Spain, Trinidad, where Bob went with a circus on a tramp freighter during the winter of 1990, and where, for purposes of his role as the nightmare narrator, he himself was now temporarily, vigorously reinvented, this time selling "lion piss" to Rastafarians so that they could smear it on themselves, in order to absorb the precious power of the Maker, the Lion of Judah.

"The centre of Port-of-Spain is as rough as hell, so they built us a compound out behind the national arena, surrounded with high chain-link fence," Bob said within seconds of reporting the bizarre denouement of his previous tale. "We had elephants and lions; Judy was there. Anyway, a lotta them black Trinidadians are Rastafarian; they believe Haile Selassie was the reincarnation of Jehovah and that his spirit resides in all male lions. All day long these guys with great big dreadlocks would stand by the fence near our lions, and they'd yell, '*Bruthhha, rise against the white man! Kill the one who commands you! Don't take his orders! Do not submit! Don't eat your food! Better you be dead than live in captivity!*'"

The terrain between Portage la Prairie and Brandon is famous not just for its wheat crops but as one of the flattest landscapes anywhere, an ancient Ordovician seabed, later glacial Lake Agassiz, now thick with soil that, during those watery weeks of 1997, was as mucky and impassable as most of the rest of southern Manitoba. The horizon in these parts is broken only by occasional stands of willow or alder, or by the lines of poplar planted along farm lanes or by houses and barns to deflect wind and snow – or by the inevitable grain elevators, the creaky aristocracy of prairie architecture.

Half an hour east of Brandon, we followed Wilson into a truck stop, where he pumped nearly five hundred dollars' worth of diesel fuel into his tanks. A scouring prairie wind had come up, bringing with it not just dust but a kind of urgency or anxiety that, during a decade away from Manitoba, I had forgotten existed in the extremes of flatland weather. In the course of lunch, one of the waitresses picked up a clue that an elephant was outside, and as we stood up to leave, a half-dozen female employees surged from the kitchen bearing a deep box of vegetables and stale bread. At the trailer, Bobby opened a vent shutter, and Judy's trunk came scoping out and plunged directly into the box, causing peels of satisfied laughter.

The Keystone Centre in Brandon is the sprawling showpiece of an enormous annual agricultural fair and is surrounded by parking lots, fields, gritty old agricultural buildings, but nothing much to bend the wind which, by the time we pulled in, was cutting through the city with the bite of fifty-grade sandpaper. The flu bug that had shown up in Dryden had by this time spread to every corner of the circus. Jill Gonçalves and seven-year-old daughter Talina, who did a turn in Daniella's hula-hoop act, had been obliged to sit out the performance the night before. Wilson and others were complaining of painful joints; and as we emerged from the van beside Dave Connors's pickup truck, we discovered Dave flat on the front seat under a blanket, his face immobile and salmon-coloured, his hand on the door handle as if clinging to the last cord. A note scribbled on yesterday's route sheet and taped to the driver's side window said: *Do not disturb – sweating it out.*

I walked with Matt to the Lunas' trailer, where nine-year-old Rolando, who had also been sick, was watching a movie on the VCR, while Rosa, as usual, was up to her elbows in suds and dust pans and cooking pots. Rolando is a bright, thoughtful kid, already in love with show business, and he and Matt latched onto one another like twins, disappearing almost immediately to check out the elephant and to tool around on Rolando's bike.

That evening, after dinner, Rosa invited us to join the Lunas, Garzas, Gadickes, and Gonçalveses, who, by the time we got there, had already jammed the trailer beyond capacity. Rosa did her best to make sure everybody had something to nibble or sip on. The gathering gave me a chance to chat with Jill Gonçalves, who was born in Yorkshire in 1954, studied acting and classical dance as a girl, and, as a young woman, chose the decidedly uncrowded career path of the sword balancer. I asked her why, and she smiled and said, "It allowed me to dance," explaining that there were times when she saw herself not so much as a sword balancer who did some dancing but as a dancer who happened to work with a sword on her forehead. During the mid-1970s, in Istanbul, on an extended gig with the Circus Williams, she had met "the king of all rola-bola," as Bill Boren invariably referred to Manuel, and the two were married before coming to America with Circus Vargas in 1980.

But even after nearly two decades in the United States, Jill was uneasy about her adopted country, enjoying its opportunities for work and remuneration but resisting the crassness of its culture and, in particular, of the American circus. "There's always this sense in the U.S. that what we're really doing in the arena is selling Coke and popcorn and balloons," she said, "and that if we weren't there, it'd be mud wrestlers or monster trucks."

Perhaps understandably, Jill harboured a particular grievance toward the Greatest Show on Earth, seeing it as the ultimate circus vulgarity, and recalling, by comparison, the European circus, in which "the floors are carpeted, the seats plush, and the patrons appreciative both of the performers and the traditions. The whole production, in Europe, is more like a night at the theatre than a night at the wrestling match."

Jill told me, among other things, that she had returned to England to give birth to each of her three children; that for years, off and on, she had kept a diary of her most personal thoughts; and that she had occasionally written verse (some of which she recited). She also said that, on arriving in the United States, in 1980, she had been appalled by the treatment afforded North American Natives in their own country. Her first hard lesson had come in an east coast restaurant, where an Aboriginal family had been kept waiting while the waitress came to Jill and her friends' table to take their order. "I said to the waitress, 'Those people were here first.' And she said, 'It's okay.' And I said, 'No, it's not okay. I don't want to be served until they're served.' So she went over and took their order, and eventually brought them burnt pancakes that their kids wouldn't eat."

Matt and I spent the night at a motel in which no measure had been spared to make the place ugly and uncomfortable. The water was tepid, the sixty-watt bulbs impossible to read by, and the bed-spreads riddled with cigarette burns.

In the morning, while Matt and Rolando tore around the floor of the Keystone Centre – Matt on a two-thousand-dollar BMX custom show bike that Brett Marshall was confident enough to let him use – I sat in a corner of the stands with Evrardo Garza Sr. and Jr., sipping coffee, listening with pleasure to Evrardo Sr.'s recollections of growing up in Reynosa, Mexico, a tough little city on the Texas border. During the 1960s and '70s he'd devoted himself to weightlifting, eventually winning a dozen or more bodybuilding titles, including "*Hercules del Norte*" and "*Señor Mexico*."

Evrardo Sr. is forty-seven, Evrardo Jr. is twenty. They are exceptionally good-looking men, with generous faces and gentle dispositions. Evrardo Sr., in particular, is fastidious about his appearance and clothing, affecting expensive leather jackets, jeans, and shoes. His hair, like his son's, is meticulously cut. Evrardo Jr. has been a part of the act off and on since 1992, when he filled in for his injured father and performed with his uncles Mario and Oscar. The act's eleven-year booking at the Flamingo Hilton Hotel in Las Vegas ended with Mario and Oscar's retirements during the mid-1990s. "My dad was really sad to see the act die," said Evrardo Jr. "Then I got serious about it, and the two of us went out and did some bookings. And now we've built a thirty-thousand-dollar portable stage for ourselves – fountains, hydraulic lifts, all sorts of lights."

These days, however, the Statues have a problem the act did not have when it came out of the backstreets of Reynosa some twenty-five years ago – namely that its popularity has spawned nearly a dozen imitators. "My dad doesn't resent them," says Evrardo Jr. "He accepts that everybody's struggling, as he once was; and if they're imitating his act, it must be because there's something worth imitating about it."

During my weeks with the show, I sometimes caught myself reacting almost too personally to the various acts – responding emotionally to their most accomplished turns, or with indignation toward an audience that did not seem to appreciate what it was seeing; or protectively toward the performers themselves, making sure that in the dressing room or on the lot afterwards,

*The Statues – Evrardo Garza Jr. and Sr. and Chunyan Ho –*
*warming up backstage in the Winnipeg Arena.*

they got at least *my* appreciation for their performance, when the audience had been stingy with theirs. That afternoon I was irritated that Ho and the Garzas did not get the response they deserved from a decent-sized crowd at the Keystone Centre, just as they had been overlooked on several occasions earlier in the tour. Larry Rothbard, whose authority on such matters was not entirely objective, suggested that they could "get more out of their audience" by abandoning the taped, synthesized music that was their accompaniment and going with live music provided by Larry and the band (they were the only act that did not make use of the band's undeniable talents). Bobby Gibbs, who had been a great fan of "the original Garzas," as he called the earlier version of the Statues, suggested that the audience wasn't quite sure when to respond because there was no obvious applause-point at the end of the performance. "They just walk off their platform after they've styled," he said, "and then walk off the floor." In the old days, Bob recalled, the prop crew had slowed down the ending by placing a large fabric draping over the Garzas' final pose. "Everybody knew it was over, and that it was time to applaud."

"The more subtle the act," said Ricky Wallenda "the more complicated the response."

Rick himself had had his difficulties that afternoon when the administration of the local Shrine had caused an acrimonious delay at intermission by insisting on holding a bicycle draw for which tickets had been sold, but for which no preparation had been made to select a winner. Finally, Ricky, whose contract called for a twenty-minute intermission and who was sensitive about the length of the show now that the Shriners were participating with their bands, ordered Bill Boren to begin the second half even though the draw had not taken place. "The local president called me just about every name he could think of," Ricky told me. "He was livid, and I didn't mind that. But when he started running down the show I got a little balky and gave him some of his own. Then, in front of the others, he accused me of cursing him out. I said, 'I did not curse you, sir. That's not how I operate.'"

Ricky's battle with the Khartum Temple would get worse as the tour pressed on. As a theatrical spectacle, however, it wouldn't come close to a battle he had been waging for months with the

Circus Producers Association of America, an organization to which he belonged and which at the moment was highly perturbed by his travels in the North. The roots of the antagonism went back to November 1996, when the Circus Producers had voted to boycott the convention of the Shrine Circus Association of North America – an annual meeting at which most of the Shrine's many annual circus dates and tours are contracted to the twenty or so producers who show up to bid on them. Their main reason for the boycott was that the Shriners had refused to lend the producers much-needed moral support in their long struggle with the animal-rights activists.

But Ricky had defied the boycott and had shown up at the convention in Omaha. Khartum Temple circus chairman David Perry explained to me one day that he had met with Ricky at that convention and had agreed on a tentative booking, not for the tour we were now on, which had been promised to Ian Garden of Garden Brothers Circus in Toronto, but for the following year. "But when we talked to Ian Garden," said Perry, "he wanted quite a bit more money than we'd paid him other years – I think in total it was twenty thousand more, or so – and so I phoned Ricky and asked if he was available *this* year, and he said he could be, and we made a deal, right there and then."

The deal, needless to say, was not appreciated either by Garden or by the rest of the circus producers attempting to sanction the Shrine. Rumours were afoot that circus producer Tarzan Zerbini's plan to be in Winnipeg with his circus and to compete aggressively with Ricky and the Shriners during the most important days of their tour was, in effect, revenge for Ricky's refusal to knuckle under to the producers. "Some of the producers wanted to kick him out of their association," Bobby Gibbs told me, "but George Cardin, who does about six hundred Shrine dates a year, told them they were crazy – that the association was weak enough as it was, and that the last thing it needed was fewer members." Cardin, a one-time trapeze flyer, who is reported to have punched

Ricky in the face during the winter of 1998 in another dispute over dates, decided with the rest of the producers to impose a fine instead. "I think they tried to collect a couple'a grand from him," said Bob, "but I heard he told them to go to hell on that, too."

On the lot in Brandon, with the wind and dust forcing its way into every skin pore and brainwave – with flu and truck problems and acrimony – the circus slipped into a late-afternoon funk, a doldrums made gloomier by news that circus owner Wayne Franzen had been torn to death by a tiger somewhere in what Pat Delaney believed to be North Carolina.

The news put the animal people into a buzz over the dinner hour, and Wilson performed that night with a stylistic tightness that neither invited nor allowed even the slightest waywardness from the cats. When he had finished the "lay down" and "go home," and the cats were back in their cages, he pasted the thinnest of smiles to his face, styled quickly, and left the Keystone Centre. Back at the trailer, he changed into his jeans, and opened a bottle of beer. Tonight, however, instead of returning immediately to the arena, he stretched out on the blue velveteen couch and closed his eyes. His nose was stuffed, and his head and joints ached. Outside, the wind had begun to drop, so that for the first time that day, the trailer was not rocking and humming in the cross-current.

Now it was eight o'clock in the morning, and Wilson and I were throttling north on Highway 10 in the cab of the tiger truck. In the sleeping compartment behind us, Rick Robinson and three-year-old Connie were engrossed in a *Beauty and the Beast* colouring book. I was travelling with them for the opportunity to chat, and would return to Brandon with Wilson later in the morning to pick up Matt, who in the meantime was with Rolando and the Lunas. As we bumped over the frost-damaged roads, Wilson described how, during the summer of 1977, at the age of sixteen, he had signed on as a prop man with Al Stensel's Royal Canadian Circus, which was on a tour of one-day stands along the Newfoundland coast. "My plan," he told me above the whine of the tires, "was to stay with the circus long enough to qualify for pogey, then go home. The problem was, about all you could do in Newfoundland in those days was fish or log, and I wasn't cut out for either."

The tiger trainer on the tour, a young Texan named Doug Terranova, who was on contract to the show from Clyde Brothers Johnson in Seagoville, recognized Wilson's interest in the cats and, when the tour ended near Toronto, urged him to return with him to the U.S. and work with the tigers full time. "I thought this was great," said Wilson, who recalled that he had been somewhat less sanguine when, at a rest stop a few miles from the international bridge at Fort Erie, Ontario, Terranova pulled off the highway and informed him that, in order to enter America without a work permit, he would have to hide in the back of the truck under a pile of forty-pound bags of sawdust carried to soak up cat urine.

During the months that followed, explained Wilson, Terranova introduced him to the variety of skills necessary to deal with the cats. "I used to line up pop cans along the seats or the boards in the arenas, and flick them off one at a time with the horse whip. Anybody can *hit* a tiger with a whip. The trick is *not* to hit them but to come right up to their face or back end, so you can get their attention and move them around."

Wilson also developed the crucial capability to distinguish one tiger from another, at a glance. "I know them from the front end, the back end, any end at all," he laughed. "Rick knows them pretty well, too, but his life doesn't depend on it."

Wilson paused to light a cigarette, inhaled deeply, and said, "It's just like being a parent with a great big family, except in this family, you can't call your tiger by three names before you get it right. If I'm lookin at Robin and calling for Rajah, and Rajah comes off her seat behind me, I'm lunch."

Outside, the sky was overcast, and the landscape was evolving from uninterrupted prairie to a mixture of rolling scrub and poplar bush, with patches of pasture and range land.

One afternoon about a year into Wilson's apprenticeship, Terranova approached him at the farm in Seagoville and asked if he felt ready to meet the tigers. "If I was ever gonna be a tiger guy," grinned Wilson, "I knew I couldn't say no."

The simplicity of the final instructions – stay on your toes, don't turn your back on them for too long, and don't show any fear – belied a volume of nightmarish subtext. Mainly, Wilson was to do exactly what he'd seen Terranova do perhaps five hundred times.

"I stepped in and closed the gate," recalled Wilson, "and my heart was doin about two hundred a minute. Doug let the tigers in, and there I was, and there they were, and before I knew it I was goin through the motions, and so were they – we were all movin around in some kinda blur . . ." Wilson is a man of relatively few words, and at this point he could find no further expression for the well-remembered trauma of that afternoon nearly twenty years ago.

"I was terrified," he said presently. "But it wasn't till it was over and I sent the tigers out that it hit me. I stood there in the middle of the arena thinkin, What the hell am I doin here? I was so weak, I just about passed out. I thought, maybe I shoulda stayed home on that fishing trawler after all."

What no one bothered to explain to Wilson was that, by some extraordinary behavioural quirk, trained tigers will allow a stranger to put them through their routines, showing the interloper a kind of feline politesse during his initial incursion into the ring. "You yourself could go in there and work the tigers once, and on that one occasion they'd play along," he told me. "But if you showed even the slightest hesitation or weakness, they'd know you weren't the real boss, and the next time they saw you, they'd eat you up."

"Why wouldn't they eat me the first time?" I asked.

"That's somethin you'll hafta ask them," Wilson said. "One thing about cats is, they're wary. They don't tend to rush into things. You've seen how they move."

I asked how common it was that beginners not be told about the hazards of the second trip into the cage.

"If they told you," Wilson said solemnly, "you'd never go back in. I know I wouldn't have. I'll tell ya, though, when I did go in for the second time, Doug Terranova was right there at the door."

For months, Wilson rehearsed with the tigers as many as three times a day. "And every time I went in that cage," he said, "I felt the same terror. I used to wake up at night wondering what it'd feel like to have those teeth go into me – or those claws. I'd dream about it. And believe me, I knew all the stories about guys getting chewed up. I just had to keep tellin myself that I couldn't let the fear show, or I'd get hit."

The most direct route between Brandon and Dauphin follows Highway 10 through roughly forty kilometres of the upland pine and spruce forests of Riding Mountain National Park. But because we were hauling the tigers, we were forbidden by law to cross the park's boundary. Our detour around it took us in a crooked easterly loop, through McCreary and Ste. Rose du Lac, then back west across the Ochre and Vermilion rivers where, during the early twentieth century, the rich farmlands had attracted

Ukrainian settlers, whose descendants still form a large part of the local population.

Coming down through the park on the return trip, running now with just the tractor portion of the rig, I asked Wilson if he thought the actions of the animal-rights activists had in any way improved conditions for circus animals. "Conditions for my animals didn't need improvement," he scoffed. "If I were a tiger, I'd sure as hell rather be in the circus than out there in the forest or jungle, where the only good tiger is a dead tiger."

Like elephants, tigers can no longer be imported from the wilds. But because they breed easily in captivity, there is no shortage of them among the relatively small number of people licensed to own them in North America. According to Wilson, a full-grown Bengal or Siberian fetches a thousand dollars at best in a legally sanctioned sale. However, its value rises dramatically on the black market, where the skin alone, particularly with teeth and claws intact, can be worth ten thousand dollars as a rug or wall hanging. The sinews, glands and organs – the so-called "medicine bones" – are worth twice that amount to illicit Oriental medicine vendors, who sell such products out of backstreet apothecaries at the risk of heavy fines or even prison sentences.

It is the black market that is responsible for much of the contemporary pressure on wild tiger populations, some of which are already within a few hundred rifle blasts of extinction. As recently as the last century, the Siberian tiger, for example, ranged in the hundreds of thousands across nearly two million square miles of southeastern Siberia, eastern China, Korea, and eastern Mongolia. Today, because of poaching and loss of habitat to logging, the once-vast population has been reduced to three hundred tigers that eke out an existence in a remote stretch of the Sikhote-Alin Mountains on Russia's Pacific coast. In the region's desolate economy, a villager's average yearly earnings are about two thousand dollars U.S., making it understandable that many would risk a fine, or even a jail term, to shoot a tiger, the carcass of which can be spirited across the border into China and sold for the equivalent of ten thousand American dollars. Practitioners of Asian medicine use almost every gram of flesh and bone to treat one human ailment or another. Some parts are believed to confer not only the animal's strength but the legendary sexual potency that allows it to mate vigorously over several days. Even the whiskers – flexible white bristles about five inches in length and prized by circus people as good-luck charms – are ground up and consumed, sometimes stirred into wine, as a general tonic for the appetites and imagination.

"Here's a whisker right here," said Wilson, reaching onto the dash and handing me one of the precious white talismans that he had recently rescued from the cage. "Mexicans braid them into rings and get a jeweller to put a little clamp on them so they don't come apart. You can keep that one."

Matt and I arrived in Dauphin at about the same time as Bobby and Wilson. But it was not until Bob attempted to get water for Judy that we learned the town's supply was contaminated with *Giardia* bacteria, present in beaver feces, which had got into the municipal reservoir. The man who answered the door at the public building behind the arena refused to provide water even for consumption by the tigers and elephant.

"Well, ain't *that* the height of intelligence," Bob protested. "If this elephant was in the wilds, the water she'd be drinkin'd be fulla every kinda piss and corruption known to the tropics."

"I'm sorry," the man told him, "all public taps are off limits."

"What am I supposta do, give her Perrier water?" Bob whined. "Lemme tell ya something," he said, jabbing his thumb backwards into the air above his shoulder. "If this elephant dies of dehydration tonight, because you won't give her water from this public facility, this town's gonna face a one-hundred-and-thirty-thousand-dollar law suit, because that's what she's worth. On the other hand, what the hell – we can just blow Dauphin and move her on to Swan River, where she *can* get a drink. But I imagine if I did that you'd have some unhappy Shriners after ya because there wouldn't be any elephant in the circus tomorrow. So I'd suggest that you figure out how to get her some water right now. We're invited guests in this town, and I'd like a little cooperation."

Bob looked at the man, and sensing that nothing he had said had made a shred of difference, ventured, "Get me some water, and I'll get ya some free circus tickets."

When the animals had drunk their fill, a dozen or more of us walked to the Thunder Country Restaurant, where we tucked into banks of home-cooking and exchanged, first, food stories, and then notes on favourite circus acts, which, among men whose big top experience totalled perhaps two hundred years, ranged from clowns to aerialists to alligators – to horses, elephants, and anacondas.

"The original Garza Statue act was as good as anything I ever saw," said Bobby. "They did the stacks and balances and stuff so smoothly, you'd sit there watching, and you really could convince yourself that they were statues come to life."

The act all the men agreed was the best they'd seen in years – "the best I've *ever* seen," said Wilson – is the work of a single young woman who walks to the centre of the ring, without props or assistants, and goes through four or five costume changes, leaving no clue as to where the new costumes come from or the old ones go. "Ya could understand it," said Bobby, "if it was just a few baggy dresses or something, but we're talking about evening gowns, high heels, elbow-length gloves. She's got this stuff on, she throws a bit of confetti in the air, and by the time it falls, she's standing there in shorts and a tank top and sandals. She steps through a hula hoop and she's got on high boots and a skirt and sweater. She's a Russian kid. Dezi Kazionov . . . Kazinovioff, something like that. Hottest act in America right now. Gets five grand for one day's work."

Bob and Wilson had worked with Ms. Kazio . . . Kazino . . . ("Kazablancanovia" Bob essayed at one point) in Pine Bluff, Arkansas, a few weeks earlier, had watched her closely at every performance, and did not have an inkling as to how she did what she does. "She bought the act from an old Russian magician," said Bob. "Musta paid a fortune for it. Actually, there's one other act like it, in Las Vegas – came from the same old Russian guy. I figure she must roll the clothes over. Then again, how do you roll an evening gown into a mini-skirt? How do you roll little flat shoes into spike heels?"

Later that evening, Matt and Bobby sat in our motel room across the street from the arena, watching a gangster movie, hooting and snorting over the action, while I sat on one of the beds addressing the agony that was my overdue income tax return. When Bob had gone, I tried to get Matt to make an entry in the journal he had sworn to keep as part of the price of taking ten or twelve days off school. "C'mon," I said, "you didn't do it yesterday either. You gotta catch up. You promised you'd do it."

"*You* promised I'd do it," he said.

"You're the one who's going to suffer if it's not done."

"You are," he said (quite astutely, I thought).

Matt is in the French Immersion program at École Gron Morgan in Thunder Bay, and had been alternating his entries between French and English. "See," he said, flinging the journal open to a blank page, "I don't know what to write!"

"Write about what interests you!" I heard myself squawk. "Write about the most interesting things that happened today – the stuff you liked!"

The long-awaited entry, completed the next morning, read:

*Lundi, le 12 may, 1997*

*Aujourd'hui je suis allé au Seven Eleven avec mes amis, Brett Marshall et Rolando. Quand nous avons allé au Seven Eleven on avez acheté les Slurpees. Brett a acheté un Mountain Dew Slurpee, et il a le renversé pour avoir un Watermelon Slurpee. . . .*

❉

I had learned by this time that one way of gauging the mood of a particular performance was to watch Manuel Gonçalves do his rola-bola act, in particular his more difficult tricks, which he tended to squeeze a little harder, a little longer, and for just a little more spritz if he felt the audience was appreciative. Which is not to say that he swung the lead even at the worst of times. He is a skilful and devoted performer, who developed his talents in the family circus in Lisbon, tried several acts as a youngster during the fifties and sixties, and settled early on the rola-bola, which he has done exclusively now for nearly three decades, throughout Europe, North America and Asia. While the essence of his gig is to balance on a board, atop a roller, atop a five-foot-high pedestal, the genius of the thing is in the brazen succession of handstands, leaps, and rope tricks that he snaps off, all the while keeping his board skimming back and forth, like a surfboard balanced not within the wave where it is stable but somehow on its crest. Jill is Manuel's assistant in the endeavour, and they wear matching costumes that she has made by hand and that suggest the finery of jungle insects. She stands below, handing him his accoutrements, prancing, posing, occasionally tensing as if anticipating a fall – generally "selling the act," as they say in the business. Manuel, too, sells it, of course, as any professional will – styling, smiling,

*Jill and Manuel Gonçalves at the conclusion of Jill's act in The Pas, Manitoba.*

grimacing, stretching out the theatrics, coming *evvvvver* so close to tipping off, *juuuuust* managing to keep things under control.

He refers to his finale as "four boards" – a trick in which he starts on a rolling plank, leaps into the air, and throws another beneath him, performing a 180-degree turn and somehow getting his feet down within the millisecond that the boards remain balanced on the roller . . . a second board . . . a third . . . a fourth. "You watch," Bobby told me one day. "If there's a decent crowd, and he's getting a good response, he'll usually miss a board, go back and try it again, build up the suspense . . . build it . . . build it until on the fourth board, he's got the crowd just cranked. Oh, yeah, if they're with him, he'll sell it to 'em."

On this afternoon in Dauphin, however, Manuel was through the trick and back in the dressing room almost before the audience had had a chance to respond. This was a reaction not just to the listless crowd but to a cheerless day, in an old arena, under weather conditions that even in frosty Manitoba would hardly have seemed remarkable in mid-February.

# 9

BECAUSE OF THE fertility of the Swan River Valley, the architecture north of Dauphin is anchored not by snow quinzees or DEW-line installations, as some members of the troupe had apparently been led to expect, but by grain elevators – and by Ukrainian Orthodox churches, little domed buildings, many of them dilapidated, but still sweetly visible across the flatlands. The fields along our route the next morning were still too soggy for cultivation, but the Duck Mountains, visible in the west, provided a tonic against another intemperate day – as did the ducks and yellowheads and magpies that made a parade ground of the ditches and sloughs within sight of the highway. During the hundred-kilometre drive to Swan River, Matt counted more than a hundred mallards in the ditches (as two days later, he would count a hundred or more loons on the open patches of water between The Pas and Flin Flon).

Unlike the arena in Dauphin, the Swan River Arena was bright and heated and carefully painted, and was such a welcome sanctuary that, after the show was erected at about noon hour, a number of the performers and crew simply hung around the stands, socializing and staying warm. I delivered Matt into the hands of his confederates and sat down inside with the trumpet player, Peter Bartels, who was nose-deep in what he referred to as a "post-apocalyptic" novel. He was dressed, as usual, in a gold leather jacket, with pencil-length fringes on the arms, chest and back. Peter is gangly, dark-haired, and affable, and his heavy-rimmed glasses give him an air of edgy intellectualism that is by no means misplaced. He had come to my attention during the early days of the tour not only because he is a brilliant performer, capable of almost anything on his trumpet, but because, unlike anyone else I have ever met, he both removed and donned his shirt and tuxedo jacket as a unit, over his head, like a piece of armour – so that, except at the collar of his shirt, he did not have to undo any buttons. He has a master's degree in music from Baylor University, in Waco, Texas. But while most of his academic contemporaries have, as he put it, "become music professors or teachers, or are playing in symphonies," he has opted for the funkier alternative of Chicago's contemporary music scene, playing in anywhere up to five bands at a time – among them an eleven-piece Latin ensemble called Jazzambo's Latin Jazz Outfit; an eight-piece "urban funk and acid jazz ensemble" called Zoogenic; and a "really hot blues band" called Hot Rod.

Peter is twenty-seven years old and works in the circus primarily to stay pumped for what he calls the next phase in his "Overall Plan" – that being to start his own experimental jazz band, replacing rhythm section and singer with trumpets, "so that we'll have maybe four horns," to go with four or five other instruments. "I need the money, too," he smiled. "If you choose the route I have, you've gotta make your money where you can."

This is not to suggest that Peter is in any way patronizing or condescending toward circus musicianship, or to the circus itself. "When I went out on my first tour, with Wayne Franzen's circus, in 1991," he said, "I got so caught up in the life that I'd be right out there on the lot, banging tent stakes, setting up with the midway crew, basically doing any job that came up, and then jumping into my tux and into the orchestra pit when it was time to be a musician."

A day earlier, in Dauphin, bored by the overture that Larry and the band had been playing at every performance, Peter quickly composed "The Dauphin Overture," which was introduced that night and would be played now at every stop on the itinerary.

Bobby Gibbs appeared in the arena, came alongside where we were sitting, and asked with Southern formality if I'd mind driving him to the Extra Foods store, where, on the way into town, he had seen a sign advertising potatoes at $2.89 for twenty pounds.

Peter turned down an invitation to go with us, and Bob and I returned twenty minutes later with sixty pounds of discount spuds, twenty of apples (bruised), thirty of bananas (black), and a miscellany of celery (shrivelled), lettuce (wilted), and onions (sprouted). We bought twenty loaves of bread (stale), and, except for a last-minute purchase of eight hundred 222s (generic), would have passed through the check out line for less than twenty dollars.

Immediately on returning, Bobby summoned Matt and Rolando and put them in charge of what, for Judy, was a kind of orgy of delectable provender, dispensed an item at a time by her obedient peons and grape-peelers.

While a show elephant will occasionally drop its feces in the ring, most have learned by the time they are five or six years old to "shit on command," so that they can be "crapped out" before a performance. To facilitate the process, the elephant is generally cued to stand on its back legs, so as to maximize gravitational pressure on its bowels. Normally the "crapping" is done outside the arena or tent. However, my own best look at the procedure came that night in the Zamboni room of the Swan River Arena, where Bobby had taken Judy to keep her out of the sleet that was falling outdoors as she awaited her turn in the ring. The room doubled as the arena staff's office and lunch room, so was far from a prudent choice as an elephant toilet. But as the time for the act approached, the two attendants on duty were out in the stands watching the circus, prompting Bob to suppose that he could just empty Judy out where she was. "How they gonna know?" he said, and he cued her onto her back legs, and in a voice that would not be heard above the band, began a low, steady petition: "Shit, Judy. C'mon, Judy. Shit, Judy. C'mon now, shit for Daddy. Daddy loves ya. Give me some shit now. Give Daddy some shit."

"C'mon now, Judy," chimed John. "Give us some shit now. Shit for Bobby. Shit now, Judy . . ." As the two of them carried on in chorus, maintaining an intense watch on Judy's anus, Judy herself poked around among the heating and water pipes twelve feet overhead, pressing nonchalantly at this valve or electrical fixture, that bit of strapping or insulation.

"C'mon, Judy," Bobby urged, his tone more assertive now, "Gimme some shit, now. *Shit*, Judy. *Shit* for Daddy. For gawdsakes, they're gonna be comin in here in a minute. Massage her asshole," he commanded. And John, ever faithful, reached out and prodded around Judy's anus with his gloved fist. "*Shit*, Judy. *Shit* for Daddy, now. Daddy loves ya."

As all of this was going on, Judy remained oblivious to everything but her interests within a foot or so of the ceiling.

"*Oo, oo, oo*, here it comes!" Bobby announced. And, sure enough, Judy's rear orifice opened to a diameter that would have allowed a five-pin ball to pass, and out it all came – four, five, six, seven turds. "Oh, good girl. Beautiful girl. Atta girl. Daddy loves his beautiful girl. That's all!" Bobby said. "No, here's another one – that's all," and John was immediately beneath Judy with the wheelbarrow, scooping up the feces and hustling them out the door, while Bob opened the valve on a nearby hose and blasted the remaining evidence – except, of course, for the smell – into the drain.

We left Swan River a few hours later on a note of accomplishment, in that Bobby, after considerable debate with Wilson, had phoned around and had managed to hire a truck and driver to haul Judy and her trailer to the remaining tour stops and into Winnipeg, where his own truck was being repaired. He had done so with such economy – a thousand dollars for the truck-tractor (a brand new International Harvester), plus a few hundred extra for the driver – that the total expense was going to be very little more than it had been costing to make each run twice with the tiger truck.

For Matt and me, the ensuing couple of days were a departure of a sort, inasmuch as our next stop, The Pas, is my wife's birthplace and the current home of my mother-in-law, Eva Carpick, and my wife's sister, Susan Carpick. This meant that, instead of checking into a motel that night, we were able to hunker down amid the comforts (if not the creatures) of home. As it happened, my mother-in-law was visiting *our* place in Thunder Bay at the time, so that when we arrived, at about midnight, only Susan, the youngest of the Carpick siblings, was waiting for us. But she had the barbecue primed in the backyard, salad on the table, and a couple of bumper steaks ready for the coals.

Like so many of the area's inhabitants, my wife's paternal forebears, the Carpicks, came to this part of Manitoba with the inundation of Ukrainian and eastern European immigrants during the early twentieth century. Her maternal ancestors had arrived some nine thousand years earlier, with the slow tide of Aboriginals that made its way gradually across the Bering Strait and fanned out across a continent recently transformed by glaciers. Betty's mother grew up in South Indian Lake, a largely Native community, some three hundred kilometres northwest of The Pas, and spent her childhood winters in a cabin on her dad's trapline in the boreal woods.

The Pas has a history of uneasy race relations, which at times have expressed themselves in open discrimination. As recently as the 1960s, for example, the local movie theatre was divided into "the white side" and "the Indian side." The town's divisions were brought to national attention a few years ago when CBC television broadcast a movie called *Conspiracy of Silence* about the slaying during the early 1970s of a Cree girl named Helen Betty Osborne by a carload of teenaged drunks, all of them white, some the sons of well-known families in the community.

There is a general feeling these days that relations between the races have improved. The symbolic separation, however, is still very much present in the wide flow of the North Saskatchewan River, which divides the town proper, with its largely white population, from the two-thousand-odd Natives of the Opasquia Cree Nation who live on the river's opposite bank.

My own restricted take on the solitudes was tested the following morning when Matt and I drove to the arena on the white side of town, under the assumption that *this* was where the Shriners would be setting up, even though the old established arena is decidedly inferior to the new Gordon Lathlin Arena on the Cree side of the river. But I was wrong. And it was not until we had crossed the bridge to the reserve that we caught up with the familiar caucus of itinerants who had come to seem pretty much like family over the last couple of weeks.

That afternoon, for the first time since the tour had begun, the circus played to a predominantly Aboriginal crowd. A member of the local Shrine club was forthright in his acknowledgement that, in part, the event was being held where it was "because the Indian kids and families are more likely to show up" – and, he might have added, "spend money," which they did with diligence:

on glo-lights, inflatable hammers, plastic tiaras, light-up swords, and, of course, popcorn, candy apples, and candy floss. It was the sort of spending that, in the light of reserve economics – which in this part of the world tend to be based less on employment than on government spending – would have outraged taxpayers of a certain perspective. But, for me, it was a joy to see such flaring contempt for the grindstone – in particular for the sort of fiscal orthodoxy that, on the other side of the river, is well on its way to wearing an entire culture to a nub.

The Cree, of course, have their own nub to deal with, and in the break between performances, I had an opportunity to chat with Rosa Luna about the local Aboriginals and their nine-thousand-year claim on the surrounding forests and lakes. Being of Mexican and Cuban background, she understands something of the friction between indigenous and "occupying" cultures, and made a point of saying that in the circus, she believed, all cultures were given a fairer shake than they sometimes were in what circus people call "the straight world."

The circus is not without its biases. According to Paul Gadicke, Mexicans, for example, prefer Canadian and American acts to those from, say, South or Central America. And it is well known that the American circus of the early century employed so-called Georgia gangs of blacks at something barely above the level of slave labour. But it is also true that in the contemporary circus, eastern Europe and Mexico, whose emigrants have often been demeaned by North American society, are a revered well of talent – and that Mexican flying acts, for example, are respected everywhere as among the finest in the world.

When I came into the arena for the evening performance with Susan, who is an attractive thirtyish woman, I went off on chores almost immediately and did not get an opportunity to introduce her to Bobby, Wilson and the rest, who were themselves busy. I was only beginning to learn that circus people, for all their mental toughness, can be highly sensitive to the way in which they are perceived by outsiders – particularly to any form of condescension born of misplaced notions that they are rough-necks or "carny" people or, as in the old days, freaks, who have wound up in the circus for lack of anywhere else to go. This, combined with my oversight in not making introductions, meant that every day for the rest of the tour (indeed, off and on for months to come, in phone calls and letters), I had to field indignant complaints over my apparent rudeness. During entirely unrelated conversations, Bob would say as an aside to Wilson or John, "At least he knows enough to keep his wife's sister away from low-life like us" or "I guess we ain't worth intro-ducin to people as good-lookin as Charlie's sister-in-law – she wouldn't be interested in us."

"If I'd known anybody cared," I said to him a few days later, "I would have introduced her to everybody on the circus."

"We didn't want ya to introduce her to *everybody*, but you might'a introduced her to your friends."

The longer this went on, the more I saw in it, and the worse I felt. Yet I can say that this seeming trifle gave me a shred of insight into the complex equation that connects the margins to the mainstream: specifically, that a self-imposed life on the edge is defined as much by a need for normality – or perhaps, more accu-rately, acceptance – as a disdain for it. I mentioned this to Bobby, who said, "Isn't that why half the hippies in America ended up as bureaucrats and bond salesmen?"

As the show wound down that night, Bobby asked me if, imme-diately after the performance, I would run him a few miles north out of town on Highway 10 to see whether the weigh scale was open. The agent who worked this particular facility was a notori-ous stickler and authoritarian, who alternated shifts between a station near Thompson and this one north of The Pas. "A truck-er'd rather see his mother in jail than see that little blinking light and the sign SCALE OPEN: PLEASE REPORT," Bob told me as we drove. "Agents like this guy are so hateful that when they see out-of-state plates, or even hear you're from the circus, they'll keep ya sittin there two hours whether there's anything wrong or not."

As it turned out, Satan's emissary was not in his tidy little booth, which meant the trucks were on the road as soon as we got back, and Matt and I were back across the river for another night of pampering.

# 10

THE NINETY-MINUTE drive between The Pas and Flin Flon is a kind of axiom for the heartland, replete with tall conifers, postcard lakes, and abundant granite. However, as you get close to Flin Flon itself, a more recent Canadian axiom spikes the tree-line in the form of the smokestack of the Hudson Bay Mining and Smelting Company, which rises to the stars and spills an endless fountain of the sort of effluents that decades ago denuded the local terrain of everything but humpy brown rock. The resulting Golgotha is more apocalyptic by far than anything the circus might have conjured as an image of the edge of the earth. Seen even in the most flattering light, there is an almost breathtaking starkness to the town, an otherworldly semblance that was considerably enhanced by the sight, in mid-May, of an enormous MERRY CHRISTMAS sign glowering from the smelter stack as we picked our way through the hilly streets toward the arena. The terrain is so entirely unforgiving within the shadow of the smelter that much of the town's water and sewer piping must be run above ground. From the social and recreational standpoint, Flin Flon is a place of good fishing, bad drinking, and the sort of hardscrabble hockey that has yielded professional trenchmen on the order of Bobby Clarke, Reggie Leach, and Eric Nesterenko.

The first thing Pat Delaney did when he reached the famed outpost was to call his mother. "Guess where I am!" he shouted into the pay phone at the Flin Flon Memorial Arena.

"Chicago," came the response.

"I'm in Flin Flon, Manitoba," shouted Pat. "I'm with Ricky Wallenda's show."

"Well you better come home," said Mrs. Delaney.

Pat told me that, in 1949, the town had been so happy to see the King Brothers tent show roll in that the women at one of the churches had served the entire circus a home-cooked feast in the church basement.

During the early afternoon, Pat and Ricky went on a souvenir-buying mission, but returned with the sort of standard-issue junk – T-shirts, coffee mugs, and the like – that said no more about Flin Flon than about any other part of the world that might have thought to have such things stitched, stamped, and packaged. When I caught up with Bobby at about 2 p.m., he showed me his new T-shirt, which was printed with a foot-high mosquito and emblazoned with the message: "Territorial Bird of the North . . . Flin Flon, Manitoba."

Determined that he have a few representative mementos, I walked downtown to a trapper's store that I had been told about and bought half a dozen white foxtails, a few key fobs beaded by local Cree women, and a "coonskin" hat (in fact made of rabbit skin but with a coon tail behind). I passed the foxtails around to Chata, Rosa, Jill, and Connie, and gave a tail and the hat to Bob, who showed up for picture-taking before the afternoon performance sporting the foxtail on his bullhook and the hat on his head.

So covetous was John McCoy of the exotic new headgear that, at intermission, Bob came to me with money, begging me to go get a hat for "poor John." I did, with the result that, by the time the

*Bob in his new coonskin hat, in Flin Flon, with a family about to be photo-graphed. Bob Bridgewater, the Grand Potentate of the Khartum Temple, is behind Judy.*

elephant act came along, Bob *and* John were out on the floor doing their surrealist rendering of the Mad Trapper on Elephant Manoeuvres in the Arctic.

By show's end, Bob's curiosity was at a pitch where nothing less would do than a personal pilgrimage to the fur store. I drove him there, and for twenty minutes he thundered around, making eighty-decibel wisecracks about Flin Flon, about Canadians, about the pathetic Canadian dollar, tossing merchandise onto the counter and buying, finally, nearly four hundred dollar's worth of fur items, native crafts, and (proving, once again, that nothing exceeds like excess) yet another fur hat, this one a big Dionysian wolfskin thing that he wore that night for the performance and that I never saw again. As he skimmed off twenty-dollar bills at the cash register, he demanded to know whether the store accepted Canadian money (his running joke was that even Canadians didn't want their own debased currency), prompting me to feign some minor disapproval of his boorishness.

Outside, he said, "Never feel you have to apologize for my behaviour."

"Somebody has to," I needled.

He said, "It sounded like you were uncomfortable."

"Isn't that the point?" I said. "To make people uncomfortable?"

As we settled in the car, a panhandler – a man of perhaps forty but with the gait and bearing of an eighty-year-old – tapped on the passenger-side window, and Bobby opened up and presented him with a handful of coins. "Some day when I need that," he hollered, "you can give it back to me."

We inched up the narrow main street, caught in Flin Flon's version of rush hour. "One thing I've never told ya," Bob said, "is that as a kid I was very shy because of my weight. I never took showers with the other guys at school, never asked a girl to go on a date. I was probably the only kid in the history of Miller, Missouri, to go to the high-school prom by myself. The reason I gravitated toward animals was that they don't care what you look like."

He went on to describe how, at the age of sixteen, in Lincoln, Nebraska, he had been asked by Gil Gray to display a truckload of elephants at a home for severely disabled children. "I'll tell ya," he said, "you oughta start every day of your life thanking God for the three kids he gave you. Some of these kids were hardly even recognizable as human beings."

The focal point of the experience had been a private audience with a highly intelligent but profoundly deformed, hydrocephalic girl. "When I got back to the truck," Bob said, "I was so shaken I couldn't even turn the key. I said, *Bobby Gibbs, you've been a fool!* Here was this smart, sensitive teenager with this shrivelled little body and this enormous, grotesque head – no teeth, no hair, bad skin – and here I was whining and pissin and moanin about bein fat. She scared shit outta people when they saw her. They recoiled. I'll tell ya, I promised myself right then and there, and promised God, too, that I'd never again feel sorry for myself or hesitate to be who I am, a fat guy with a bad attitude. People were just gonna have to deal with that. And that's why I do what I do, and am the way I am. I ain't gonna keep my candle under any bushel – for you, for the woman in the fur store, or for anybody else."

That night, in an echo of Fort Frances, the lights went out just before intermission, but came on of their own accord the moment Ricky jumped up from the lighting board, where he was filling in for Patty Alexander, who had been sacked out all day in a hotel room a couple of blocks from the arena. Patty explained to me later that she had been injured during her clown appearance in The Pas, when a boy out of the audience had walloped her with an inflatable hammer. The blow itself would not have done damage. But she had not seen it coming until the last instant, and had jerked her head with such violence that she'd damaged a nerve, temporarily paralysing her right hand and arm.

When the show was over, Matt and I returned to The Pas for one more night, this time with Paul and Chata, who Susan installed in an unused basement bedroom. In the morning, as Matt and I quarrelled over his continued reluctance to keep his journal, our guests sat as quiet as clothes pegs on the living room chesterfield and watched television game shows. Paul is not inclined to reading. He had told me so on the day I asked if he had read Malcolm Lowry's *Under the Volcano*, which is set in Cuernavaca, where he and Chata live, near Mexico City. But he is fanatical about crossword puzzles, and had his nose in a book of them during the first hundred kilometres of the drive eastward across Manitoba to Thompson, where two shows were scheduled for the following day.

Just east of Grass River Provincial Park, on Highway 39, Paul moved into the front seat, and we talked at length about the

Mexican circus, most of whose four hundred shows are what he called "tiny family operations" that require little in the way of licensing, and tend to perform "anywhere they can find a bit of open space." Paul said there were probably a hundred such circuses in the Mexico City area alone and described one he and Chata had seen, in which twelve of the thirteen performers were brothers and sisters.

Understandably, most circus performers, particularly those in high-risk acts, prefer to work with family than with non-family members. "The other guy may be just as talented or more so," Rick Wallenda had told me, "but in the crunch it's the guy with the same blood who cares most for your safety, and who's most likely to risk his life for you. My grandfather's brother, Herman, was always in charge of my grandfather's rigging. Then I did it. I've sometimes thought that if I'd been in Puerto Rico with him, the wire would have been rigged properly, and he'd still be alive – or at least wouldn't have died down there."

Paul always rigged Chata's hair-hang. Enrique rigged for Liliana. And Liliana refused to perform her somersault to the web unless Enrique was spotting beneath her. "That's the way it's always been," she said. "And when the day comes that he can't be there, I'm not sure I will be either."

When we arrived in Thompson, Matt and I treated ourselves to the best hotel in town and immediately stocked the room with fresh fruit, as an antidote to the flu bug that by this time had caught up with both of us.

During the evening, Bob and I drove to the local mall, where I saw the arguments against the circus's employment of animals reduced to a level that would have sent even the hardest strokers in the animal-rights movement swimming for the bottom. We had gone into a fur store, where the walls and shelves were a costly profusion of fox, wolf, bear, lynx, and beaver pelts. Bobby, who had bought as much fur as he needed in Flin Flon, took a liking to a book of photos of boreal mammals, and took it to the cashier, who said amicably, "Are you with the circus?"

"How did you know? I don't stand out, do I?"

"A little bit," she smiled.

"Ya gonna go?" said Bobby.

"I don't know. I've heard they don't treat their animals very well."

The shriek of contempt that emerged from Bob's throat turned heads a hundred feet down the mall, and he leaned onto the counter and said, "Ma'am, did I understand you right?"

"I don't know, did you?" she said, apparently unsure as to what she had said to set him off.

"Here you are in a store where the walls are hung with intelligent fur-bearing creatures that I'm gawdam sure didn't die peacefully in their sleep, and you're tellin me that the circus doesn't treat its animals very well? What exactly is it you heard?"

"I heard they beat them," she said.

"First of all, 'they' is me," said Bobby. "I've got the elephant. And, yes, I admit it, I do beat her three or four times a day with a tire iron, just to show her how much I love her. And, ma'am, do you know what she said to me after I beat her this afternoon?"

The woman, whose only desire at this point seemed to be to get the massive infidel before her off the premises, said quietly, "I don't know."

"She said, 'I don't care if you beat me ten times a day, boss, as long as you promise you won't leave me in Thompson – I've heard the people here catch animals in traps, and let 'em freeze to death, and then hang what's left of 'em over there in the mall. And I sure as heck don't want that happening to me.' How much is this book, ma'am?" said Bob.

"Twenty-four, ninety-five."

"Well, that's twenty-four, ninety-five that'll stay right where it is in my pocket, instead'a goin into yours." Bobby slapped the book onto the counter, turned, and, as he left the store, hooted, "*I hear they don't treat their animals very well! I hear they beat them.*"

The next morning, as I waited for an oil change in a little cinder-block garage, a middle-aged Native man came in with his three children and told me he'd driven a hundred kilometres from Nelson House for the circus, but that the assistance cheques on which many people in the area depended had not arrived from Ottawa. The result was that he'd had to hock his new Sony television for two hundred dollars at the local pawnshop. "Now," he said stoically, "I gotta drive all the way back here on Tuesday when the cheques come." He was less philosophic, however, about having to miss three days of televised NHL playoffs in the meantime. By coincidence, Bobby's driver, Jim Unger, was an old friend of the pawnshop owner, and told me later that between nine and noon that day some ninety families, both local and from surrounding reserves, had come in and pawned televisions, VCRs, tools, appliances, boat motors, as well as an apocryphal hearing aid and prosthetic arm, in order to raise the money to get them and their kids into the C.A. Nesbitt Arena for the matinee show. "You must like the circus," I said to the guy in the garage. "Go home broke every year," he laughed – a prophecy well on its way to fulfilment when I saw him and his family that afternoon, the kids festooned with the sort of merchandise that, in the words of Pat Delaney, was "sold at a mark-up of between five hundred and fifteen hundred percent" – in this case to consumers who had spent the better part of the week's grocery money to acquire it.

By this point on the tour, I had made a habit of asking two or three kids at every performance what it was they liked about the show. Almost invariably they mentioned the elephant, tigers, and bicycles. Girls of a certain age liked Daniella's hula hoops – in part, I imagined, because of the participation of seven-year-old Talina. That day, in Thompson, a little Native girl, perhaps four years old, thought for a moment about the question and said confidently, "I liked the lady who hung by her neck and I liked the whale."

At about dinner time, between shows, the whale, ostensibly under John's care, wandered across the field behind the arena, into the spruce woods, where, in the veiled light, she was indistinguishable from any of the countless Precambrian boulders that had been scattered across the landscape by the receding ice fields some ten thousand years ago. Several of us poked helplessly along the edge of the woods, calling Judy's name, and fifteen minutes later she reappeared, several hundred metres upwind, surrounded by kids in the unfenced backyard of a row of townhouses. "Get her to stand up," one of the kids said to Bobby as he fetched her, and, without hesitation, he cued her onto her back legs, prompting her to drop a half-dozen turds at the perimeter of the yard. "Spread that on the lawn," Bob told the kids. "The dandelions'll be as high as your ass."

That night, after the show, which took perhaps forty minutes to pack up, Dave Connors and the prop men hit the road for the ten-hour haul to Winnipeg – a journey that, in the end, would take twenty-four hours and leave them pale, pink-eyed, and speculating on how close they had come to being savaged by bears.

Bob, Matt and I celebrated at the Poseidon Restaurant with a torpor-inducing meal of, among other things, roast pork, mashed potatoes, homemade bread, and lemon pie.

Wilson, John McCoy, and Rick Robinson headed out for a night in the bars.

A hodge-podge of reports the next day – from Jim Unger, from Rick Robinson, from John McCoy – confirmed that, at about one a.m., Wilson had got into a pool game with a man described to me both as "a three-hundred-pound Indian" and "a three-hundred-pound asshole." Wilson was notably uncommunicative about the affair, but his accomplices volunteered that he had refused to acknowledge his losses at the pool table, had made a wisecrack to his opponent, and, for his troubles, had been sucker-punched with such force that the blow knocked him ten feet across the room, from where he was picked up by bouncers and thrown another ten feet out the door.

John took it as an almost mystical sign of Wilson's resilience – as I did – that ten minutes later he had recovered to the point that he was "back in the bar ready to party." However, when we caught up with him at the service centre at Pelican Narrows at about noon the next day, he looked anything but resilient and was decidedly out of the party mood. He had sent Rick Robinson into the store for snacks, and, I suspect, would have been quite happy to avoid face-to-face contact. But when I went up to the truck and knocked on the door from below, he had little choice but to roll down the window.

I said, "Are ya okay, Wilson?"

"I'm okay," he said.

He was wearing sunglasses, so that I could not see his eye. But his temple and cheek were swollen to the point that the left lens of his glasses resembled a black coin pushed into mauve plasticine. Otherwise, it looked as if a kilo of calf's liver had somehow been slipped beneath the skin on the left side of his face.

"Have you taken anything for it?"

"No."

"Do you want some two-twenty-twos? I've got some in the van."

"Don't need 'em."

"How are you doin, Connie?" I said.

"We got tigers!" she called above the rumble of the engine, keeping a sentry's eye out for Rick, who would be returning with the chocolate bars and drinks.

Wilson and I looked at one another for a second, and I said, "You're sure you're gonna be okay?"

"It's happened before," he said cheerfully, "and it'll happen again."

The plan for the morning had been that Matt would travel in the elephant truck with Jim Unger and John, while Bobby, Paul and Chata would ride with me. However, by Ponton, two hundred kilometres out of Thompson, where we stopped for a mid-morning breakfast, Matt had wearied of truck-riding and changed places with Bob – but not before I had had the pleasure of pointing out a great grey owl to Bob, Paul, and Chata; had felt the fleeting humiliation of mistaking a German shepherd dog for a timber wolf; and had experienced the modest high of taking my passengers down a quarter-mile trail to see one of the glories of northern Manitoba, Pisew (Pee-soo) Falls, which were still under forty feet of elaborately sculptured ice.

After filling the van with gas at Pelican Narrows, I gave my only functional credit card to the teenaged cashier, who ran it through his machine, handed it back, and (for reasons I understood well) said, "I'm sorry, sir, the system won't take it." I saved face by pulling out just enough cash to cover the gasoline, and, when I checked the bank machine on the premises, found that there was just $103 in a chequing account that I share with my wife. I withdrew a hundred of it, bought a couple of fruit juices for Matt and myself, and hit the road, feeling remarkably unencumbered.

The truth is, I had expected the credit card to collapse long before it did, having piled one expense after another onto it for three weeks, knowing that it was already at its limit and that a required payment on it had been missed perhaps ten days ago. "Do you know what we're going to do tonight?" I said to Matt as we rolled south.

"What?" he said.

"We're gonna call up Terry and Jane Gray and see if we can use their spare bedroom. We haven't seen them for a long time."

"Let's stay in a hotel," he said.

"I'd like to see Terry and Jane," I said, calculating that, when we got to Winnipeg, I would call home and get Betty to endorse any cheques that might have come in, to apply a payment to my Visa debt in the morning, and put the rest into the chequing account, with hopes that the latter would be above mortgage level at the beginning of the month.

"What's the matter?" I said to Matt. "You like Terry and Jane."

"I like hotels," he enthused.

About ten kilometres north of Grand Rapids, on Highway 6, we came up behind the prop truck, marooned on the shoulder, with no one in sight. We found the prop crew a few kilometres south at the truck stop at Grand Rapids, the four of them sprawled in Dave Connors's half-ton, in various degrees of despair, waiting for a wrecker to arrive from Winnipeg to haul the prop truck four hundred kilometres into the city. Roy MacFee and his nephew Mike MacFee, who had been driving the vehicle when it sputtered, had shambled to the service centre on foot in the middle of the night, where they had later been found by Dave Connors and Tim Weaver, who had been driving in the half-ton. Mike, according to Roy, had predicted a deadly succession of bear attacks as they had navigated blind down the highway, hypersensitized to every snapped twig and bird twitter that came out of the forest. Ricky Wallenda had passed them during the morning, apparently in a less-than-sterling mood, and had dropped them a thousand dollars in cash to take care of the tow. "One thing my wife could never get used to," Ricky had told me a few days earlier, "was the way the circus ate up money, and how you could never tell when it was going to eat."

We sat in Grand Rapids, comforting the casualties, until Bobby announced that he was going to ride in the van again if we didn't mind, and a minute or two later we were back on the road. "Here, put this on," he said, and he handed me a tape of the Stamps Gospel Quartet.

Above the sweetly harmonized singing, he mentioned that the Shriners had been disappointed by the lack of clowns in Ricky's show.

"Ricky told me they were supposed to supply their own clowns," I said.

"Yeah, but that's amateur-hour stuff. But it ain't his fault. The clown he *did* have got hurt. *He's got your comedy trampoline*," Bob shouted into the back seat, to Paul.

"I thought he coulda used a clown act," said Paul.

"The problem these days," said Bob, "is clowns all come outta these clown colleges, like the one Ringlings runs in Florida. I call them McClowns – they're widgets! Who's gonna pay 'em? Ringlings won't even pay the good ones any more. They use David Larible five or six times a show – one of the best in the business. Run 'im ragged. And I'll bet they don't pay 'im half what he's worth."

"Did ya know he's Chata's brother-in-law?" I said.

"No kidding!" hollered Bob into the back seat. "You *know*, then! I'll bet they don't pay him more than fifteen hundred a week."

Paul exchanged thoughts with Chata and demurred, suggesting the figure was probably considerably higher. "I was told they only payed Gunther Gabel Williams fifteen hundred," said Bob, "the best animal trainer in America."

"When was that?" said Paul.

"I dunno, ten, twelve years ago."

The Ringlings-bashing continued for several minutes before veering into an area in which Bobby gave the Greatest Show on Earth unqualified praise: elephant breeding. "Let's face it," he said as the spruce trees sped by, "the elephant is still the bottom line in the traditional circus. But the numbers are dropping, and you can't bring any more in. So, here come's Kenneth Feld, the owner of Ringlings, and he decides to make his own elephants – and that's what he's doing."

Bobby predicted that twenty years from now, Ringlings would be one of the few circuses in North America that owned *any* elephants. "It's a very smart, very forward-thinking move."

Jim Unger had followed us out of the truck stop, hauling Judy, and I watched in the mirror as the big International Harvester closed from behind.

Bob explained that a couple of smaller breeding operations were afoot in the U.S., including Dory Miller's at the Carson and Barnes Circus, and that a pair of Canadian breeders – Mike Hackenberger at the Bowmanville Zoo, east of Toronto, and Charlie Gray at African Lion Safari in Dundas, Ontario – were running modest but successful programs.

"The problem with all of it," said Bob as a pair of mallards buzzed up out of the ditch, "is that it's so damn expensive! You've got your barns, your employees, your vets, your health care, all your research and technology. Maintaining the males is *very* expensive. Once they're sexually mature, every damn one'a them has to be kept in a half-million-dollar, hydraulically operated crush that they use to move them around. You can't even go near 'em or they'll kill ya. Imagine what it costs just to *feed* the elephants in a program like Ringlings – five males, twenty-six females multiplied by about fifteen thousand dollars a year each. There's half a million right there."

Bob estimated that a million dollars had been invested in each of the seven babies born so far at the Ringling farm in Florida, and pointed out that one of the greatest difficulties faced by breeders is that, unlike the females of most species, a female elephant in heat will not breed with "any old" male. "She has to be *courted* by him, and if she doesn't like him, no copulation – just like human beings." He explained that, in India, female elephants in the logging industry are released into the wilds when they begin to ovulate, so as to provide them the widest possible selection of mates. "The owners never lose one," he said. "It's like clockwork. Three or four months after they're released, every one of them gets to thinking about all the lovely groceries she used to get in captivity, and one day she'll wander back into the logging camp, pregnant, and her mahout'll climb back up on her and work her for maybe a year and a half until he figures she's ready to have her baby, and then he'll turn her loose again."

What happens next in the breeding cycle has been understood for centuries in Asia, Bob reported, but was, until recently, a mystery to those attempting to breed elephants in captivity in North America. "For an elephant, giving birth is extremely traumatic," he said. "So, the first thing she does when she's ready to pop is find herself a midwife, usually an old matriarch, a sort of 'aunty' elephant, who's seen the birth process many times, and can comfort her or, if it's her first time, can teach her what it's about as she's going through it." Studies have shown that during delivery, any number of female elephants will gather with the midwife and add supportive wailing to the mother's own stressful vocalizations. "This is all nature," said Bob. "The midwife bites off the umbilical cord, cleans the baby up, stands it on its feet, because all through this the mother is in shock; she's out of it. And as she comes round, the midwife introduces her to mothering, shows her what to do."

By this point, Paul and Chata were leaning forward from the back seat, Paul listening intently and translating the commentary quietly into Spanish. "Breeders in North America gradually caught on to the necessity of providing a midwife," Bob said. "What they didn't understand was that the female is as choosy

229

about her midwife as she is about her mate. She doesn't want just anybody attending to her in that intimate way. It has to be an elephant she trusts." Somehow, even in the old days, he said, a circus elephant would occasionally get pregnant. "But when the time came to give birth, they'd put the mother in a barn or tent or someplace by herself. She'd have this baby and wouldn't even know what it was. She'd be completely freaked out. And of course her first reaction would be to kill it, and that's often what happened. Nowadays, they wouldn't dare put an unfriendly elephant anywhere near one that's approaching its time to give birth. They watch them constantly – know exactly who likes who. And it's working. They're getting elephants."

As we approached Gypsumville, Bob described a census initiated during the 1980s by Bill Woodcock Sr. that tracked the arrival and fate of every elephant that had been brought to North America since the first arrived in 1796. "More than three thousand came in," he said, "and there are four hundred left – about a hundred and eighty-five of them with the circus."

He had barely finished speaking when one of the sweetest and best-loved of those elephants – certainly one of the best-travelled – roared past us in her mobile residence.

"What I wanta know," Paul called from the back seat, "is how many guys like you are still operating out there."

"Maybe twenty, twenty-five," Bob shrugged. "We're dyin off faster than the elephants."

"How many elephants are there, period?" I said, to which Bob responded that there are five hundred thousand Africans and perhaps forty thousand Asians. "What makes me totally wanta puke," he said, "is that, in Zimbabwe, hunters cull thousands of elephants a year outta the herd – shoot 'em dead. In Zambia, over the past thirty years, poachers have reduced the herd from two hundred and fifty thousand to about twenty-five thousand. And we can't import a few because it's supposed to interfere with their propagation. If you've got the money, you can go over there from *here* and shoot elephants. 'Course, if you've got lotsa money, you don't have to pay attention to *any* of this endangered species stuff. The Sultan of Burundi will sell you a permit to shoot a bongo, which is on the A-one endangered list. You can shoot a little four-teen-inch dik-dik if you've got the money."

Bobby described going to the "big annual hunting show" in Dallas and discovering a company selling expeditions to the Canadian Arctic, including helicopter transportation to the ice floes, where a "hunter" was guaranteed a polar bear kill, all taxi-dermy, first-class accommodation, and meals. "I said to the guy, 'I make a living with live animals, and this is offensive to me.' He said, 'How's that?' And I said, 'If the circus can't show a polar bear because it's endangered, how do you get off shooting them?' He said, 'The Canadian government issues a certain number of permits a year to the Natives up there to shoot bears, and they sell them to us for ten thousand dollars each, and we sell them to our clients.' *We sell them to our clients!* I'm thinkin, Who the hell are your clients? – a buncha currency speculators and plastic surgeons who don't give a shit about the state of our animal populations. Oh, I was steamed. I said, 'I guess if I had enough money, a guy like you could take me to east St. Louis, and we could shoot a couple'a little nigger kids.' He didn't like that – he said, 'Get away from my booth. Get outta here.' When I was in Hawaii, I was taken to a big warehouse filled with piles and piles of exotic reptile skins. I said, 'How do you get this stuff, when it's against the law?' The guy said, 'These skins were taken in Indonesia, where reptiles are a pest. The people eat the meat, and we make boots outta the skins.' Yeah, I'm thinking, and sell them on Fifth Avenue to the same bimbos who shoot the polar bears! And the conservationists and animal-rights people are worried about me having an animal do a few tricks!"

# 11

DURING THE LATE nineteenth and early twentieth centuries –
the circus's golden age – it was not uncommon for rival shows
to engage in fierce, strategic battles for the attention and atten-
dance of circusgoers. In those days, a circus's publicity machinery
consisted not of a press agent in an office in New York or Sarasota,
as it might today, but in ambitious, sometimes ruthless, gangs of
advance men, bill-posters, who moved into a town or city as much
as a couple of weeks ahead of the show they worked for and plas-
tered every available fence, hoarding, and unprotected building
with provocative publicity posters. Competition was so intense
that, even before the bill-posters were finished, another circus's
men were often at work pasting up their own sensational advertisements, directly overtop of those already in place. Within days,
choice spots could end up under as many as a dozen layers of competing notices. If a particular city meant a lot to a circus, or if an
owner felt especially combative, an advance team would often
leave behind a few of its toughest members to make sure its posters
remained undisturbed. Just as often, competition among advance

men led to street brawls in which the combatants were left bloody and toothless and, on occasion, seriously injured.

It is a long-standing irony of circus life that the participants in such battles would often change shows between seasons and, a few months later, fight just as hard in the interest of a former rival.

The competition was frequently more devious than brutal, as when agents for, say, the P.T. Barnum show would enter a town where a rival was about to open and urge audiences: "Wait for Barnum, with his Much Larger Show!" or "Don't waste your money on Robinson, when Barnum is on his way!" Sometimes a show's "rat sheets," as hostile posters were called, were directly disparaging of a rival, although seldom honestly. When Barnum installed electric lights in 1879, for example, Adam Forepaugh's posters denounced the innovation as "hazardous" to the eyes, "harmful to the brains of children," and "potentially fatal" to those with breathing difficulties. "Watch their street parade, but don't go near the lights," declared one notice. On another occasion, Forepaugh announced publicly that Barnum's claim to having "a hundred cages" and "hundreds of costumed beauties" in his street parade should actually read "23 cages" and "25 people in costume."

It was considered a rollicking coup to be able to sneak a wagon into a rival's street parade, and then to roll out rat sheets denouncing the circus whose assets the crowd had gathered to see. One year, Forepaugh outmanoeuvred Barnum by secretly renting Madison Square Garden in New York for exactly the dates on which his arch-rival traditionally used the arena for his spring opening.

But the spirit among circuses was by no means always malevolent. As these competitive skirmishes were being played out in public, shows frequently went to considerable lengths to support and assist one another behind the scenes. If a circus lost tents, props, or animals in a fire or train wreck, for example, it was not uncommon for a rival show to do its best to provide replacements. Longstanding grievances were regularly resolved when rival owners shook hands and joined forces. Forepaugh's treachery at Madison Square Garden was mitigated when he and Barnum agreed to open the 1887 season together on the site, with unprecedented extravagance. The storied union between Phineus T. Barnum and James A. Bailey was itself a marriage of two bitterly contentious rivals from the late nineteenth century.

It is unlikely that Ricky Wallenda and Tarzan Zerbini will ever shake hands and join forces. But in the realm of circus warfare, the battle brewing between them as the Great Wallenda Circus straggled into Winnipeg on May 18, 1997, conceded little to Barnum and Bailey in terms of gimmicks, strategy, and animosity. While Zerbini's Royal Canadian Circus – which is in fact owned and headquartered in Joplin, Missouri – would not arrive in the Manitoba capital until mid-week to prepare for its five-show tent stand at the Garden City Shopping Centre, its selling effort had already fixed media and public attention and was working wonders on the hackles of the local Shriners. The show's newspaper advertisements, were manipulative little masterpieces, promising in script half an inch high a "Big Top Seat Sale of $4.00," before revealing in type virtually impossible to read without jeweller's lenses that the four-dollar figure was not in fact the *price* of admission but a mere reduction in the price, which was disclosed in even smaller letters as twelve dollars per seat. More galling to the Shriners was Zerbini's widely bruited promise to donate a dollar a ticket to the Manitoba Flood Relief Fund – this on tickets that were already priced two or three dollars higher than ticket prices for the Shrine Circus. "It really plays on people's vulnerabilities," lamented the chairman of the Shrine circus, Dave Perry. "And of course people forget that while Tarzan may end up giving a few thousand dollars to flood relief, we give a hundred and fifty thousand every year to children's hospitals. It's easy enough for a circus to give a dollar back to the community when it's extracting a dollar more to begin with."

It also bugged Perry and the Shriners that, while money raised by their circus over the years had benefited numerous Manitobans, most of what was grossed by Zerbini – as much as forty thousand dollars a show – left the province on the milk run and did not return.

Matt and I spent the night not in circumstances befitting the beggars we had become but as the pampered envoys of adventure, indulged by our friends Terry and Jane Gray, who even went so far as to listen with sympathy to my mewling about credit cards, bank accounts, and such.

Late the next morning, Matt and I returned to the arena's back lot, a barely habitable asphalt compound, heavily secured by arena guards and battered chain link, where the troupe was camped out, unable yet to get into the building but at least able to spread the props and ring mats and to begin cleaning up for the opening of the nine-show stand on Wednesday night. As I stood talking to Bobby Gibbs in the parking lot, where Judy had apparently been greeting well-wishers since early that morning, Rick Wallenda, with whom I was to have lunch, walked by at a distance and hollered in Bob's direction, "Get that elephant cleaned up before Wednesday."

"You take care of your responsibilities, I'll take care of mine!" Bob hollered back. "For starters, you could get us into the building!"

An hour later, a block away, I sat down with Rick in the near-empty restaurant of the Polo Park Inn, where he ordered a glass of water and a cheeseburger. He looked exhausted – as well he might have with his physical pain escalating, with the Shriners at his neck, and with the new stress of impending competition.

Not that he was answerable for the competition itself – or for the way in which the Shriners chose to deal with (or avoid) it. But the reduced crowds that would be its inevitable result would do him little good in the Shriners' overall assessment of his performance or in his attempts to secure future contracts, either here or with other Shrine clubs. At the moment, Ricky was both frustrated and offended that Zerbini was being hailed publicly as a philanthropic benefactor for offering money to flood relief, while the Shriners had, in Rick's words, "blown ten thousand dollars' worth of good publicity" by refusing his offer to have the Great Wallenda Circus perform free for the many Canadian troops in the area, on the date they would have been doing the (cancelled) Selkirk performance, just north of Winnipeg. "It wouldn't have cost the Shriners a dime!" he complained, "and we would have had media attention all over the continent – coulda tied right into all the coverage the flood's getting."

The decision not to hold the circus had not, however, been the Shriners' alone (the Shrine had resisted the idea for what David Perry referred to as "legal reasons"). The armed forces, too, had rejected the idea, on the grounds that they did not want the troops to be seen "lolling around a circus" when the flood was taking such a toll.

"We could have held the circus outdoors for *everybody* to come to," said Rick. "We had the permits, we had insurance. There's no law against going to a town and doing a circus. If the Shriners had had the foresight, *we* could have been the good guys right now, instead of looking like pikers. It's the kind of publicity you can't buy."

That morning, as a test, Rick had presented both circuses' ads to a clerk at the Polo Park Inn and had asked which one she would prefer to attend. "She told me she'd go to the one that was giving a dollar to the flood," he said in disgust.

I asked Rick about the Shriners' complaints about the show, and he acknowledged that they had some legitimate beefs. "We didn't have the dog act I told them I'd bring," he said. "I thought the dog people were gonna come through for me, but they didn't. My sister got sick. My clown got hurt. One of the elephants was in quarantine. We lost three tigers. But, hey," he perked up, "we had a lotta good stuff they didn't even expect – the trampoline act, the hair-hang, the Lunas; we put the swords in. None of that stuff was on the original display list. And they know we can't do much aerial stuff in those little arenas."

Ricky was less sanguine about the charge that his equipment and props were dirty. "They were clean when we got to Thunder Bay," he protested. "I had the guys mop the ring mats twice a day. You've got a thousand people coming down outta those hockey bleachers and tramping across them – of course they get dirty. I've got the guys out there painting them right now."

Given the insignificant level of most of the Shriners' complaints, I came finally to understand that the local temple executive simply wasn't partial to Ricky, although I believe the circus chairman remained loyal to him.

If there was a poignancy to all this quibbling it was, first, that, despite perceptions, Ricky *had* tried – had, in my opinion, done everything he could have done – to put on an attractive show. Half a dozen times during the run, I had heard him deliberating about whether this or that part of the show was working, whether the Shriners liked what he was doing, wondering what might be done better, or to better effect. More touching yet, I thought, was that Ricky craved the approval of the very Shriners who seemed determined to run him down. Above all, he wanted a renewed contract, a chance to do it again the following year, more to the liking of those who no longer cared.

"Have they said anything?" I asked him.

"They told me they didn't want to make a commitment," he said.

"The problem with dealing with the Shriners," a senior trouper had told me, "is that the circus isn't their *business*, it's their *party*. And they don't take kindly to suggestions about how their party should be conducted. And Rick is the sort of guy who'll do what *he* thinks needs doing. The other problem with the Shriners is they do most of their contracting on price, not quality – if a producer says he'll bring in a circus for a certain dollar figure, often nobody thinks to ask about the specifics of the show. The Shriners'll tell him they want tigers, elephants, and maybe one more animal act; beyond that, anything goes – in some shows, you get some real stiffs. But that wasn't the case here – there was nothing junky in this show. You had nine or ten performers here who could work in any show in North America."

Despite the disagreements, any rational observer would have expected the Shriners and Rick to bury their differences at this point, and to unite what remained of their energies and acumen, the better to compete with Tarzan Zerbini, who, by now, posed a significant threat to their success.

But the differences held.

As for Zerbini's motivation in choosing his Winnipeg dates, Ricky remained resolute in his belief that it was all a retaliation for Rick's refusal to boycott the Shrine Circus convention the previous autumn. "Everybody in the business knows I got these dates away from Ian Garden, who is a Canadian, and who is friends with Tarzan," Rick said as we ate. "They were both part of the move to get me thrown out of the Producers Association for attending that convention. I understood the producers' grievances with the Shriners, but when they decided they were gonna try to hurt the Shriners by staying away from their convention, I just said I didn't think that was a wise thing to do, that the producers' relationship with the Shriners went back a long way, and that, despite the problems, the Shrine was doing a lot of good work, and that I felt I wanted to go. They said, 'Don't go.' But I did – and now, it's payback time."

"At least Tarzan had the grace to put his show out in the suburbs," Bobby Gibbs would tell me that afternoon. "If Ricky'd taken the dates from some guys, they'd have moved in right across the street, outta spite, and been willing to take a ten-thousand-dollar loss to be there. It's a cutthroat business. And if your rival happens to be a Wallenda, that makes it even more cutthroat. There are producers out there who, whether they admit it or not, will never forgive Ricky that name and the advantage the name gives him. They couldn't care less about his accident, or losin his family, or that he's gettin over alcoholism, or anything else he's up against. Their attitude is: Kick his ass – we don't want 'im in the sandbox. But Ricky's tough. He's hangin in there. And I'll tell ya, he's not gettin by just on his name. He's sure as hell earned every cent he's made on this tour. You've seen him work."

When the earliest rumblings of conflict had sounded ten days or so earlier, Bob had explained to me that Zerbini was a one-time cat trainer who had made his mark during the 1960s and '70s and then had gone into circus production during the 1980s. "His name is John," Bobby said, "but people started callin him 'Tarzan' because he always worked in a loincloth, nothin else. And before long he was callin *himself* Tarzan, until Edgar Rice Burroughs's descendants got wind of it and told him the name belonged to them, and that he'd better ditch it fast. So he had his name legally changed to Tarzan, and there was nothing they could do about it. He's French."

"He *claims* to be French," said Ricky as we pecked at our lunch. "He's actually Algerian."

Rick told me that, during the 1960s, Tarzan had often worked in circuses produced by his grandfather, and that his act was the only cat act in the world that Ricky had been willing to watch as a kid. In those days, he explained, his grandfather employed an act called the Diano elephants. "One of them was a huge male with tusks," he said, "and somebody had the idea to put Tarzan up on this elephant for his entrance. The ringmaster'd announce him, and he'd come bounding in on this big tusker, and they'd throw him one of the webs and he'd grab it and swing right up to the top of the cage and perch there, then down he'd drop inside. He had great showmanship and great animals, and on our show he was a star. As long as my grandfather wasn't around, Tarzan was king of the hill." Rick sipped at his water, and said, "The problem was that when he *was* around, Tarzan was upstaged, and he didn't like that – the one thing he had besides a big talent was a big ego."

Of the Zerbini ego stories I heard, perhaps the most revealing was Pat Delaney's recollection of a date in Grand Rapids, Michigan, during the 1970s, when, in front of eight thousand spectators, Tarzan, who had been chatting with Pat as he waited to perform, put his arm around him and said, "Pat, do you know how many women out there are dyin to see what's under this loincloth?"

"I told him, 'Probably none, John. But even if there's five thousand, I guarantee ya you're the only one in the world who gives a crap.'"

Ricky explained that, because of the tension over Tarzan's status on the show, "a certain amount of ill will" often built up between Zerbini's men and Karl Wallenda's. "One day," Rick said, "I guess my grandfather's guys agitated Tarzan's guys a bit too much, and they all met out by the trailers, and there was a big fistfight, and I guess the Zerbinis got the worst of it. This was in sixty-eight or sixty-nine, and Tarzan's held a grudge against the Wallenda family ever since."

I asked Rick how he thought Tarzan himself would characterize either his relationship with the Wallendas or his motivation for coming to Winnipeg, and he shrugged and said amicably,

"Why don't you ask him when he gets here? I wouldn't mind knowing myself."

Five days later, I would indeed ask Tarzan for his views on the subject. In the meantime, I wanted to know if Ricky had a strategy for coping with the combined pressures of internal criticism and outside competition. "All I can do," he told me, "is try to give them the very best show I can" – a response that I found superior, both tactically and ethically, to the entire course of the debate and antipathies thus far. Even as we spoke, Rick was anticipating with gusto the arrival of the Nerveless Nocks, one of the preeminent aerial thrill acts in America, and the Flying Redpaths, a family trapeze act that he described to me as "a guy and four totally gorgeous women." Here, too, however, there were stresses to deal with – doubts, for example, about whether these splendid new acts would get to Winnipeg on time for Wednesday night's opening performance, given the potential both for immigration problems (visas, work permits, and so on) and for flood delays (at the moment, the highway from the border crossing at Emerson was under five feet of water, necessitating an extensive cross-country detour for those driving to Winnipeg from North Dakota). More troubling yet for Rick was a simmering concern that, because the patriarch of the Nock family, Eugene, was a brother-in-law of Tarzan's partner, Joe Bauer, the Nocks might ultimately refuse to support Ricky in competition against Zerbini.

Even as Ricky doubted, however, seventy-year-old Eugene, a former sway-pole star who had passed his act along to his sons, was driving the I-75, north through Georgia and Tennessee, toward Wisconsin Dells, Wisconsin, where he would meet his son, Gene, and nephew, Timo Nordstrum, who would accompany him to Winnipeg, where Gene and Timo would perform happily on Ricky's behalf.

In the meantime, the Great Wallenda Circus was on a three-day break. Given the opportunity, I decided to travel briefly to Thunder Bay, in order to get Matt back to school, before returning alone to Winnipeg for the last eight performances of the tour. After the opening on Wednesday, Rick would be off to Florida, where he had put together another show that was to begin in Tampa on Friday. He would be back in Winnipeg Saturday night for the last couple of performances of the Canadian tour.

For now, in the restaurant at the Polo Park Inn, thinking this might be my last chance to do so, I thanked Rick for all he had done to help me and wished him well, and we agreed that we would be in touch. I stood up, while he remained slumped on the banquette, apparently in thought. Then he lurched forward, pushed himself up with his hands, and said, "Right now, I'm about as tired as I've ever been."

I told him I'd been impressed by his energy and his capability to keep things together.

As we crossed the hotel lobby, he said, "I hope you can find some good things to say about us."

I assured him I could.

"You've seen us at our worst," he said.

This was not quite true. But I was happy enough that, when I returned to Winnipeg from Thunder Bay three days later, the "worst" was over, and things were more or less back to normal. The reports lingered, however, of how at Wednesday's rehearsal for the big opening-night performance, stress and weariness had finally gotten the better of Ricky, and he had, in the words of one crew member, "just kinda lost it. Suddenly, after all these weeks, it was as if nobody but him understood a single thing about how this show should operate."

When Enrique Luna had questioned Liliana's obliged participation in the aerial ballet, using a crescent-shaped metal prop on which she was decidedly uncomfortable, Ricky had apparently informed him that the family should stick to its contract, which made certain requirements of Liliana, or move on.

"He was tired, he was in pain, he was stressed out," said Patty Alexander, one of Rick's most consistent supporters.

The result of his lapse was that a couple of his key crew people quit – and then, according to Patty, "sort of hired themselves back," when the dust had settled.

Happily for the show, not everyone was affected equally by the stress of the impending finale. For the performers, these were the dates that brought forth their best – the extra bit of risk-taking, the longer arc, the newest and brightest (and, in some cases, briefest) costuming. Faces that, for weeks, had appeared crumpled and immobilized by cold seemed to stretch and enlarge, an effect dramatically abetted by "bigger" hair, darker make-up, and longer lashes. Larry added a sax and a horn to the band.

When I arrived back on Thursday evening, I walked through the performers' entrance just in time to see the Flying Redpaths – Michael, Linda, and their three daughters (the women as fetching as promised) – ascend smiling and waving into their rigging in the arena's south girders and charm the audience with a series of lyric leaps and loops. Even ten-year-old April made the well-grooved trip from the flyers' perch, out into space, into her dad's sure hands, and then back to safety with a tidy kip and salute. Twenty-two-year-old Gail, who is capable of a triple somersault, the *coup de grâce* of the trapezist's art, is the troupe's most ambitious flyer these days. On this night, however, she came up a fraction short on her "full-twisting" double, and boinged gracefully into the net before rejoining the family to participate in a flawless "passing leap," a dangerous and difficult trick in which two flyers cross in mid-air, one leaping from the flying bar to the catcher, the other from the catcher to the flying bar. The trick is in a sense the finale of the family's act, although, like all flyers these days, the Redpaths make a production of descending into

*The female component of the Flying Redpaths. Left to right:*
*Alecia, Gail, and April, with their mother, Linda.*

the net at the end of their performance – dropping, bouncing, doing a variety of layouts and somersaults, Gail coming off last, in the tradition of the lead flyer, occasionally rebounding so high that she returns briefly to the catcher's bar, to the crowd's great pleasure and applause. It is part of the appeal of a flying act that, if it has done its job, the crowd is left with an almost aching desire to see just one more leap, one more somersault. I would watch the Redpaths' ten-minute performance seven times during the next three days, and, on each occasion, would be left with the feeling that I could quite happily have watched for an afternoon or evening.

When the show was over that night, I made a point of catching up with Michael, a most genial and articulate man, who sat chatting with me in the stands beneath the family's rigging for the better part of an hour. He is a one-time soldier and surfer, who, as a child in South Africa, lost both his parents to tuberculosis and spent his teenaged years in a strict Catholic residential school in Cape Town, learning fairness, toughness, and, at times, coping with what he calls "fierce punishments and disciplines" meted out by the school's senior boys or prefects. His introduction to flying came during his late teens, while he was living in a Cape Town YMCA, where a group of amateur acrobats had hung a flying rig above an abandoned tennis court. "I'd go out and watch these guys trying to do the tricks," he recalled, "and of course everybody wanted to fly, not catch. So, one night outta the blue they asked me if I'd like to try catching, and I got up there and started swinging upside down in the catcher's rig, not expecting anything to happen, when, suddenly, a guy came flying right over, and I caught him – and that was that, I was a catcher."

Michael eventually became part of South Africa's first professional flying troupe, the Flying Ostlers, who performed in northern Europe and Scandinavia and, in 1969, took a contract with Ringling Brothers and Barnum & Bailey in the U.S., where Michael met his wife, Linda Easey, a Milwaukee gymnast who was at the time performing in Ringlings' aerial ballet and production numbers.

"Linda and I worked in a number of flying acts – good ones, too," said Michael. "But, at a certain point during the late seventies, after Gail and Alecia were born, we decided that we eventually wanted to do an all-family act. And by the late eighties, that's what we were doing."

Perhaps because of his own dire losses as a child, Michael has an almost mystical belief in the importance and power of the family. "The only thing in life I've always known I wanted was a wife and children," he told me. "You hear a lot these days about corporate strength, financial strength, political strength – but I've always felt that all of those things are pretty pale, measured against the strength that exists in a good, loving family. The circus has been good to me in that it's given me the chance to spend more time with my wife and kids than most people get to spend."

In 1996, the Redpaths worked eleven consecutive months with Ringling Brothers. But, during most years, they work no more than twenty to twenty-five weeks. More work is available, according to Michael, but the family will not perform in, say, amusement parks because of the seven-day-a-week, three-show-a-day grind that is expected. "Flying is extremely hard on the shoulders," explained the Sarasota-based catcher. "When a flyer comes out of, say, a triple or a twisting double, she's moving maybe sixty miles an hour – and then, *whomp*, into the catcher's hands. You can blow a shoulder out, and basically your career's over." (It is said of Tito Gaona, the pre-eminent flyer of the 1960s and '70s, that his failure to complete the quadruple somersault, which he attempted on hundreds of occasions, was, in part, the legacy of a dream he had had in which the pressure of the catch was so great that it tore the arms off his brother and catcher Lalo.)

Michael said, "I'm lucky, I have good shoulders – so does Linda, so the girls may be all right, too. But, believe me, I've known flyers that have burned themselves to the degree that they can't even stand up in the morning for pain; they have to roll out of bed, get onto all fours and gradually get to their feet."

The conversation turned to Michael and Gail's inability to complete the double-twisting somersault earlier in the evening – something they normally do with ease – and Michael explained that the troupe had been idle for several weeks, and that Gail's timing, which was flawless through the remainder of the run, was just a trifle out of sync with his own. "I probably could have been a little more aggressive with her and reeled her in," he said. "But one thing about working with the family is, I'd rather see them go safely into the net than make the catch at any cost and risk a collision or strain." He held out a pair of tanned, muscular hands, working his fingers as if to receive a flyer. "You catch them by the wrists," he said. "There's a feel when it's right, and another feel when it's *almost* right and you know you can make the catch with a little extra effort. And there's another feeling yet, when the timing is off, like tonight, and you tend to lay back a bit, so you don't come up hard into the flyer and put them off, so they go into the net with their neck. You have to give them the opportunity to rotate and fall properly on their backs."

Thanks in part to Michael's experience and sensitivity, the Redpaths have had no serious accidents, although Michael has had teeth knocked out and has had his nose and ribs broken, while working with other acts.

His greater concern these days is that his specialty, like others in the circus, is gradually, imperceptibly dying. "For one thing," he said, "the pay hasn't kept up with the costs." He recalled that on returning from a season of work during the 1970s, he had been able to go to a car dealership and purchase a new vehicle with cash – a possibility as remote to him today as that of turning the quadruple somersault. "That same vehicle now costs five times what it did," he shrugged. "And we're making maybe twice what we did." Michael ran off a litany of familiar costs – breakdowns, fuel, capital expenditures – and pointed out that he had paid more in insurance on the family's mobile home over the years than the vehicle was currently worth. "That's why there aren't many big acts out there," he said. "Part of the problem is just logistics, of course. Unless you're a family, it's extremely difficult to keep a troupe together when they're only working half the year. It's hard enough *as* a family – getting the kids educated, allowing them to develop job experience. Alecia works in a yogurt shop, in

Sarasota. They wanted to make her manager, but she can't take the job, because she's not there enough."

While nineteen-year-old Alecia has a perhaps less strenuous role in the flying routine, she makes up for it with her solo "cloud swing," a preposterously daring performance in which she climbs into the rafters to a cotton web strung as a swing between two hooks, pumps the apparatus to maximum height and speed, and then embarks on a series of dramatic flips and hangs, each freer and more daring than the last – all performed without safety line or net. Her finale is a kind of free fall that she performs at the height of her forward arc, perhaps sixty feet above the crowd, by throwing herself suddenly from the swing, so that the audience, unaware that she has slipped her ankles through a pair of straps that will catch her at full extension, is momentarily, gapingly convinced that she is on her way to the floor.

"The first time I did it in the backyard on the practice swing," she told me, "I was so scared, my father had to beg me to jump. I just kept swinging and swinging, and he kept calling to me, but I couldn't commit myself to those little straps. Then, finally, I did it – I'll tell ya, I screamed."

Now, explained Alecia, the crowd does the screaming for her. "I love hearing that gasp," she said. "Some people can't watch. Or they duck. I get a real thrill out of their reaction."

Alecia is tall and well-proportioned, with copper-coloured eyes and an exotic, aquiline face. Like so many of the circus's best – and despite her talents and intelligence – she is disarmingly modest. The most extravagant thing she would say about her act was that she "guessed" it was "a little harder than it looked," proceeding to show me the calluses on her ankles and wrists caused by the straps, and several vivid bruises on her arms and legs, the result of recent performances. "If you don't leap with the flow," she said, "you can get an awful jerk when you hit the ends of the straps."

The Redpaths would be moving on to dates in Nebraska, Ohio, and Virginia. But Alecia, for one, was in no hurry to hit the road. The circus is notorious for getting in the way of its performers' love lives, but on this particular weekend it was the agent of romance, and Alecia spent every possible moment in the company of her boyfriend, Shane Hansen, a Danish roller skater who happened to be performing with his father and sister in the rival Zerbini Circus, a twenty-minute drive away at the Garden City Shopping Centre. Indeed, all weekend long, there was a steady stream of visits back and forth among friends on the competing shows. "For Shane and me, it's great," Alecia told me. "But it's also kinda weird in the sense that, once the season starts, we don't see one another in Sarasota for months on end, and here we happen to meet up in Winnipeg, Canada, where neither of us has ever been in our lives."

On the lot that night in the darkness, I gave Connie Barnes a good-sized bag of toys and stuffed animals, as well as some children's clothing, that I had brought with me from Thunder Bay. She was greatly taken by a white stuffed bear and a rubber doll, and, for the next couple of days, I rarely saw her without one or the other in her arm. As for Wilson, the swelling in his face had gone down. But, in performance, he was still wearing make-up to hide what he could of the bruising.

Where was Matt, everybody wanted to know. Why hadn't I brought him back? Bobby could barely forgive me for what he called "betraying a kid," and Liliana told me that she had planned to take Matt and Rolando out for dinner and to a movie, and seemed genuinely chagrined about losing the opportunity. "We were going to have him sleep in the trailer with us," she said. "Rolando was really looking forward to it."

The truth was that, by this time, I was disappointed in *myself* for not bringing Matt back. Before I left Thunder Bay that morning, we had had a mutually painful battle over his having to go back to school – the effect of which was that, at about midnight that night, under a burden of guilt, I went into the arena, called home, and asked Betty what she thought of putting him on the overnight bus to Winnipeg the following day. But we couldn't come to an agreement over it, and when I spoke to Matt himself on the phone the next day, he seemed resigned to being where he was. We agreed, however, that, in the future, we would visit the circus as often as we could (a promise I was able to make good on several times during the upcoming summer and then again during the spring of 1998, when Bobby brought Judy and Betty into Grand Forks, North Dakota, and Matt and I went out for the four-day run).

That night, in an attempt to wring the most out of my last few days with the tour, I slept on the lot, curled awkwardly in a sleeping bag on the floor of my van, and awakened in the morning feeling much like one of those flyers Michael Redpath had described, unable to walk for stiffness, and having to roll and crawl until my joints and muscles loosened. The van, achingly cold overnight, was, by the time I awoke around 8 a.m., as hot as a desert solarium.

I showered in the dressing room in the arena and went to Perkins' restaurant with Bobby for breakfast. There, he described an animal-rights rally that had drawn eighty or more activists to the arena on opening night and at which police had arrested a protester. "Of *course*, it made the front page of the newspaper," he scoffed. "Every little scrap of propaganda those people put out gets printed verbatim. And not one damn reporter bothered to come around the side of the building to see what was actually going on."

An old media acquaintance of mine, Morley Walker, reviewing the show in the *Winnipeg Free Press*, noted its slender reliance on animal acts and questioned why more hadn't been made of the Wallenda name, history, and performers, perhaps not realizing that there were no Wallendas in the show, a circumstance Ricky had hoped to avoid in his unsuccessful attempt to have his sister, Rietta, and her daughter, Lyric, along on tour. Still, Bob tended to agree that a name as recognizable as Wallenda was being unnecessarily sublimated, and that the Shrine might do well to offer Ricky to the media as a general agent of their ambitions, assuming he had some interest in being offered.

If Rick's doubts over the commitment of the Nock family had been anything more than a figment of his weariness, which I suspected they were not, he betrayed those doubts with flying colours in appointing Eugene Sr. his stand-in producer before departing for Florida on Thursday morning. The producer's assigned "office" was an airless concrete bunker, apparently a kind of trainer's room for the Manitoba Moose hockey franchise, that smelled discernibly of liniment and old jock straps. But it was here, on Friday night, during the fifth performance of the run, that Eugene Sr., one of the circus's most respected and successful citizens, chose to chat with me about his career. When I entered, he was dining with medieval vigour on a whole barbecued chicken that he immediately invited me to share.

When we had polished the thing off, he described to me how, in 1979, at the age of fifty-two, he and his family were about to climb their ninety-foot sway-poles for a performance of the Shrine Circus in Nashville, Tennessee, when he had been knocked on his backside by a heart attack that, had it occurred a minute later, would have thrown him from his pole and killed him.

And how, in 1945, in Geneva, as he made a headfirst slide down what was, in those days, a wooden sway-pole, a sixteen-inch splinter of white pine, as big around as a finger, had broken loose from the pole, entering his chest just below the neck and emerging near the navel.

And how when his sister's pole snapped in mid-performance, in 1959, her husband, Joe Bauer, had grabbed her "by the clothing," saving her from a ninety-foot fall to the concrete.

He proceeded to tell me that, when each of his four sons turned two years old, he had taught him to stand on his hands and to stay that way for half an hour, before rewarding him with a lollipop. "If you can't do it," he said, "you don't have the control you need for the tricks – or the strength. My wife is Italian; she's tougher than I am, always wanted to make them do it. I never forced them."

When we had talked for perhaps fifteen minutes, Eugene informed me without preamble that, in 1996, when he and his sons Bello and John and their families had travelled to Heidelberg, Germany, to perform for four months, they had gone one day to the city courthouse to try to discover the whereabouts of a branch of the Nock family that had lived for a while in Germany during the 1940s. "What we discovered," he said, "was that, in 1944, all six of them, children included, had been put to death in the gas chambers in Auschwitz. The clerk gave us their death certificates and said, 'I'm sorry, but they no longer exist.' They weren't Jews – weren't even Germans. They were on their way from Switzerland, through Bavaria, to Berlin, performing as they went. They had even named their baby Adolf, so they wouldn't be harassed."

When I asked what Hitler might have had against circus people, Eugene raised his palms, opened his eyes wide, and said, "Nothing. He just didn't like anybody who wouldn't make a good Nazi – travelling performers were considered too free-spirited."

Eugene is short and sturdy, with a bald head, pinkish skin, and a gnome-like smile. He exudes good will and optimism bordering on the preternatural. "I survived a heart attack," he smiles. "I could be dead. The Big Guy likes me. Of course I'm happy to be

*Circus veterans Eugene Nock (left) and ringmaster Bill Boren minutes before show time, in Winnipeg.*

in Winnipeg. Happy to be working for Ricky. Happy to be talking to you. Happy to see the show."

Eugene was happy to note that his family's circus involvement can be traced to 1840 in Switzerland, where there is still a Nock Family Circus, and where Eugene learned his turns before emigrating to America with his wife, sister, and brother-in-law, to join Ringling Brothers in 1954.

"In those day," he explained in his Swiss-German accent, "Americans knew nothing about an act like ours." And the Nocks knew nothing of Americans, who, when they saw the four scramble like monkeys to the tops of their poles and begin their great metronomic arcs – their handstands, "exchanges," and "hangs" – applauded and whistled with such force that the Nocks, believing the whistles to be derisive (as they would have been in Europe), considered their performance a failure.

"Education has always been as important to us as the circus," said Eugene, noting proudly that when his four sons had obtained their college degrees, they returned to the circus, and now operate four separate touring units, some hauling up to thirty-thousand pounds of equipment. "The boys do stuff that scares *me* out of my wits," he said, citing in particular the "globe of death" (three motorcycles travelling a hundred kilometres an hour inside a twelve-foot-diameter steel-mesh sphere) and the helicopter trapeze, from which a daredevil performs without safety gear at up to five hundred feet above ground.

As we chatted, one of those sons, Eugene Jr., a helicopter and jet pilot, and his cousin, Timo Nordstrum, were preparing to scramble up the towering steel sway-poles at the north end of the arena. Bill Boren had, in fact, just begun his extravagant introduction of them when there was a knock at the trainer-room's door, and Eugene bid entrance to two swarthy gentlemen whom he leapt smiling to greet, turning to me and introducing his brother-in-law, Joe Bauer, and his old friend, Tarzan Zerbini, a man I might have expected to have horns and a forked tail.

But, in reality, he looked more like a middle-aged *bocce* ball player than either the devil or the intrepid young cat trainer who, at this point, had been conjured for me by three or four separate descriptions. He was grey-haired, puffy-faced, and, where he had once sported his loincloth, now struggled to keep a pair of expensive wool dress pants aloft beneath a decidedly bulgy middle. He wore Gucci loafers and, like Bauer, a black team-style jacket, the chest of which bore the embroidered initials TZ, while the back was emblazoned with the words Tarzan Zerbini Circus.

Bauer, who has dark brown eyes, leathery skin, and hair the colour of ravens' feathers, entered bristling with criticisms of the Great Wallenda Circus – "not the acts," he was careful to point out, but the presentation. "They haven't spent any money for lights or scenery! They've got no special effects! On our circus, we spend thousands of dollars on all that. This should have been better. Producers have to do more."

Bauer next embarked on a personal disparagement of the owner, beginning with the words, "I've always liked Ricky," and ending with his belief (a refrain now familiar to me) that the one-time wire walker had taken a long, leisurely ride on the Wallenda name – a name that, in effect, he did not own, because his mother, not his father, was the Wallenda in the genetic picture.

"Now, now, now," said Eugene, whose good nature was clearly being tested. "Ricky owns the name if he *wants* to own the name. His grandfather is Karl Wallenda. Some people call themselves 'Tarzan,'" he said, aiming a wink in my direction.

"I've *always* supported Ricky," responded Bauer. "I used to book Karl into the stadiums for his skywalks. He was like our uncle. And when he died I booked Ricky. You ask him if I haven't supported him."

Bauer recalled Winnipeg circuses of the 1950s and '60s, when, as he put it, "We used to come in here advertising 'twenty star circus acts,' and we'd bring along one mediocre movie star, the Rifleman or the Three Stooges or something, and you couldn't get a seat in this building. The show went eleven days. Every night, they'd have limousines outside, and the Shriners would take all the performers to the Temple and put on a big fancy buffet. It was one of the finest dates in North America. And now this," he said, pointing toward the arena. "Six thousand people in a sixteen-thousand-seat house. The Shriners haven't kept up."

I pointed out that they were expecting ten thousand tomorrow, had had nine thousand on opening night, before inquiring as to what role television might have had in the changing fortunes of the circus.

Eugene Jr., who had completed his sway-pole performance and had come into the room without fanfare, piped up that he thought television had actually improved the circus's fortunes. "It's educated people," he said. "They see it up close. I think it stimulates them to want to see it live."

Joe said, "We're the only clean entertainment left in the world. We don't need the violence or the sex. All I'm saying is we have to do better. We can't let it go downhill."

Tarzan, who had been more or less silent to this point, said, "Circus existed before television, before boxing, before any kind of sport that we now know. And I guarantee you that circus will exist three hundred years from now, when a lot of these sports are history."

I asked him as diplomatically as possible if he didn't think part of the responsibility for the reduced crowds in the arena belonged to him.

"Why?" he said, unperturbed. "There's lots of people in this town for two circuses. I can only put thirty-two hundred in my tent; they can put as many in here as they can get."

I mentioned the reports that he had lined up against Ricky and the Shriners because of a producer's quarrel, or over an old grievance against the Wallendas.

"Look," he said softly, "For forty years the Shriners in this city have held their circuses in March. I've been coming to Winnipeg in May for ten years. This year they decide to go in May. And I'm the one who's supposed to be competing?"

"Competition helps everybody," called Eugene Jr. from behind a screen where he was pulling off his costume. "I figure we're both gonna kick ass tomorrow."

When Bauer, Zerbini, and Eugene Jr. had left to gamble at a

downtown casino, Eugene Sr. said to me, "Don't take what they say about Ricky seriously. He's a young man with a big name – bigger than anybody's. And some of the people are jealous." He threw the remains of the chicken in a garbage can, wiped the table with a plastic bag, and said, "What's the matter with a young guy coming in? You can't have all old guys. And don't listen to what they say about the Shriners. They do good work. They care about crippled children. Tarzan used to do lots of Shrine dates. So did Joe. The Shriners have done more for the circus in North America than anybody. We've all made lots of money with them."

I stopped by Bobby's truck as I came out of the arena and told him I had met Tarzan and that he had not been entirely forthcoming in explaining his Winnipeg agenda.

"He's not gonna say *nuthin* about why he's here," Bob laughed. "As it stands, he can't lose. If his purpose was to hurt Ricky, he's succeeded. If his purpose was nothing more than to take advantage of all the Shriners' publicity, he's done that, too. If he had no purpose at all, except to put on a circus, well, he put one on. I still say that he chose his dates deliberately, and that the choice stems directly from the business with the Shriners."

The next morning, at about nine, I picked up Bobby, and we drove seven or eight kilometres into northwest Winnipeg, to Garden City Mall, where Tarzan's Cannobio Italian tent – perhaps a quarter-million-dollars' worth of tenting, in predominating red and yellow stripes – was gleaming in the parking lot. "Isn't that beautiful!" exulted Bob as we drove past it on our way to the mall entrance. Behind it, among the mobile homes, was a pair of half-million-dollar customized buses, one of which Bob recognized as Zerbini's, the other as Joe Bauer's.

We walked through the front-end concessions canvas, through the tent proper, into the menagerie at the back, where Bobby spotted a youthful acquaintance, Mike Donohue, an elephant trainer who was travelling for the summer with the show. They exchanged elephant talk as the three of us walked single-file down a narrow roped pathway that might have passed for the valley of the shadow of death. On one side were four immense Asian elephants, staked and chained, and separated from any possible contact with the likes of ourselves by a couple of strands of high-voltage electric wire. On the other side, within eighteen inches of us, were fifteen caged "white" tigers – genetic aberrations prized by circuses ostensibly for their beauty but I suspect, too, for the ghostly ferocity that is implied by their pallor. For those aware of the ancestry of such cats, there is an added spookiness in the knowledge that almost every "white" tiger is the product of a degree of inbreeding (necessary to achieve the desired chromosomal combinations), and is thereby a little crazier, a little less predictable, than the average Bengal or Siberian.

Bobby described one of the elephants, a fifty-year-old female named Peggy, as "a horrible elephant" that would "kill ya in a heartbeat." He had taken care of her once when her former owner Ed Witterman had gone on holiday in Texas. "I bet she remembers me to this day – and she'd still love to stomp my ass," he laughed. "Ya won't see no little old ladies walkin up to those elephants with peanuts. They ain't like Judy. That's what that electricity's about. Mike has no confidence in 'em – he's livin on the edge. They can turn on him, and he knows it. In the ring, no problem. Out here, watch out."

We walked out onto the lot, where a family of Afghanistanis who had been brought to America by Ringlings but now did business on their own were tending to their equestrian and bear acts, watering the animals and cleaning out the U-Haul trucks that were their road homes. "You'd think the protesters'd be over here instead of at our place," said Bob. "They've got half a dozen animals for every one we've got."

As we strolled back through the menagerie, Bob grabbed at my shoulder and yelled, "*You're too close! How many times do I have to tell ya? They can reach out and grab ya!*"

*Writer and friends. Left to right: Gail Redpath, Daniella Gonçalves, "First of May," Liliana Luna, and Jill Gonçalves.*

I walked chastened to the van, where, on the way back to the arena, it occurred to me to ask Bob how many of his friends and acquaintances had been killed by their animals in, say, the past decade. "One this month. Five in the past six months," he said. "Probably twenty or twenty-five over the years."

That afternoon, when our own show had ended, I drove with Manuel, Daniella and Talina Gonçalves, and Alecia Redpath to see an hour of the Zerbini show, catching, among other acts, a first-rate Russian trapezist, the Hansens' roller-skating feats, and Mike Donohue's elephants, which, in the ring, were as pliant as lambs, at times stepping to within a metre of the ringside spectators.

When we got back, I drove Bobby to the Cummins dealership to pick up his truck. He was carrying a plastic grocery bag stuffed with small bills totalling twenty-two thousand dollars Canadian, and as we walked through an upstairs warren of corridors on the way to the comptroller's office he announced to anyone who would listen that he was not to be trifled with because his body guard was a black belt in karate and that I could kill a man eight ways with my bare hands. By comparison, the hands of the comptroller, who had a touch of palsy or Parkinson's disease, trembled like aspen leaves as he counted out the bills on his desk (causing Bob to remark later that the man had been so nervous in my presence that he had shaken "like a dog passing a peach pit"). Bobby was greatly relieved to have his truck back – not to mention his documents and a number of personal affects, including old photos, that he had inadvertently left in the cab.

That night as I sat along the boards watching the flying act, I caught a glimpse of Ricky Wallenda standing in a corner of the arena, at floor level, wearing a suit and tie and carrying a briefcase, apparently just back from Florida. I wandered that way and told him I thought the show looked good, and asked him how things were going. "All right," he said. But he was in no mood to talk.

After the show, I hung around the lot, chatting first with Dave Connors and then with Brett Marshall, who had emerged from the arena with an attractive young woman named Kim Villeneuve whom he had met in Brandon a couple of weeks earlier and who had travelled to Winnipeg for the weekend (it was the beginning of a relationship that was going strong a year later when Matt and I saw Brett with the Clyde Brothers Johnson Circus in Grand Forks, North Dakota, where Kim, too, had shown up for a visit). I told Brett that I appreciated his friendship toward Matt, who, to this day, regards him as a hero, both of athleticism and style. The night air was warm, and a few muted stars were visible in the east. For a while at around midnight, as the prop hands chawed into their customary all-protein barbecue, a hint of the aurora borealis wavered in the north and disappeared. The lights in the trailers had been extinguished.

❧

"A circus travels and never stops," wrote Edward Hoagland. "This is the point, and it is addictive. The mud . . . the privation, the gypsy allegiances and easy goodbyes, the chaotic glory and whirl, all mix together and fix a man into the troupe. As long as he's traveling he need never stop and take stock; his situation is fluid, in a sense his life is ahead of him; things may look up. Even if he's young, the ashes of his past are well behind him and he's in a new country this week, next week, and forever on."

I'll say that, when it all ended, late the following afternoon, it happened fast and without ceremony, and that I was unprepared for the suddenness and finality of it. There was no party, no last gathering of the performers, no sentimentality or fond farewells. Even the taking of the cast photo, which required no more than five minutes, induced benign mutterings about delays and obligations and the pressure to keep moving.

When the photographer had done his job, I climbed to the arena's top row of seats and sat for a while observing the teardown. The previous night I had asked Michael Redpath if he'd mind if I tried the trapeze. But he had persuaded me not to, on the grounds that most people he had allowed onto the rigging over the years were unaware of the tremendous tug on the arms that occurs when the flyer leaps from the platform. "Most of them lose their grip and smash into the net face first," he said. "It's a good way to break your neck."

I took Bobby for dinner at a nearby Chinese restaurant, and, on the lot, at dusk, made a tour of the trailers, to say goodbye. By the time I had finished, the cook-out had started by the tiger truck, and I stood for a few minutes with Wilson and Bobby and the others. The coals from the barbecue made a pale orange glow in the middle of our circle.

Eventually, I said, "I gotta go," and I shook hands with Wilson and wished him luck. I told him I admired his courage.

"Uh-huh," he said.

Bobby walked me to my van, and when I got in stood at the

open window with his arms folded in front of him. Behind him, by the elephant truck, Judy was poking selectively at a mountain of popcorn and old fruit.

I told Bob I appreciated what he'd done for me.

"I didn't do nuthin," he said.

"There's not much I can do or say to thank you."

"I didn't *do* nuthin," he repeated.

We shook hands through the window, and then I got back out and gave him a hug. We promised we'd keep in touch, and before I knew it he was walking away from the van.

"See ya," I called out.

"See ya," he called without looking.

I had a momentary urge to get out of the vehicle and keep talking, keep listening, keep being a part of this thing I had begun to love. Instead I just watched while he unhooked Judy and led her to the back of the truck. As he was about to open the doors, he stopped and looked over. "Don't sugar-coat it!" he called. "Tell it like it is!"

"I'll do my best," I yelled out the window. But by then he had disappeared into the truck.

I cranked the engine and gave the quickest of toots on the horn, so as not to waken those who had distances to cover in the morning, as I did.

And, with that, I was gone from the lot.

# Epilogue

Two days later, at the International Peace Garden south of Brandon, where Highway 10 crosses the border into North Dakota, Bobby, Wilson and the rest were detained by U.S. Immigration officials determined to prove that Bobby, who had eight hundred dollars in his pocket, was carrying more than the ten thousand in cash that can legally be brought into the U.S. without a declaration. They were strip-searched and harassed. But a seven-hour combing of the trucks and their contents turned up no illegalities, other than two bottles of 222s (three hundred pills beyond the limit of one hundred that can be brought in). The pills were confiscated.

John McCoy, I learned, returned to the U.S. with thirteen dollars of the roughly fifteen hundred he had earned in Canada.

The tour, as it turned out, was Bobby's last as an elephant trainer, and for a variety of reasons, including differences with his boss (in particular over the handling of the trucks) began a temporary breach in his twenty-year relationship with Clyde Brothers Johnson. In July, he started with the King Royal Circus, driving an animal truck, until the show was taken off the road in late August.

In December, pressed for cash, Bobby took a transport-driving job with a big interstate trucking operation. Throughout the winter, we talked regularly by phone, and exchanged frequent letters.

Bob often predicted that the traditional circus would be gone within ten years. But during February, a tiger on the Ringling show bit a grapefruit-sized chunk out of the head of its trainer, provoking the trainer's brother to shoot the animal in its cage. The incident was closely reported in the media and caused a significant stir among animal-rights activists, who clamoured for the withdrawal of Ringlings' licence to own and display animals. As a result, Bob revised his doomsday estimate to five years. "Maybe even three," he said. "What you're seeing is the end of the circus as we know it."

He told me there were times when he would be just as happy to be done with it himself, and that the steady thousand dollars a week he was earning as a trucker was worth as much to him as the fading pleasures of being part of the show. "I see more circuses right now than I ever did as an elephant guy," he told me one night on the phone. "Everywhere I go, I get to visit my old friends. Besides, it's time to think of some security for Rosa and me."

In early April, he phoned to say it was official; he was done with the circus for good. "I don't even miss it," he said.

Four days later, he sent me his route for the summer – first with Clyde Brothers Johnson, in Kentucky and North Dakota, and then with Circus Leonardo, a Canadian show, with which he would tour New Brunswick, Quebec, and Ontario. He was finished in the ring, he explained, "but Donny needed somebody to drive Judy and Betty around, and to take care of them." Donny's son, Shane, has been handling their performances.

In early May, Matt and I travelled to Grand Forks, North Dakota, to spend a weekend with Bob, and found him as surly and delightful as ever. He was fed up with the circus, he told me, and looked forward to returning to truck driving.

Like Bobby, David Connors swore off the circus during the autumn of 1997 and took a job installing doors for a contractor in Gainsville, north of Dallas. It was a job he had had before, and, when he took it, he was informed by the boss that if he left again for the circus, his days as a door installer would be over.

His days as a door installer are over. When I talked to him in the spring, he told me the "lure of being out on the road and making some decent money" had been impossible to resist. During April 1998, he was the prop boss for a Wallenda date in Nebraska, and for Clyde Brothers Johnson dates in Tennessee and North Dakota, on each of which shows, he also worked the centre ring with his unicycle and rola-bola acts.

I have heard nothing from the Garzas or Chunyan Ho. Nothing from Bill Boren. The Gonçalveses, I was told recently, are on the road with the Hammid Circus, somewhere in the United States.

Wilson and Rick Robinson spent much of the 1998 season touring western Canada with Circus Gatti. Connie is living with her mother in Dallas.

I received a Christmas card from Paul and Chata, including a photo of our stop at Pisew Falls in northern Manitoba. They are performing regularly with a family tent circus in Mexico City.

Brett Marshall performed with a number of shows during the 1998 season, and, like Bobby, toured with the Leonardo Circus in Canada.

❀

Liliana Luna eventually got the call she had wanted from Ringlings – but turned down their offer. For one thing, they wanted her not as a specialist on the rings but as a kind of generalized aerialist and showgirl, part of whose work would have been in the elephant displays. "She's afraid of elephants," her mother told me. "And for all the years she's spent perfecting her routine, she didn't want to do something less challenging." The contract, what's more, called for considerably less pay than she had become accustomed to making. And Ringlings did not want her family along. "She likes her family with her," said Rosa.

So, instead of touring with the Greatest Show on Earth, Liliana worked the winter as a receptionist with Steven Spielberg's DreamWorks studio in Los Angeles. She also became the lead singer in an alternative Latin rock band. In her dreams, she told me last June, she is "still out there on the rings."

Rosa Luna recently completed training as a registered nurse's assistant in Sarasota, and Rolando is attending school and working on his performance routines. When I spoke to Enrique in March 1998, he was looking forward to getting out on the road.

❀

Ricky Wallenda was not rehired by the Khartum Temple for the 1998 tour. He also lost his Shrine date in Chicago – a show controlled by Pat Delaney. He told me in January 1998 that he and Delaney, once good friends, had severed ties over a dispute about the division of the concessions money that our tour had accumulated up north.

The cast, crew, and musicians, preparing to have their photo taken after the tour's last performance. Standing, left to right: David Connors, Roy MacFee, Patty Alexander, Wilson Barnes, Paul Gadicke, Tim Weaver (partially hidden), Chata Olvera, Timo Nordstrum, Mike MacFee (partially hidden), Gene Nock, Evrardo Garza Sr., Alecia Redpath, Bill Boren, Gail Redpath (partially hidden), Michael Redpath, Baby Redpath (Gail's), Linda Redpath, April Redpath, Daniella Gonçalves, Jill Gonçalves, Manuel Gonçalves, Rolando Luna, Liliana Luna, Enrique Luna, Eugene Nock. Kneeling, left to right: Brett Marshall, Ronnie King, Pete Bartels, Larry Rothbard, two unidentified musicians who joined the band for the Winnipeg dates, Doug Pashuta. Judy the elephant can be seen in the background.

In March of the same year, a troupe of Wallendas headed by Rick's cousin, Tino, remounted the seven-person pyramid in the Coliseum of the Michigan State Fairgrounds, in Detroit, where the fall had taken place thirty-five years earlier. When I spoke to Ricky during the weeks before the event, he said business was tough and that he was tired. But he was optimistic about the future. In recent months, he had recreated a nineteenth-century German circus wagon that he now takes on tour as a kind of totem of the family's past.

In June 1998, Pat Delaney informed me that he and Ricky were back on good terms and were about to head out on tour.

❀

David Perry, the Khartum Temple Circus Chairman, from Winnipeg – a nice man, without whose help I might never have travelled with the circus – died of cancer in early 1998.

❀

In the wake of their differences with the Great Wallenda Circus, the Khartum Shriners returned the contract for their annual tour to Ian Garden of Garden Brothers Circus in Toronto. Again, in May 1998, Tarzan Zerbini met the Shriners head-on in Winnipeg.

❀

My own interests at the moment tend to the Mexican circus, which, before long, I hope to experience first-hand. In the meantime, my son, Matt, and daughters, Georgia and Eden – aged four and two – are practising their acts.

They have all met Bobby Gibbs, who commands a status beyond legend at our house – and my ongoing gratitude and affection. As do many of the others from the tour.

For the better part of the past year, I have thought about them, talked about them, and written about them. I consider myself both lucky and privileged to have spent a month of my life with them.

I believe I am a changed person for having done so.

# Acknowledgements

Many people made valued contributions to the creation of this book. For their varied assistance and advice, I would like to thank Jake Macdonald, Larry Krotz, Dan Diamond, Jane and Terry Gray, Joan and Emil Dolphin, Susan Carpick, and Hume Wilkins – and Charles Stuart, who so capably copy-edited the manuscript.

I would like especially to thank my agent, Jennifer Barclay, of Westwood Creative Artists, for her faithful and upbeat support from the beginning, and my editor at McClelland & Stewart, Dinah Forbes, who piloted the book through development and publication and provided countless insightful suggestions about its structure and language.

My thanks are due to many people from the circus, but in particular to Ricky Wallenda, without whose openness and understanding I could never have become part of the show – and of course to Bobby Gibbs, a great teacher and friend.

As always, I owe an inexpressible debt to my wife, Betty (my on-site editor and inspiration), and to my children, Matthew, Georgia, and Eden, for their forbearance and love through the writing-caused chaos that so often seems to swallow up our lives.